Later Chapters of my Life

THE LOST MEMOIR *of* QUEEN MARIE OF ROMANIA

DIANA MANDACHE

FOREWORD BY DOMINIC LIEVEN

SUTTON PUBLISHING

First published in the United Kingdom in 2004 by
Sutton Publishing Limited · Phoenix Mill
Thrupp · Stroud · Gloucestershire · GL5 2BU

British Library Cataloguing in Publication Data
A catalogue record for this book is available from the British Library.

ISBN 0-7509-3691-6

Typeset in 11/14.5pt Sabon.
Typesetting and origination by
Sutton Publishing Limited.
Printed and bound in England by
J.H. Haynes & Co. Ltd, Sparkford.

Contents

Foreword

In the history of the modern Romanian monarchy queens were more interesting than kings. That was true of the author of these memoirs, Queen Marie. It was also true of her aunt, Queen Elisabeth, and daughter-in-law, Queen-Mother Helen. This makes the belated publication in English of the last and long-lost volume of Queen Marie's memoirs of particular interest.

To be sure, as will always be the case with crowned heads, there is much that is not said in these memoirs. Most notably, the scandals caused by Marie's son, the later King Carol II, and the anguish this caused his family is barely alluded to. Moreover, though there is much that is political in these memoirs, this is disguised in a narrative that flows from one personality and impression to the next. These are very consciously the memoirs of a society lady – one feels more like a reader of *Tatler* than of solemn political autobiography. Though this style makes the book extremely interesting and amusing to read, it would even so be a mistake to think that its author was superficial, silly and uninfluential.

On the contrary, in Paris and London in 1919 Queen Marie was very important in gaining publicity and sympathy for Romania's cause. Never before or after was she to have an international role of such significance. Her memoirs bubble over with excitement and pride (but never smugness) as she recounts the story of her efforts to gain for Romania the attention of the statesmen who were deciding Europe's fate at Versailles.

The Queen had real literary ability. Her vignettes of places, atmospheres and people command the imagination and are vivid and sensual. Though proud of her influence and of the role she was playing successfully, the book is also shot through with an awareness of the ambivalence and tragedy of the immediate postwar months.

This stemmed partly from her own direct and acute experience of suffering in and just behind the lines in 1916–18. Even in 1919 she expended great effort in trying to mobilise foreign aid for Romania's destitute population, still reeling from the effects of war and foreign occupation.

It also owed much to the fact that her own family loyalties were divided. Her Russian uncles and cousins were massacred in large numbers between 1918 and 1919. Her mother, daughter of Alexander II of Russia, not merely had to contemplate this tragedy but also the defeat of her adopted Germany and the overthrow of its monarchs. Queen Marie's reminiscences of the triumphant receptions of Paris and the somewhat smug security of Buckingham Palace are tempered by moving passages on meetings with her Romanov relatives and even with tsarist Russia's former Foreign Minister, Alexander Izvolsky.

It is high time that the memoirs of the most important period in the life of this intelligent and sensitive woman saw the light of day. Diana Mandache is to be congratulated for making this possible, and so are Sutton Publishing.

Dominic Lieven

Acknowledgements

I would like to gratefully acknowledge the kind assistance from the
Romanian National Archives in Bucharest in identifying materials
pertaining to the country's royal history, which ultimately enabled
me to find this remarkable document written by Queen Marie. I
received invaluable help and support throughout my research for
this book from Valentin Mandache, my husband, who is also a
historian. I would also like to express my thanks to Jaqueline
Mitchell, senior commissioning editor at Sutton Publishing, for
accepting and preparing for publication a historical document which
will further illuminate an important period from the turbulent
history of Romania and south-east Europe following the First World
War.

Diana Mandache

Introduction

Of the Romanian monarchs, Marie was the most charismatic, admired and publicized by the world media. The recollections of the diplomats, politicians and writers of those times present her extremely favourably. During the First World War, she gained the peculiar aura of a courageous woman. Her nonconformity was often criticized: she was reproached for her vanity and exaggerated wish to remain in the spotlight. However, this worked to Romania's benefit, as many of her contemporaries believed, 'Romania has the face of Queen Marie'.

This final volume of her memoirs, *Later Chapters of my Life*, a previously unpublished manuscript, was for a long time believed to have been destroyed by King Carol II after his mother's death. Marie's last private secretary, Christine Galitzi, knew 'of the new book the Queen was writing as a sequel to *The Story of My Life*'. She believed that 'after the Queen's death Carol ordered the manuscript to be destroyed'.[1]

The writing of these last memoirs was undertaken on the basis of notes from the Queen's diary. A short time after the publication of the first volume of *The Story of My Life* the queen was asked to continue to write her captivating recollections. The first mention of starting the fourth volume appeared during 1934 in the correspondence between the queen and Ray Harris Baker, a pen-friend, librarian at the Library of Congress and the founder of Queen Marie's Collection (today deposited at Kent State University, Ohio).

The completion of this volume of memoirs by the Queen continued with many difficulties stemming from pressures from her son Carol II.[2] He was envious of the Queen because of her widely recognized prestige. The result was that she decided to hide her private papers. Also from 1931, as a precaution against Carol's intrusions, she arranged to receive some of her correspondence via King Alexander of Yugoslavia, her son-in-law, in Belgrade and in Bucharest at the Yugoslav Legation.

Documents[3] confirm Marie's fears during the 1930s and her wish to place the diaries and other personal papers in a safe place at the British Legation in Bucharest. This was a politically sensitive action and was possible only for a short time. The intention to keep her papers – material for her memoirs – in a safe place was paralleled by a similar situation in respect of Empress Frederick and her son Kaiser Wilhelm II. The same kinds of restrictions and pressure resulted in her memoirs and Kaiser Frederick III's personal papers being smuggled out of Germany by the British Embassy in Berlin and stored in England.

From his first days as a king, Carol II impressed upon his mother that she should not concern herself with politics. There were often quarrels between them, with the result that the king resolved to send her away from Bucharest. In order to diminish the queen's political influence, Carol ordered close surveillance of her so that all her private conversations taking place at Cotroceni Palace were reported to him. Carol had also tried with some degree of success to prevent the queen from receiving her old friends at the palace, because he was obsessed by the possibility that they might criticize him. However, Marie was careful to avoid any open conflict with her son. Despite that, Carol had placed restrictions on whom she could meet and play host to at her residences, on her correspondence and even on her movements. In such circumstances, it was difficult to write anything that might upset some politicians and the new royal camarilla that had seized power in Romania since the return of Carol II.

Prince Barbu Stirbey, an old counsel of King Ferdinand and close friend of Queen Marie, was also forbidden to come to the Court. Stirbey knew many unsavoury facts about Carol from the time when he wanted to renounce his rights as heir to the throne in 1919. Now Carol had a special squad of informers with the task of finding incriminating evidence against Stirbey. In these conditions Stirbey went into self-imposed exile.

In this tense environment in which the queen found herself, Marie's literary executor, Stephan Gaselee,[4] advised her in October 1937 not to write the fourth volume because of the difficulties arising from King Carol's restrictions.[5] On the other hand, in January 1938 Ray Harris Baker encouraged her, stating, 'there are so many personal tasks that I know it would give you joy to turn to – the completion of Volume IV, the book on flowers which you once mentioned, one of your children's stories with the Sulamith Wülfing illustrations, and other happy undertakings of the Queen-Artist, which have in the past, and will in the future, enrich the world'.[6] Marie decided to write on, prevented from completing the fourth volume of her memoirs only by a fatal illness.

The memoirs were produced in at least one typed copy, sent outside Romania for safe keeping. Nothing has been revealed about where this manuscript was kept.

In 1939, after Marie's death, the *Cornhill Magazine* published extracts from these memoirs in three parts, in a slightly different form from the manuscript published here. In the *Cornhill* version the titles – 'My Mission. I. In Paris', 'My Mission. II. At Buckingham Palace', 'My Mission. III. Paris again' – differed from the original.[7] As the periodical stated,

> during her lifetime Queen Marie of Romania, daughter of the Duke of Edinburgh and the Grand Duchess Marie Alexandrovna, published three volumes of reminiscences under the title *The Story of My Life*, which won wide popularity. A fourth was in preparation but was unfinished at her death and has never been published. In this and the two succeeding issues will be found Her Majesty's own account of the unofficial diplomatic mission to Paris and London that, at the request of King Ferdinand, she undertook on her country's behalf in March and April, 1919.[8]

The original manuscript contains sections entitled 'The Peace Conference', 'England' and 'Back Again to Paris'.

Introduction

In 1942 Ray Harris Baker mentioned this unfinished manuscript in a booklet entitled *A Collection concerning Marie Queen of Romania and the Romania of 1866 to 1941*. He claimed to have a typewritten version, together with 'a letter signed by the Librarian of the Foreign Office, London, attesting to the authenticity of the manuscript'.[9]

After the war there was silence regarding the memoir's fate; its existence was very uncertain. It seemed that we would only ever have the extracts published in the *Cornhill Magazine*. But in the mid-1990s, when I had read thoroughly the correspondence between the queen and Ray Harris Baker and also many other materials from different archives containing documents pertaining to Queen Marie, I became convinced that the manuscript or typescript version of her memoirs was deposited somewhere in the Romanian, American or British archives. Obviously this was like looking for a needle in a haystack. Finally, after seven years of research I struck lucky at the Romanian National Archives in Bucharest. There, after a re-reading of inventories, I decided to have a look at a file with no apparent importance and unexpectedly found the lost manuscript among many other innocuous documents.

What I found revealed for the first time was an account of the life of Queen Marie from 1918 to 1922, and the new political reconfigurations witnessed by her after the First World War. There she was speaking about her informal visits to Paris and London and the role that she played in the Paris Peace Conference, the importance of her connections in post-war Europe with the British and European royal families, and the last meeting of Marie with her mother, the Duchess of Saxe-Coburg. All these recollections, published here after nearly seven decades, constitute a prime historical restitution. The importance of this document consists in the fact that it was written by a gifted writer who in her position as a monarch was best situated to appreciate and chronicle defining moments of Romanian and European history. Not much is known by the Western public about her adopted country, and the present memoirs contribute to an understanding of the aftermath of the First World War in Romania and south-east Europe.

Princess Marie was born on 29 October 1875 at Eastwell Park, near Ashford in Kent. She was the daughter of Alfred, Duke of Edinburgh and Marie Alexandrovna, née Grand Duchess of Russia. A granddaughter of Queen Victoria and Tsar Alexander II of Russia, Marie became Princess of Romania through her marriage to Ferdinand of Hohenzollern-Sigmaringen, Crown Prince of Romania, on 10 January 1893. She became queen of Romania, her adopted country, on 11 October 1914 when Ferdinand assumed the throne following the death of King Carol I.

Queen Marie is known worldwide for her charitable efforts and for her work nursing wounded soldiers on the front lines during the First World War. She took part in the political and diplomatic efforts that led to Romanian national unification in 1918. But Marie also turned out to be a well-known writer, especially after the war.

Even in childhood Princess Marie of Edinburgh possessed a vivid imagination, and used to take pleasure in telling fairy tales to her sisters. She was brought up in the Victorian age and knew Shakespeare from the theatres of London and from the Coburg stages. She was also familiar with the dramas of Goethe and Schiller. However, she was even more fascinated by the English poetry of Tennyson, Shelley, Keats and Yeats.

During her later education Marie was captivated by philosophy, and had a particular interest in reading and quoting from Nietzsche or Rabindranath Tagore, and later even used such texts in her writings, as in *The Real Regina Maria: The Story of a Soul* or in *The Dreamer of Dreams*. In Marie's correspondence with the Lebanese poet Khalil Gibran, in connection with the publication of *The Prophet*, she displayed a keen interest in the philosophy of the tragedy of existence. The real creative work for Marie was the understanding of truth through her own symbols.

Marie had regularly read the Scottish and Scandinavian sagas and the Bible. All these helped transform her into a sensitive writer. She saw emotions in a visual way and had a unique narrative style.

Regarding her first attempts at writing, she recorded: 'I knew nothing whatever about writing, about style or composition, or about "the rules of the game," but I did know how to conjure up beauty, also at times, emotion. I also had a vast store of words'.[10] In this way she noted the reminiscences of her brother, entitled 'Souvenir of Alfred's last stay with us',[11] depicting scenes from the autumn of 1898, and they are a part of Edinburgh's family history, Alfred being the hereditary Prince of Saxe-Coburg-Gotha. After his premature death in 1899, these pages remained an interesting story of the Edinburghs, in which the artistic aspirations of the young princess are shown to Alfred.

As a young mother, Marie used to tell fairy tales to her children. Prompted by one of these children, Marie began to write the tales down. One influence in this was the staging of plays at her residence, the Cotroceni Palace. On 22 May 1904, Princess Marie organized some performances in the Cotroceni Park in support of the 'Materna' orphanage. One of these was 'The Princess's Dream', a pantomime directed by Alexander Davila.[12] It was a custom of the age that the aristocracy acted in such plays. In 'The Princess's Dream', Marie played the title role and her children, Carol and Elisabetha, played the part of pages. Romanian aristocrats took the other parts. All these theatrical events helped inspire her early compositions.

At that time she believed that she would write only fairy tales, but she gradually evolved an original style. In time she realized that she had the ability to write novels and poems. Another major step came with the war years, when Marie wrote for the soldiers and for the press. In the same period she wrote for the benefit of wounded soldiers and orphans.

The publication of her autobiography, *The Story of My Life*, coincided with her maturity as a writer. Marie's memoirs are far superior to those of any other royal figure from the epoch.

The European press saw the literary queen as part of the traditions of the Romanian Royal House established by Queen Elisabeth.[13] It was a happy coincidence that both were so talented. From the very beginning, Queen Elisabeth (Carmen Sylva) encouraged Marie's writing when she noticed her real talent. 'When I first suddenly discovered within myself a gift for writing', Marie recorded, 'I wrote sad stories instinctively, irresistibly. None other came naturally to me. And when I wrote "A Vision of Joy" amongst my thirteen visions which were all sad, I instinctively made it end upon a sad note because it enhanced its beauty.'[14]

Marie's first published book was *The Lily of Life*. The English edition was printed in Bucharest by A. Baer in 1912, and in the following year Hodder & Stoughton published an edition in London with illustrations by Helen Stratton. In the foreword, Carmen Sylva wrote, 'A young mother, who is a true artist, relating a fairy tale, is one of the greatest joys in this world.' Marie remembered this work as 'the first book I wrote, written for my children because my heart was bursting with the love of beauty'.[15] The book was translated into Romanian in 1913 by Elena Perticari-Davila, and was published by Socec. A film adaptation was produced in Bucharest by Loie Fuller and Gab Sarère. In 1919, Marie recorded in her diary: 'I worked with Loie Fuller, and we prepared all the details for *The Lily of Life* which will be on stage in England in December, directed by Loie Fuller together with her dance company and Mărioara Voiculescu.'[16]

The queen continued to write, and during her lifetime published over thirty books. There were many subsequent editions in many languages, including one book in Japanese. She covered a large range of styles from children's fiction to short stories, novels, memoirs and poetry. Moreover, some of the short stories were adapted for theatre, ballet and even film.

Marie wrote in many different genres, but not all her literary work is known. In her writings, her diary contained in 100 notebooks, her correspondence with friends, family and officials of that time, she emerges as a strong personality and an accomplished and skilful writer.

Queen Marie's friends knew very well her custom of writing early in the morning. Marie noted in her diary the time she allowed for writing, either in the golden drawing room or in the brown room – also known as the Norwegian room – in the Cotroceni Palace. These were her favourite places for writing. But during the war she felt little inspiration. As William T. Ellis observed, 'before she discovered her gift with the pen the queen expressed her love of nature with the brush. "I think in colours", she said. As her writing shows, she is an artist first, observing accurately, and reproducing both the spirit and the letter of a place or a scene. The Romanian translation of her work has become very popular with the people.'[17]

She usually wrote in English, but there are also texts in Romanian from the First World War when she suffered alongside the Romanians.

QUEEN MARIE'S MEMOIRS: *THE STORY OF MY LIFE*

The writing of Queen Marie's memoirs, which were finally published in three volumes in 1934–5, had begun a long time before their publication. During the twenties Marie wrote several works containing autobiographical material. These include 'The Real Regina Maria. The Story of a Soul',[18] written in 1922–3 and 'A Book of Remembrances', written in 1925–6.

At the end of the 1920s Stephan Gaselee, the queen's literary executor, began negotiations with several publishing houses and editors. In December 1927 Gaselee recommended that the memoirs should be placed with agent Curtis Brown.[19] The publisher received the manuscript of the first volume. In 1929 Gaselee informed Marie that they had received an offer from Cassell in London.[20] The negotiations in both Britain and the United States dragged on over several years, with further offers being received in August 1933.[21] Among the editors who had received the manuscript had been Curtis Brown and Lee Keedick, the latter being the queen's literary executor in the United States. The *Saturday Evening Post* serialized chapters from her memoirs entitled 'My life as Crown Princess' during 1933–4, and in March 1934 Gaselee announced that a contract had been concluded with the publisher Charles Scribner. In the autumn of that year, Cassell in London and Scribner in New York simultaneously published the first two volumes.[22]

The publication of all three volumes of *The Story of My Life* in 1934–5 made Marie famous. The memoirs rapidly appeared in several languages, including French, Romanian, German, Polish, Czech, Swedish, Italian and Hungarian. In Romania, the writer D.V.

Barnoschi noted that 'in the near future this book will remain alongside the memoirs of the great writers'.[23]

After the first American edition in 1934, there was also a later reprinting. In 1935 Scribner published a second volume entitled, *Ordeal, The Story of My Life*.[24] The memoirs were reprinted in facsimile in New York in the 1970s, showing how the book's success had lasted several generations.

The British edition of *The Story of My Life* was immensely successful, going through several editions between 1934 and 1936. By July 1936 the first volume was into its sixth impression, and the second volume was up to its fifth impression by December 1935. The third volume, published in March 1935, was already into its third impression by the following month. The income obtained was deposited in the queen's account at Coutts.[25]

A Romanian translation by Margarita Miller-Verghi was published in 1936. After the fall of communism in 1989 there was great demand for a book that had been forbidden by the communists for almost fifty years. The Moldova publishing house, Porţile Orientului at Jassy and the Eminescu house in Bucharest published three new editions in 1990, 1991 and 1998.

The Story of My Life shows the queen at full maturity as a writer. After it was published Marie was invited to preside at the 145th anniversary dinner of the Royal Literary Fund in London. Proposing 'Prosperity to the Royal Literary Fund', she expressed her pleasure at being asked to attend. It was for her a special honour, as she realized that she was the first woman to receive such an invitation. She remembered how kindly her books had been received and felt that she would like to tell people how very grateful she was for their reception. It was a great joy and rather an astonishment to her to occupy that position, because when she started out in life she never thought that one day she would be called a 'writer'.[26]

The success of her memoirs brought her great prestige. In January 1938 the artistic director of French state television, Georges Dilmare, sought her approval for television and radio adaptations of her 'Stealers of Light', 'Voice on the Mountain', and of her memoirs.[27]

In *The Story of My Life* she gives a good description of her early years of adjustment, years full of conflicts and difficulties and a sometimes heart-rending struggle against obstructions of every sort . . . No doubt she does not tell us everything, but we can admire her unusual fairness of judgement, she takes her own share of blame with the rest. She does not try to whitewash herself and there is a generous spirit running through the whole book. Though she criticises those who complicated her young existence, she never maligns them. Her sense of humour often runs away with her, but there is no malice in her laughter; irresistibly she sees the funny side of things and does not spare even herself when she laughs.[28]

These are the queen's remarks written in the third person, in a biography of King Ferdinand. She considered it easier to tell her own story in this way.

Mary Colum wrote in *The Forum* in 1935 that the queen's autobiography was as interesting to read as that of H.G. Wells:

Like him, the queen is a vigorous, unified personality without any obvious complexes, and like him she has got nearly as much of what she wants out of life as anybody can . . . She has the same sort of power of portraiture in words that Wells has and gives vivid and memorable pictures of the royal figures of Europe, so that her book will be a storehouse for the historian.[29]

The book offered a series of portraits, including: her mother Marie Alexandrovna, her grandmother Queen Victoria, her sister Ducky, Carmen Sylva (Queen Elisabeth of Romania), 'Unchiul' – her uncle, King Carol I of Romania – her cousin Charly, Princess of Saxe-Meinnigen, the Romanian prime minister D. Sturdza, the historian N. Iorga, Albert Thomas, her old grand-uncle the duke of Coburg, 'tante Ella', Kaiser Wilhelm, Countess Tolstoi Alexandrine, the Romanian liberal Ion I.C. Brătianu – or I. Kalinderu, head of the Romanian Crown Domains – her husband King Ferdinand and Tsar Ferdinand of Bulgaria. There are also some portraits from the war, but the most impressive are of Tsar Nicholas II and Tsarina Alexandra. Marie did not forget the tragic murders of so many relatives by the Bolsheviks. Her reminiscences about their fate in 1917–18 are valuable documents. She also wrote about people outside royal circles. 'There are many names and descriptions of servants and quite simple persons, I do not wish these suppressed, my life would not be real nor complete were I only to speak of the great ones of this world.'[30] The most affectionate was the remembrance of her nurse Pitcathly, 'a splendid old Scotch woman. It would stand out in all its combed beauty, for indeed Nana groomed and cleaned and polished us up like pampered horses, and I can still feel in my shoulders the little twist I would give to be able to catch a glimpse of my own shining mane.'[31]

Marie hoped the work would be 'descriptive enough to hold my readers' attention'. She was adamant that every word was based on fact, claiming, 'All portraits I draw are true to life. When I have disagreeable things to say about anyone, even if he or she is no more alive, I suppress their names.'[32] Her initial wish was to have both 'the English and Romanian arms' on the cover,[33] but the editors persuaded her to use the Romanian coat of arms alone as a cover illustration.

The first volume of the memoirs was divided into two parts: 'Childhood' and 'Youth', each having six chapters. The first part portrayed the places of her childhood: Eastwell Park, Osborne, Clarence House, places in Scotland, Russia, Malta, Coburg and Devonport.

Her birthplace, Eastwell Park, the Edinburghs' home for twelve years from 1874, is depicted with joy and nostalgia. As she wrote,

However old I may grow, the smell of dry or damp autumn leaves will ever bring the old English home before my eyes . . . That scent of autumn leaves, no matter where I may be, still evokes the vision of Eastwell Park and its woodland paths that our childish feet once trod. And in the kitchen garden there was that perfume of violet leaves mingling with the mouldy smell of potatoes and old sacks . . . and a little farther on the rather bitter scent of the high laurel hedges we would slip through, which seemed to us darkly mysterious passage to dream places to which we must finally come. And the huge cedar tree on the lawn in front of the house, with its lowest boughs sweeping the ground under which we would crawl. This tree was a wonderful cathedral-like mansion in which we children each possessed a room.[34]

Marie displayed the same sensitivity in describing childhood places when writing about Osborne House and Swiss Cottage on the Isle of Wight. For her, nature was the perfect retreat:

Osborne – Grand mama's summer residence with its lovely terraces, and the dear old lady sitting out for breakfast under a giant green-fringed parasol, fixed into the ground, Grand Mama Queen surrounded by collies and sky-terriers attended to by kilted Scotchmen and silently moving Indians of which we were slightly in awe. The air was full of a delicious odour of coffee mixed with the irresistible smell of a certain biscuit which we children greedily loved and were sometimes allowed to taste . . . Then above all there was the 'Swiss Cottage' where Papa and his brothers and sisters when children had each planted a little garden. These nine wee gardens were kept abloom just as in those far off days when an earlier generation were children, and still today the perfume of the Madonna Lily reminds me of the 'Swiss Cottage' garden where first it burst on me with all its fragrance. It was wonderful to me then as it is still wonderful to me today.[35]

In Malta she was on very friendly terms with Prince George, the future King George V. In a version of her 'Story of My Life' she later wrote:

from the age of thirteen I do not remember not having some man or boy in love with me! My first adorer was George, my cousin, now King of England. I was then but a flat, innocent bit of a thing with a thick mane of golden hair, and yet I remember thrilling to his unmistakable love for me. Already then I felt the great temptation to give, to bestow the best of myself, to be generous and responsive. What could I give? About that I was very vague, all that I knew was that I wanted to make others profit from that rich abundance of love and life which rushed through my being and which welled up in my heart like a bubbling fountain of joy, with the irresistible desire to spend it upon others, share it with them in glorious fraternity.[36]

Prince George used to call her 'Missy the Cat'. In March 1888 he wrote to her:

I thank you a 1000 times for your dear little letter I got this morning & for the little violet which I shall put in my Prayer book & always keep. I can't say how sorry I was to say good-bye to darling aunt Marie & all of you . . . I am so sorry to hear that you & 'Ruby' fell down together how funny you must have looked, but I am so glad you did not hurt yourself. So Capt. Bourke is allowed to ride with you now, I hope he looks after you as well as I did.[37]

Their friendship lasted a lifetime, and as George's correspondence with Queen Victoria reveals, there was even talk of a marriage between him and the princess of Edinburgh.

For Marie, education meant discipline but also happiness:

If excessive innocence had been the family tradition at home, there had also been another happier tradition, that of the joy of living; young people were there to have a good time, to run wild with companions of their own age, to ride, swim, play tennis, laugh, sing, romp and be happily foolish to their heart's content.[38]

The first volume of her memoirs ended with the moment when Marie changed her destiny by her betrothal and marriage to Ferdinand, Crown Prince of Romania. Marie Alexandrovna, her mother, did not want an English marriage for her daughter. She did not want a marriage between first cousins, as this was forbidden by the Russian Orthodox Church. Ironically, this prohibition was ignored when her other daughter Victoria Melita – Ducky – married Ernest of Hesse, a first cousin on the paternal side; also, her second marriage was to a first cousin from her mother's line. Another possible reason was political: namely to settle territorial disputes between Russia (where her brother Alexander III was Emperor) and Romania over Bessarabia.[39] Obviously, this matrimonial relationship could provide the basis for a good understanding between Russia and Romania.[40]

Some memories that did not appear in the published memoirs recall anxieties over the wedding, as she wrote, 'I did not look my best and was very disappointed with myself. My crown did not suit me, my figure was too flat under my rather heavy dull white silk dress, and my veil had been arranged in a too-complicated way.'[41]

As a writer Marie considered it a perfect choice to end the volume with her departure to Romania, 'considering that if I have been able to interest my public they will be willing to follow me into the "far Country" in the next volume'.[42]

During the negotiations for writing the first two volumes, Curtis Brown advised Marie 'to concentrate the first years and give much more circumstantial details' from the period from when she became queen up to the king's death. She agreed to this, but was worried in case 'the book becomes rather weighty, for there it a great deal to relate'.[43]

The second volume was also in two parts: 'Early Wedded Days', and the 1906–14 period. The first part covered her arrival in Bucharest and her first acquaintance with Romanian high society; the birth of Prince Carol (the future King Carol II) and the other children (Elisabetha, Mignon and Nicolae); the coronation of Tsar Nicholas II of Russia; the illness of her husband Crown Prince Ferdinand; and encounters with Romanian politicians, the advisers of King Carol I, and also Marie's friends – the Earl and Countess Larisch, Waldorf and Pauline Astor, Maruka Cantacuzino; Marie's first return visits to England, then journeys to Darmstadt, Rosenau, Coburg, Tegernsee and Sigmaringen in Germany; and the coronations in Moscow in 1896 and London in 1902 and 1911. Part two of the volume covers her years as crown princess. The chapters 'Royalties visit Romania', which dealt with the visit of Emperor Franz Joseph on 28 September 1896, together with Count Goluchowsky and General Beck, and 'Sarajevo and after,' which described the murder of Franz Ferdinand and the beginning of the war, the declaration of Romanian neutrality in 1914 and the death of King Carol I, contain significant material on the history of most of the royal families of Europe.

In an unpublished manuscript, a variant of the printed memoirs, Marie shows the discontent of her first years in Romania much more directly than in the published text. In this manuscript, written in the third person, she wrote that she 'had not been brought down to Romania to be adored and spoilt and made much of; Marie had come to be part of the machinery King Carol had wound up. She had been imported to be trimmed, educated, cut down and trained according to the great man's conception of things.'[44] In the same context she also recorded: 'And now the family circle had shrunk to almost nothing, consisting only of old Uncle Carol, the King, and my husband, his nephew, who stood in mighty awe of the iron old man, forever trembling that any action of mine might displease that duty-bound head of the family!'[45]

After her separation from family and friends, all seemed cold and strange to the princess, the architecture of the city, the Royal Palace:

> For long hours would I mope, whilst my young husband did his military service, all alone in rooms I hated, heavy German rooms, rich, ornate, heavy, pompous, with no cozy nook in which to take shelter. Everything was 'Altdeutsch' and not of the best! . . . All the treasures brought from home were lost, out of place, did not fit in, almost absurd, as I myself was a lost, absurd, miserable, piece of humanity, torn out by the roots, away from the home-soil and unable to adapt myself to the new.[46]

In this unfamiliar place Marie had unpleasant visions of the old home, beloved and abandoned, and the old liberty. In comparison with Britain, Marie felt that Romania was a new country, 'one in construction, a country without old traditions, with a dynasty which had to make itself respected, therefore no risks could be taken, friends were not always good counsellors, besides favouritism created jealousies, so it was safer to have no friends'.[47]

'She found herself' – the *Times Literary Supplement* recorded – 'from the hour of her arrival in Bucharest under the tutelage of that stern disciplinarian King Carol I. Of this unbending Hohenzollern prince, who did more than any other man to make modern Rumania, Queen Marie paints a portrait from which future historians will draw their inspiration.'[48] Marie put this portrait in 'juxtaposition to an exceedingly clever sketch of another remarkable Balkan monarch, King Ferdinand of Bulgaria'.[49]

The royal duties brought the new crown princess into the thick of various events, which belonged to the protocol of the Romanian Royal House. One of these events was the move to the new official residence at the Cotroceni Palace (Bucharest) in the spring of 1896. At this palace, Marie recreated some features of her childhood. Her golden drawing room recalled Celtic traditions, especially the Celtic cross, and the lily, the symbol of purity, but also a symbol of Osborne House.

The year 1897 brought much anxiety to the Cotroceni Palace. Ferdinand fell ill with typhoid fever and hovered close to death for many days. A steady stream of telegrams passed between the Romanian and British royal households. Had the crown prince died, Marie's life would have changed completely, even though she had children, among them Prince Carol, the future heir to the throne. However, Ferdinand recovered.

His illness prevented the couple from participating in Queen Victoria's Diamond Jubilee, the last great family meeting of the nineteenth century in London. Romania was represented by the envoy Balaceano, and the Romanian Royal House sent General Pencovici as a special envoy, together with the king's aide-de-camp, Colonel Georgescu.

The third volume of the memoirs is entitled *The War Years*. Marie covered all the major events of the war in Romania: the period of neutrality; the death of Queen Elisabeth, of whom she wrote a unique portrait; the decision to enter the war on the Allied side; the

German invasion; the death of Prince Mircea; the retreat to Jassy; the difficult life at headquarters; the Russian Revolution; the typhus epidemic; her work in hospitals together with her daughters Mignon and Elisabetha; the infamous peace with Germany; the end of the war and the emergence of Greater Romania.

Despite the highly political nature of these events, Marie felt that 'All through I have endeavoured to be fair without being tiresome or over-political. Having a kindly feeling towards humanity in general, I do not think that I have ever been spiteful, anyhow never intentionally.'[50]

This volume includes various entries from Marie's diaries; for her, the great difficulty was the selection and, because of this, the style is different from the previous two volumes. She admitted that 'each page is so alive with the events of the day that they all seem to need to be quoted, but I shall pick out those most character-revealing, those which best express the stress of the times'.[51]

A *Times Literary Supplement* review stated that the queen was 'the heart and soul of Rumania's defence throughout the bitter and tragic winter of 1916–17', and that 'her adopted country owes her a debt of gratitude for her tireless efforts on behalf of the wounded and the sick'.[52] Nevertheless the third volume attracted some criticism in Britain. The *Illustrated London News* warned that 'some readers may find the extremely personal character of the memoirs a little embarrassing, the consciousness of royalty they everywhere confess a little overwhelming'.[53]

During the war, the Romanian Prime Minister Brătianu encouraged Marie to seek improved relations with the Allies. As she recalled:

The Emperor of Russia and the King of England being both my first cousins, it was easy for me to keep in touch with them unofficially, and of course I was ready to serve my country in every way. Being entirely trusted by both the King and his Prime Minister, I was more initiated into State affairs and secrets than is usual for queens. I was considered a valuable asset and therefore expected to do my share.[54]

Having been coached by Brătianu as to Romania's history, geography and economy, Marie supported Romania's interests through her correspondence with George V and Tsar Nicholas II. As she stated in one of the letters: 'Even before Uncle's death, the country began to worship in me one whom they considered the supreme supporter of their national dream.'[55] The third volume of memoirs contains a selection of correspondence with her two cousins, including the tsar's last message from 1917, which Marie regarded as a blessing: 'May God grant you final victory and the fulfilment of all your hopes.'[56]

After long negotiations with the Entente and the conclusion of separate political and military conventions, Romania declared war on the Austro-Hungarian Empire on 27 August 1916. Marie was influential in this. According to the Comte de Saint-Aulaire, the French minister in Romania, Queen Marie 'embraced the war, as others might embrace religion'.[57]

She set up the Queen Marie Organization, which ran a network of hospitals in the province of Moldavia and an ambulance service. Marie promoted co-operation with organizations such as the British and American Red Cross, and she published several books, such as *My Country*, the proceeds of which supported British Red Cross operations in Romania. The queen cultivated support for Romania in the United States, and held frequent meetings with the Allied ambassadors in Romania.

Despite Marie's endeavours, the Romanian press was divided between the official line, which favoured the Entente and stressed Marie's charity work, and the Germanophiles. These were opposed to the queen. As the liberal politician I.G. Duca confirmed, they 'blamed her for our entry into the war'.[58]

Marie felt optimistic about the victories in the summer of 1917.[59] As she wrote, 'In spite of the bad example of the Russians, who had mostly turned Bolshevik and were daily abandoning their positions by the thousand, our soldiers, underfed, insufficiently armed and hardly ever relieved, remained staunch to a man, unshaken amidst the débâcle of their erstwhile allies.'[60] The complete disintegration of the Russian army prevented the Romanians from following up their successes.

At that moment, Marie wrote that 'to stay still and die suffocated among the Russian and German traitors who hate us is really a very unworthy death'. Her main fear was that the Entente might make a separate peace and leave Romania's territorial ambitions unfulfilled. She declared,

> if we are to die, let our Allies at least know that we do not die like blind fools, but as conscious heroes, knowing that we have been sold and betrayed, and that at the moment when, through the failure of others, our front is becoming useless, our big protectors begin to haggle and bargain with us, as to whether they will be able to keep any of the promises given to us when we were still prosperous, before the Russian revolution cut our throats![61]

Even Marie could not prevent the Romanian surrender, but she was able to extract telegraphed promises from the British government 'to uphold Romania's interest and claims, regardless of how much she will presently be forced to give way'.[62] On the insistence of Brătianu, the Allied ministers gathered in Jassy signed a note acknowledging that 'Romania, having battled heroically to the extreme limits of the possible', had been forced to make peace following the 'betrayal of the Russians', and therefore 'the armistice should not affect the allied agreements with her'.[63]

Marie was opposed to the 'infamous peace' with the Central Powers in 1918, and felt she had no choice but to abdicate. This did not happen because of some later events. With the departure of the Allied missions and the enemy take-over of the telephone and telegraph, Ferdinand and Marie found themselves isolated. In a cable to George V, she asked him not to forget her family and Romania, and complained that the 'peace was not peace; it is foreign occupation, it is living death, it is strangulation'.[64]

The American *Literary Digest* ran an article entitled 'Marie, Queen of Conquered Romania, Defies the Kaiser'. It stressed her unwillingness to rule a 'country under German domination', and claimed that she had 'refused to acknowledge the peace agreement between her small country and Germany'.[65]

The Imperial Counsellor Hortmann in Bucharest confirmed this.[66] As a precaution, the Foreign Minister was advised that the Kaiser's wish was that her correspondence should be monitored, including that with her sister Beatrice, the Infanta of Spain.[67]

Romania's re-entry into the war on 10 November 1918 marked the achievement of the union of the Romanian provinces, and guaranteed international recognition at the Paris Peace Conference.

The third volume of the memoirs ended with the return of the monarchs to Bucharest on 1 December 1918. As Marie remembered 'all the world over there are so many dead . . . who today cannot rejoice over the hour of victory, nor weep over the hour of defeat'.[68]

LATER CHAPTERS OF MY LIFE

Queen Marie decided to write the fourth volume because of the success of the others. As she noted in the foreword, 'I have been asked to write a fourth volume of "The Story of My Life", and because of the generous interest with which my first books have been received, so to say, I have given in to the temptation of putting pen to paper once more.'[69]

She also hinted that she could not given a proper account of Romania's problems after the war, because of the restrictions imposed by Carol II. She ended the foreword by saying 'I must, because of others, keep silent, and holding fast to my sense of humour which has carried me through so many vicissitudes, I shall only relate certain chapters, leaving it to history to complete a story I alone could really have told!'[70]

One insight comes from a letter to Marie written by Ray Harris Baker in 1934. He wrote, 'you speak of the difficulties about planning for your fourth volume. You mention the one awful event, which saddens all your recollections of those years. I do not know if it is a tragedy about which you feel that you can write. If it can be told, I should imagine that it would add great power to this fourth volume of your Story and make it the most poignant climax of your entire work.'[71]

This 'awful event' was probably the morganatic marriage of the Crown Prince Carol to Ioana (Zizi) Lambrino. In the summer of 1919 Carol had left the army, trying to marry Zizi, against the wishes of his parents Ferdinand and Marie. Marie saw this as betrayal, and asked him whether he had 'lost all sense of honour and duty'. She went much further, suggesting it would 'be better to die, a bullet in your head, to be buried in the good Romanian earth than to betray your country.'[72] Carol returned to the family fold and was sent on a long trip around the world during 1920.[73]

All these matters made for an anxious life for the dynasty in Romania. Trying to resolve Carol's problems, the queen used her best friends such as Joe Boyle, Barbu Stirbey, and the army officer Mugur, Carol's friend. It is possible that this is the chapter that is missing from these recollections. According to Ray Harris Baker, the typewritten manuscript had thirteen chapters, but in the archives there are only twelve.

The last volume of Marie's memoirs describes events after the end of the First World War, when Europe changed its political configuration, and new states appeared on the map in the aftermath of the collapse of the Austro-Hungarian, Ottoman and Russian empires.

Among most of the defeated states, such as Germany, Austria and Turkey,[74] the old monarchical regime was abolished and replaced by a republican one. The exception was Hungary, which kept its monarchy, but was a kingdom without a king, the head of state being a regent,[75] Miklós Horthy, elected by the parliament for an indefinite period. Among the new sovereign states there were republican and monarchical regimes. Poland and Czechoslovakia became republics, while in the Balkans the Kingdom of Serbs, Croats and Slovenes emerged.

The Kingdom of Romania, being among the winners, fulfilled in 1918 its dream of the unification of all Romanian-populated territories. Thus Bessarabia, former Russian province, annexed by the tsar in 1812, became part of the kingdom, while Bukovina and Transylvania, annexed by the Habsburgs in 1775 and 1687 respectively, became Romanian.

Bulgaria, a defeated country, maintained its monarchical form, but Tsar Ferdinand, forced by the Allies, abdicated[76] in 1918 in favour of his son Boris III. Greece, also a winner in the war, swung between monarchical and republican regimes. Here the monarchy survived until 1924, when a short-lived republic was proclaimed; in 1935, by a military coup and a plebiscite, the monarchy was reinstalled and King George II regained the throne. Albania regained its independence in 1920. The monarchy had been maintained with a regency since 1914 when the Prince of Wied renounced his leadership of the country.[77] In 1925 it was proclaimed a republic and a local chieftain, Ahmed Zogu, was elected president. Albania was proclaimed a monarchy in 1928, and Zogu declared himself King Zog I.

After the fall of the Tsar's empire, the new Soviet Union emerged, and for a while the Bolshevik regime threatened to take over in Hungary and Germany. The Hungarian soviet republic of Bela Kun was quickly defeated in 1919 by the Romanian army.

On European thrones fundamental changes thus took place in Germany, where the Kaiser was forced to abdicate in November 1918. Wilhelm II sought exile in the Netherlands, a neutral power in the war, where he lived for the rest of his life.[78] In Austro-Hungary Karl of Habsburg, emperor of Austria and king of Hungary (under the name of Charles IV) abdicated in 1918 and went into exile in Switzerland. The newly created states of Austria and Hungary adopted constitutions and special laws[79] which abolished the right of succession for the Habsburgs. The peace treaties did not include reference to the House of Austria and its problems. But in February 1920, at the Conference of Ambassadors, the Allied Powers declared that they would not accept a Habsburg restoration.[80] After some unsuccessful attempts to regain the throne in Hungary in March and October 1921, Karl went into exile in Madeira, where he died in 1922. From among all monarchs the most tragic fate was that of Tsar Nicholas II and his family, who were murdered by the Bolsheviks.

In Romania the monarchy came out of the war as a stable state institution with very high prestige among its people. King Ferdinand

and Queen Marie ensured the relative political stability of the country, compared with other Balkan states.[81]

The manuscript of the final memoirs is in two parts, of which the first is more reliable. Queen Marie wrote an ample description of the aftermath of the war ('Postwar Readjustments'), and of her family and relatives in Russia ('Effort'). She wrote about her unofficial visits to Paris and London, her return to Bucharest, her visit to Transylvania and a special encounter with her mother, Marie Alexandrovna, in Switzerland after many years apart. The other part of the memoirs is much shorter and betrays an evident tiredness caused by her incurable illness. Here she writes about the first parliament in Greater Romania, about social reconstruction and her charitable activities, and about the new political context in 1919–22, giving brief portraits of Romanian politicians.

The chapter referring to the Peace Conference and visits to Paris and London is a page of personal history, with impressions of European royalty amidst the events of high society. At that time Marie was an important ambassador for Romania. This is a fact worth stressing. Regarding her visit to Paris, Prince Stirbey had advised Marie not to 'object to the word unofficial or even incognito, because once there, everything will turn into an official reception'.[82]

As already noted, Romania's re-entry into the war had ensured international recognition at the Paris Conference. Despite the presence of the official Romanian delegation, it was felt that Marie's presence would be helpful. On the initiative of the Comte de Saint-Aulaire, the French Minister in Bucharest, and Prime Minister Brătianu, Marie undertook an unofficial diplomatic mission to Paris and London. Marie's diary makes it clear that Brătianu had prepared her for her meetings with Clemenceau, Lloyd George and Woodrow Wilson, in order to persuade them to honour the conventions Romania had signed in 1916. As she later wrote, 'so many diplomats and politicians were having their say that it was difficult to get a hearing. It needed an exceptional ambassador to plead for a country which did not enjoy special popularity.'[83]

She was also advised to go to Britain to speak with her cousin King George V and contact various politicians and businessmen. She noted in her diary that Brătianu 'considers that my best work here [London] is to be on excellent terms with the royal family'.[84]

Although the famous Romanian liberal politician Ion George Duca claimed Marie's role was insignificant, the historian Iorga acknowledged that Marie's intervention won valuable friendships, something that Brătianu admitted he could not have achieved himself.[85] Clemenceau recognized this, and Brătianu himself confessed that Marie 'accomplished in a few days more than they did in a month'.[86]

Marie's visit to Paris was part of Brătianu's new strategy in the diplomatic game. As Marie recalled, 'we, the little countries, were anything but pawns in the big game'. At a time when important decisions about the new Europe were being made, Marie's unofficial visit had well-defined aims. When Marie met the French President Raymond Poincaré, he confirmed that 'Clemenceau's attitude to Romania had changed after you acted for your country'.[87]

In Paris, Marie raised Romania's cause in meetings with Herbert Hoover and Woodrow Wilson. After her encounter with Wilson, she noted, 'I spoke of the hopes of the smaller countries, whose defender he especially was. He declared that it was especially the smaller countries that would profit from the League of Nations.'[88] After the meeting with Marshal Foch, Marie obtained a convoy of Red Cross aid for Romania.[89]

During her mission Marie stressed Romania's geographical and strategic position, pointing out that 'we are the outpost against Bolshevism in the Near East, a barrier against Russia's pernicious propaganda'.[90]

Marie did much to help Romania's cause in those years. A Foreign Office report noted that 'the Queen is loved in the country, and in political circles she is considered an excellent ambassador and the government was happy to use her qualities in missions'.[91] Walter Long, from the British Legation in Paris, pointed out that 'propaganda was a most delicate art [and] countries spent thousands of pounds upon propaganda, with, very often, poor results', but Queen Marie was 'the most astonishing propagandist he had ever met'.[92]

This was no mere socializing but a diplomatic action meant to bolster the image of Romania. As she recalled,

> I had shunned no fatigue, had allowed no doubt or discouragement to sap my energies. I had endeavoured to grasp situations, to face difficulties, occasionally, even, hostility, intent upon lessening any prejudice held out against Romania. I had brought forward the needs and aspirations of my people. I had pleaded, explained, had broken endless lances in their defence. I had given my country a living face.[93]

What Marie accomplished was to put Romania on the map. As a diplomat she earned the title of 'irresistible ambassador'[94] and later that of 'mother-in-law of the Balkans'. As a patriot, she won the deep love and gratitude of the Romanian people for her war work. And 'like her uncle, King Edward VII of England, she knew how to use her personal charm and popularity to gain influence'.[95]

A later chapter, 'Transylvania', dealt with the visit of the royal couple in May and June 1919. This was particularly significant in the context of Bela Kun's Bolshevik coup in Budapest and the subsequent Romanian military intervention to topple him. The 'Royal march' was not always regarded favourably by the Allied leaders, as the official border was not fixed until 11 June 1919.

James Mills, correspondent of the Associated Press, who witnessed the royal visit, recorded:

> One of the most striking developments of the visit of the King and Queen has been fact that in almost every town they have visited they have been assured that if it were not for the presence of the Romanian army, Bolshevists would have secured control of the country. Bolshevism had spread into Transylvania from Austria and Germany and was checked only by the timely arrival of the Romanian army, which not only had a tremendous stabilizing influence but did much to relieve the condition of the population. In the town of Bichis Csaba, a delegation of Hungarians headed by Countess Almassy, a cousin of Count Tisa the famous

Hungarian statesman, called on the king and thanked him for the presence of Romanian troops, which she said had saved the city from the terrors of Bolshevism and had protected life and property and restored order.[96]

Marie gave another account in her journal, noting that even the Hungarians 'came to thank us for having, with our army, delivered them from the danger of the Bolsheviks'.[97] She 'also visited a military hospital where some of our wounded soldiers are. Everywhere our troops have behaved first-rate and everybody and all nationalities praise them which makes us very proud.'[98] In 1920 the Treaty of Trianon officially recognized the union of Transylvania with Romania.

The chapter on the last encounter between Marie of Romania and her mother, Marie Alexandrovna, Duchess of Saxe-Coburg-Gotha, is very thrilling, and shows how the war divided the European royal families. Marie Alexandrovna died in the autumn of 1920. For the duchess, the war meant also the loss of her Russian imperial family and of a considerable sum of money left in the Imperial Treasury in Moscow, a sum arising from the marriage treaty of 1874.[99] Marie enquired whether anything could be done in this matter, even approaching George V. As Britain did not recognize the Bolshevik government at that time, there was no way to pursue the matter.

After visiting Switzerland, Marie spent a holiday in Florence with her mother and daughter, Elisabetha, Princess of Romania. These recollections of Marie Alexandrovna are the last ones the queen wrote.

In her final months Marie stopped writing her memoirs. But in the last chapter of her life, she tried to remain lucid. From the Dresden sanatorium, she wrote to a friend saying that: 'Going home will not be quite easy, but I'll try to be as calm as possible, and not to let myself be upset.'[100] Arriving home in Romania, she died on 18 July 1938 at Pelishor Castle, Sinaia, and was interred in the Curtea de Argeş cathedral, in the tomb of the Romanian royal house.

Diana Mandache

Later Chapters of my Life
by Queen Marie

With flattering insistence I have been asked to write a fourth volume of *The Story of My Life*, and because of the generous interest with which my first books have been received, so to speak, almost all over the world, I have given in to the temptation of putting pen to paper once more.

However, I consider that I can hardly give the same title to this fourth volume, so I have chosen the above as most suitable. There is still much to tell, my life is still brimful of events and faces – but – as I advance in years, it becomes less and less my own life and ever more involved in other lives, younger lives, but which are so closely bound up with mine as to be inseparable. So inevitably there will have to be gaps, certain omissions, certain silences, certain discretions.

'In wisdom is much grief and he that increase the knowledge, increase the sorrow.' Little by little we all learn this truth, but saddest of all is to gradually have to realize that it is often those we love best who give us the greatest sorrow. This is part of life and has to be accepted with so much else; nor can we always help those nearest and dearest – those with whom and for whom we have lived.

So this book will just be chapters out of my life – and even if they can no longer follow closely one upon the other, there is still much to tell.

It is said that, as we become older, we remember most clearly that which lies far behind us, whilst more recent events slip from our minds. Perhaps. But probably I have not yet reached that age, as I still retain the faculty of seeing everything in pictures, almost startlingly distinct with every accompanying detail: form, colour, sound, smell, touch; a long series of changing events which join one onto another; great and small, sad or gay, funny or tragic, some even absurd; a long string of events: Life – My Life.

When young, we are so busy living that we have little time to ponder the 'reason why' of things; we do not pause to consider that each act, even the most insignificant, engenders its own direct consequence, that nothing ever stands still, neither time nor events. We hasten along, we hurry impetuously so as to break our way through, and we take our knocks as a necessary part of the game; hope is always with us and the future is ours to gain!

Life is like a great puzzle made up of but small bits: at the outset we are little interested in the pattern it makes, we only want to rush on, impatient at every hindrance; everything must be according to our wishes, immediately, at once! Therefore the many blunders, the many falls, all the heart-ache, the disappointments, disillusions – and yet how wonderful it all seemed, how splendid, how worthwhile.

Then there comes a moment when all the pieces fit into the puzzle and it suddenly lies complete before us: a picture – We gaze – and understand.

But just when my puzzle is completed, when with almost cruel lucidity, I see the real meaning, the real explanation of my life, when it lies before me most logically, most tragically clear, I must, because of others, keep silent and, holding fast to my sense of humour which has carried me through so many vicissitudes, I shall only relate certain chapters, leaving it to history to complete a story I alone could really have told!

ONE

Postwar Readjustment

I closed my third volume on our return to our capital, on the evening of that day when, after a tremendous reception, I stood in the old church[1] beside Mircea's grave.[2]

Yes, we were actually back! The long nightmare was over, we had returned to our home victorious: Greater Romania was a fact, and we were hailed as the first King and Queen of all the Romanians – undoubtedly an achievement, but – well, the whole world was one great 'but'. Everywhere new situations had sprung up, the map of Europe had changed, thrones had crumbled, and readjustment after such a frightful upheaval was, as I had foreseen, uneasy work; nor was it a small thing to knit together again so many broken threads.

Those who had remained in the occupied part of the country had almost become strangers. There was something painfully haggard about their appearance; it was as though, underfed and terrorized, they had shrunk to half their usual size. Besides, there was something almost furtive in their look – a reflection of past dread was still with them. Having had to bow their heads while the invaders were masters, it was not easy to hold them up again. Those who, out of fear or want of conviction, had temporized with the enemy, did not dare meet our eyes, and those who had suffered because of their fidelity, although today triumphant, were still cowed and worn out by two years' subjugation.

It was best not to enquire too closely into the secrets of men's hearts and conscience; there are occasions when there is no benefit in complete knowledge. All men had suffered, some with more dignity than others, but one and all needed encouragement, a helping hand.

We in Moldavia, although living in continual distress, had been free, and had therefore been spared certain humiliations. Our sufferings had been of another kind, but this must be a period of healing and rebuilding, nor would it have been wise to separate too severely the sheep from the goats; a certain tactful blindness was best just then.

Of course we had to submit to any amount of festivities. Our people wanted to express their gratitude for our return, and to demonstrate their delight in having us back in their midst, but neither the King nor I wanted unnecessary money to be spent in this way. There was so much else more important to be done, but we had still Allied troops in our city: we desired to show them every honour and our people wished to entertain them with the proverbial Romanian hospitality.

It was a wonderful feeling to be among friends once more, but only very gradually could we readjust ourselves to joy. I still felt more at home wandering through the hospitals or among the poor than sitting at official banquets or submitting to festive receptions.

The Spanish flu was raging everywhere and I was continually visiting the English, French and Romanian soldiers down with this horrible malady. The doctors warned me that it was exceedingly contagious and that I ought not to allow our men to kiss my hands. Having for two years lived fearlessly amidst every form of epidemic without ever taking any precaution, I was deaf to their injunctions, firmly convinced that I was immune. But this time, unfortunately, it was not the case, and quite shortly after our return I fell ill and had a very bad time of it, paying at last my tribute to sickness just at the moment when everyone wished to glorify me for what they so kindly termed my bravery and heroic resistance. I believe there was even, for a few days, great fear that they should lose their still so necessary Queen.

I believe I was more exhausted than I knew: the immense straining effort was at an end and it was as though I could not properly adjust to peace and plenty. Laughingly I declared, 'I belong to the old canons, so I suppose my time is over.' Anyhow, for about three weeks I was very ill indeed.

I had never been ill before, except that once I had phlebitis, after the birth of my sixth child,[3] and confess that I have a terrible recollection of those twenty days' misery.

I had just been planning, with great enthusiasm, a large banquet we wanted to give the English, French and Romanian soldiers in the great ballroom of the old palace. Soldiers and officers alike were to sit at our table, over which we ourselves would preside. All was ready; I myself saw to every detail, but just the evening before, that wretched and treacherous flu laid me low. I meant to get up next day, certain that my usual energy would put me on my feet and carry me through, but this was illusion: I could not lift my head, I could hardly see, yet I still insisted upon personally supervising the dressing of my daughters for the great occasion. But next day, when they wanted to tell me about the tremendous success of the banquet, I turned my face to the wall, begging them to say nothing; the very word 'food' was more than I could bear. I felt as though I would never again be able to put a morsel into my mouth. For thus does the celebrated Spanish flu treat its victims!

During my illness I had strange hallucinations – I continually had the sensation of being two personalities, and my second self, lying in bed with me, took every sort of shape. Even the separate parts of my body seemed to have faces! It was horrid, especially as quite casual acquaintances, noted more particularly for their ugliness, became my companions. I could not get rid of them!

Then there was also that other queer sensation of dissolving into nothing: I felt as though I were melting into my bed, becoming bodiless, and withal struggling not to quite disappear in that uncanny way. I actually used to ask General Ballif,[4] my 'Fearful One', as I called that severe, austere military follower and adviser, to sit by my bed and hold my hand; his very 'fearfulness' was a sort of guarantee against the invading shadow which seemed to creep upwards to annihilate me.

Everybody was very kind; my little lady-in-waiting, Simky Lahovary, spent several nights in an armchair in my bedroom so as to be near in case of need. Through the mist of fever I dimly saw faces leaning over me: Nando,[5] the children, old Nini, different friends, different doctors, but it was all like a bad dream.

Deadly also was the gradual crawling back to life. Everything overwhelmed me, tears came too easily; it felt as though I would never again be my own vigorous self, and the ache in every limb was next to unbearable . . . But after a period of abject weakness and almost morbid discouragement, I did finally climb back to face life and its many harassing obligations.

One of the last things I had been able to arrange before giving in to that Spanish fiend was that our Nicky[6] should go off to England with Mr Mişu[7] (our minister in London) and Colonel Boyle,[8] as I had secured, through the kindness of King George,[9] that the boy should be taken to Eton – a great privilege as it is very difficult at short notice to enter that school of schools. It was a terrible wrench to let Nicky go so far, at a time when regular communications had not yet been re-established, when the post could not be counted on, and letters took weeks to arrive. But I had at once grasped the fact that, owing to the present, chaotic and dislocated state of our country, the boy would have a better chance at school than at home. Besides, Colonel Boyle, who was going to England, had guaranteed for Nicky with his head. I knew that my faithful 'Backwoodsman' (as he liked to call himself) could be entirely relied upon, and I was aware of what an almost fearful energy he had when he meant to carry a thing through. Then there was no standing up against him: he would stick to his word no matter what the difficulties. So when I came back to life again, my jolly little Nicky was no longer there to be my fun and recreation!

Events had not stood still during my illness; Transylvanian deputations had been received by the King, who had taken up contact with his new subjects, and the moment I was strong enough, lying on my sofa, I also received them: Maniu,[10] Vaida Voevod,[11] Goldiş,[12] Popp[13] and the bishops, Miron Cristea[14] and Hossu.[15] Great emotion, a sort of hushed joy and many hopes for the future . . . Ardent assurances of eternal loyalty.

Also my little cousin Marie Putiatin, Uncle Paul's[16] daughter, had arrived as a refugee, having escaped from the terrors of Red Russia.

In this case also, Colonel Boyle had brought his influence successfully to bear. Her experiences had been terrifying, and the moment I was well enough to receive them, we asked her and her young husband to accept our hospitality. Marie had arrived literally without a stitch of clothing, and my own, just then rather meagre wardrobe, had to be ransacked so as to dress her as well as I could.

It must be remembered how absolutely and hopelessly disorganized our country was just then. After two years' occupation, Romania had been mercilessly plundered; the enemy had laid hands upon absolutely everything. Food was becoming scarcer and scarcer; we were once more facing famine. The shops were empty, even the most elementary necessities could not be had for love nor money. No material for clothes, no shoes, no soap, no medicine! Our oppressors had raffled everything and owing to disastrous communications, nothing came our way: we were as destitute as in time of war. Between our country and those of our allies lay the lands of the defeated, with uncertain frontiers and Bolshevism raging all around us. The old order of things had been overthrown and the new map of Europe had not yet taken definite shape. And we lay between these countries in complete chaos, standing up as well as we could against overwhelming difficulties.

My diary speaks in detail of the long-drawn-out effort to reconstruct, to help, to reorganize, to build up, get into shape again what had been dislocated and destroyed. That first year was a continual struggle against overwhelming odds, and certainly 1919 and the following years can be looked upon as the busiest period of my life.

During our exile in Jassy,[17] it had become the habit to appeal to me for everything: people had got accustomed to look upon me as the centre of every effort. I had got into the bad habit of receiving them at all hours of the day; nor did anyone pause to consider if I was equal to the effort, or if it was my job or not. I was in harness, exhausted or otherwise, I just had to go on. There were days of excruciating physical fatigue, of almost superhuman strain, but it just had to be endured and lived through, without holding anything back, without ever showing discouragement or anxiety.

Added to all the rest, I was still harassed by our own private grief, which we had to carry secretly, showing to the world at large a brave front while in reality I was torn to pieces by an unbearable sorrow, which threatened to overthrow all our work.

The sunnier side of the picture was that interesting people were continually coming to Romania. I made many pleasant acquaintances and gained several excellent friends. For the moment everything was still entirely military: fighting had stopped but it was not yet disarmament or peace!

Our army, because of conditions in Hungary, was still mobilized, and finally we were asked by our Allies to march into that unlucky country so as to fight the Bolsheviks who, under Bela Kun,[18] were overthrowing everything and plundering the land. Everywhere confusion, obstruction, hindrances: a boiling state of discontent and unrest. The war had lasted too long, too much had been dispersed, destroyed, torn up. In all things there was change, rebellion, different currents; nor was there any master-word with which to allay disorder. Kings and emperors had been done away with and nothing had as yet taken their place: no form of government had properly crystallized, every man's hand was against every man; everywhere there was chaotic disarray and discontent.

General Berthelot[19] remained for several months in Romania with many of his staff. His solid presence was a reassurance. There was also a charming British general, Greenly,[20] who was a staunch upholder of our cause, as well as a personal friend. After General Berthelot's departure, General d'Enselme was with us for a while as military adviser, to be replaced, when he was sent to Odessa, by General Pathé. These military gentlemen kept in continual contact with me and I was given much unofficial, and mostly disagreeable information, which I was expected tactfully to pass on, in small doses, to the King,[21] who had not always time to listen to everything. It was considered that I could be told the full truth, even those things which would have overwhelmed less robust natures; but, because I never complained, nor asked for mercy, few ever knew how often I inwardly staggered under the many terrible things brought to my hearing.

I could always meet with outward calm the most appalling situations and none guessed how often my knees shook beneath me while I never dared let the smile leave my lips.

News filtered slowly down to Romania, but soon rumours reached us that there was to be a peace conference in Paris and, of all astounding announcements, that Wilson[22] was to come to Europe as a sort of arbiter to help unravel the European confusion. This was indeed an unheard-of event. Brătianu became very anxious, wondering how Romania was going to be treated by the Great Powers. I also, holding my breath, listened anxiously for all tidings coming from either England or France.

Another continual distress was our internal politics. Instead of joining hands in a united effort to build up strength, our political parties were shamefully disunited, mutually accusing and fighting each other, frustrating the King's every attempt to bring about a national government in which all sides would collaborate. I had to sit for endless hours while our various 'big men' poured into my ears their unreconcilable detestation of each other. I even had a certain chair which I called 'the chair of the opposition', and many a hopeless confession did I listen to from those on that chair. And yet if ever there had been an hour when all parties might have come together, it could and should have been then, when Romania's most far-reaching aspirations had been fulfilled. But it did not come to pass, neither then nor later . . . And I begin to think that I shall go to my grave without seeing that union, which alone would mean strength, health, prosperity and progress for the country I love.

TWO

Effort

It was in my house that poor Marie Putiatin[1] heard of her father's death.

We knew that Uncle Paul with three other grand-dukes had been thrown into the prison of the Peter and Paul fortress, and that their lives were in danger. News from Russia came irregularly and was maddeningly conflicting, but when it did reach us, it was of terror, persecution, overthrow. In those days the white armies were still desperately hoping to get the upper hand, but there was no unity, and although the Allies threatened, no country felt capable of offering effectual military aid. Everybody was tired of war and Russia was a problem too vast, too difficult to solve. There would be volumes to write about all the mistakes that were made, about eternally defeated hope, misunderstood situations, about all the ghastly suffering endured, but the telling of it is beyond my competence; I must leave it to others to unravel the tale of defeated possibilities and of a state of affairs no human intelligence was large or far-seeing enough to grasp.

Princess Paley,[2] Uncle Paul's morganatic wife, has written her own story, of how, heroically but in vain, she tried to save her husband's life and to get him released from prison, as he was a very ill man. Many a promise was made, but the Bolsheviks keep no promises, so the terrible day dawned when all four grand-dukes (my old friend George Mihailovitch who had been with us in Jassy was among them) were taken out of their cells, early one morning, and secretly shot, without warning, one of them holding in his arms a little cat that had been his prison-companion.

The news reached us through England: a telegram sent by brother Dimitri, who, ever since the Rasputin murder, had been in Persia

12

and was still there under British protection. I shall never forget that evening. Dressed in my smartest clothes, I was just getting into the lift, having been asked to preside over an official concert. Marie had come to the door with me to wish me good night when a telegram was put into my hands and I quite naturally opened it: 'Papa has been killed . . .' and a few details of the murder. The open telegram in my hand, I looked at Marie – I was trembling; all the blood had left my face. Marie guessed immediately what the news was; she had been expecting it. And I had all the same to go to my concert; everybody was awaiting me, for such are the lives and obligations of queens; they must forever tread on their hearts.

Marie remained with us for some time – I helped her as much as I could. She was still very much in her grief, but I understood what she was going through; the dreadful picture of her father's violent death must have been continually before her eyes. And Uncle Paul had been such a gentle, chivalrous man, and had never said a harsh or unkind word to anyone. The Putiatins felt safe and at ease in our house, and Marie liked Romania because, in many ways, it reminded her of Russia, especially the wide plains around Bucharest with their funny, untidy little villages. Whenever the weather permitted I would take her for long drives in an open motor. The snow had melted, the mud was indescribable, the roads awful; but accustomed, since Jassy, to going everywhere by myself, I kept up the habit of driving about the poorest quarters to enquire personally into the people's needs. I always had great sacks of sugar with me to distribute among the children, who during the occupation had been quite deprived of this luxury.

I thus came into contact with many who, now demobilized, had known me either in the hospitals or at the front, and everywhere I was greeted with loud exclamations of delight. My face was known to them all.

One day I had stopped my motor in a faraway and particularly poor slum. Crowds of pale-faced children were pressing round my motor, eagerly clamouring for their share of sugar, when an old man, full of pleasurable excitement, came running out of one of the houses, manifesting great joy at seeing me.

'From where do you know me?' I asked.

'Don't you recognize me?' exclaimed the old fellow 'I was one of the old men you used to feed at Coţofeneşti;[3] I belonged to the commissariat, to those to whom no one pays attention, because we are non-combatants, but you, you came up the hill every evening with sugar and cigarettes, don't you recognize me?'

Of course I had to act as though I recognized him and to pretend that this was as joyful a meeting for me as it was for him. He covered my hands with kisses, and then turning to his neighbours who had gathered about us, he cried, 'Look at her well. She is our Mother, and she would not allow our fallen sons to be put into a common grave; she stood there and insisted that each soldier should be buried separately; I heard her myself!'

The old man was a bit confused in the telling of his tale; he exaggerated a little, but I was touched by his enthusiasm, even if in memory he magnified my virtues.

That same day, on the way home, our motor stuck in the mud. It was promptly surrounded by eager faces and strong hands ready to help. On the side where I sat was a young man in an old military coat who was pushing with all his might. I noticed a small cross dangling from his neck and asked him whence he had it. With a fine show of very white teeth he smiled back at me: 'You gave it to me', he said. 'I lay wounded in hospital [here he mentioned a number] and you came to see me and hung this cross round my neck. I have worn it ever since.' So here on the same day was another anonymous friend looking at me with grateful, affectionate eyes! I felt a lump come to my throat. And thus all through the years I have been enthusiastically greeted by many subjects in all the four corners of my country, and each time I felt that it was I who ought to be grateful, grateful for the humble homage of their remembrance, and I knew then that no effort had been wasted; I could not remember all their faces, but one and all they remembered mine.

That loving remembrance of my people was the happiest side of the postwar picture: the warm, sunny side, the side of the heart. Less pleasant were the eternal political conflicts, the general intolerance and discontent, the groping about in distrustful uncertainty. As though tired of heroism, today everyone was over-ready to criticize his neighbour, to discover in others the faults he did not like to recognize in himself. There was no indulgence, but a mutual tearing to pieces, instead of a brave and steady unity for the common work. The King and I suffered sorely from our people's quarrelsomeness and their inability to pull together; it made our work a thousand times more difficult, more discouraging.

The age-long dream had been realized: Greater Romania was a fact, but it must not be allowed to stand still at that. All that lay before us was uphill work, bristling with unsolved problems, with the necessity of reorganization, of amalgating the different units.

Our country had nearly doubled in size, our people were no more so homogeneous, new elements had to be reckoned with, and these had to be tactfully handled, to be attracted towards us, to be gradually absorbed into one state; many also had to be sieved. There was no longer complete unity of law, coin, or religion. It was all very well to talk of the brothers beyond the mountains – these certainly had the same language, the same aspirations, but they also had their own habits, their pride, their susceptibilities. For centuries they had been oppressed, so they were easily suspicious, very much on their guard, ready to see offence in every approach, and fraternal feelings did not always prove very strong!

Nor must it be forgotten that we were living through a period of acute social upheaval: everywhere new values, new measures, new desires, new hopes, and all this in a world exhausted by four years of appalling carnage which, having emptied Europe of some of her best elements, had brought a new untried generation to the fore, an unseasoned generation, liberated from old traditions, eager for something new, on tiptoe, awaiting some marvellous message, some splendid change which was to open the door to a different and of course better future.

Bolshevism was rampant, destructive propaganda was spreading through every country and with it a stealthy underground effort to overthrow the existing order and institutions, to incite anarchy, to foster the spirit of revolution and discontent.

And added to all this a sort of inhibition seemed to have taken possession of the victorious countries, a sort of blind impotence to cope with the advantages gained, a tendency to waste precious time and opportunity in a sort of aimless groping about instead of bravely tackling the great work of reorganizing, remoulding and rebuilding which lay before them. There was too much spirit of revenge, too great a tendency to look for fault in others, a want of unity, of generosity and spontaneous good understanding. High-sounding words were pronounced and broadcast, but they carried small conviction as they were too little believed by those who pronounced them, so they sounded as empty as they were. Something was wrong somewhere, but what?

Unconsciously I felt all this, but my belief and enthusiasm were not to be killed in a day. I was full of faith, I believed in my mission, and still pursued my ideal with unwearying persistence, so it was excruciatingly disappointing to run up always against closed doors and a despairing lack of understanding and ignorance of essentials. I sensed blindly that a wrong turn was being taken, but my voice was not strong enough to carry among the selfish a truth for which they had no use. Besides, I still hoped that this short-sighted rush, each man for himself, would be but a passing phase, due to a natural state of exhaustion after having been heroic too long, and in my invincible optimism there was even a time when I thought I could help!

But this was not a time to sit still and philosophize, or to deplore that things were not as they should be, nor must I be unfair: even if those who were considered the most important were disappointing, there were many, though there is no special record of their names, who were doing brave and excellent work.

The food question was the most acute; also the hospitals: their disorganization was total, and in leaving, the retreating enemy had laid hands upon all they could, and so, as in Jassy, the work had to be begun all over again, immensely difficult, needing enormous efforts to accomplish very little.

Luckily, about this time, both the American Red Cross and the Hoover organization for feeding poor children began to come our way. They were greeted with the greatest joy, for we were almost as destitute as our beaten neighbours and urgently needed to be helped. I was sending out SOSs in every direction and was also greatly helped by material sent by both the British and the Canadian Red Cross, but the cruel difficulty was that, being so far off, all transports reached us very slowly and uncertainly, so that some of the generous donors were unable to get their gifts shipped to us.

I came together with excellent and efficient workers from these precious American units and they were all willing to co-operate with me and under my direction. I received all who came; we saw each other often and became excellent friends. I called together my most charitable ladies, such as Mme Hélène Pherekyde who all her life had been a relentless promoter of good works, Mme Vintilă Brătianu and her sisters-in-law, Didine Cantacuzino,[4] Olga Sturdza, Simky Lahovary, Mme Popp, and countless others whom it would take too long to enumerate. Also my fat friend, Minister Alecco Constantinescu,[5] was again well to the fore. Rotund and practical, he was ever ready to lend a helping hand, although occasionally party feeling got the better of his charity, which would make me fume and use language more energetic than strictly polite. But for all his annoying little particularities he was a loyal friend and through many years we were firm allies. But I am not going to weigh down these pages with long descriptions of our various useful efforts. They were laudable, and were just then our principal preoccupation, but it would make dull reading.

There is, however, still a pet work I would like to mention, as it was my own private and quite unofficial little undertaking. With Carol's aid I planned an organization for using my 'Regina Maria' ambulances also in time of peace. As all public services had been thrown into confusion, transportation was one of the sorest points. With my *camionettes* [pick-up trucks] we were ready for each and every emergency, we transported the sick, and in times of epidemic we were nearly run to death. We also had machines that transported wood, fuel being a terrible problem that winter, and once, when there was a strike, we even distributed bread throughout the whole town, especially in the poorer quarters. We had no pretensions, we made no propaganda, not even any claims to recognition. We were entirely independent, but the whole thing was run with love and enthusiasm and untiring good will. We never refused to help, and the most unexpected services were asked of us, but we never considered anything beneath our dignity. I ran and ran my brave little Fords for over a dozen years, until one by one they fell to pieces. *Tout passé* . . .

While I was straining every nerve to help stem the ever-increasing tide of distress, Brătianu,[6] accompanied by Mişu and General Coandă,[7] had gone off to join the Paris Peace Conference, whence tidings began to reach us that our prime minister was not exactly having an easy time. Our main allies were inclined to slight us. Having been obliged to treat with the enemy, because of revolutionary Russia's attitude those great ones were ready to drive a hard bargain, trying to ignore our claims, and to put us aside.

I listened to these rumours with clenched fists and racing heart. Knowing what my country had endured and how bravely we had borne overwhelming misfortune, I was filled with overflowing indignation and would have long conferences with faithful friends still in our country, such as General Berthelot and General Greenly, and also with others more lowly, but none the less ardent defenders of our cause, such as Evans Griffith, my Welsh friend of the armoured cars. On all occasions when I defended the rights of my country, my speech waxed eloquent, my cheeks flamed and my eyes became hard, almost fierce – what my children used to call 'Mama's wolf's eyes'. I was well aware of the force of my language, I did not spare my words and I knew how to kindle an answering flame in the eyes of those who were listening to me. And then, all of a sudden, one day, the King asked me if I would consider going to defend our cause abroad. Would I have the courage to do this, to take it upon myself? It was Brătianu who was asking for me. The ardour of my enthusiasm was known to my people and there was no one like a woman for speaking up when deeply stirred. Would I do this?

'I, go to Paris and London? I? To uphold our cause? Unofficially, of course, but all the same, called upon because my people considered no one better than I could do this for Romania?' A shiver of pride shuddered through me. 'I? Yes of course; I was the one designated – yes, I think I felt capable of holding my own, even with the "great three"'!

'What would be the pretext?'

'A visit to Nicky[8] at Eton.'

'Yes, that was a good idea, and what a joy to see Nicky! But would I be allowed to take our three girls with me? I could not leave them alone just now. Our life was too disorganized, nothing as yet was going smoothly, I really could not leave them at home!'

Yes, I could take the girls with me.

'And when must I start?' I was terribly unprepared, ill-equipped for such a sudden departure, so much work on hand, so many dependent upon me. I felt like both laughing and weeping, a thousand tumultuous thoughts and emotions surged through my mind. I had not been abroad for five years! And now this sudden unexpected offer, and such a prospect opening out before me, I . . . chosen to defend my country!

A pardonable excitement took hold of me. Go abroad on such a mission! Right into the heart of things. I felt a little giddy, I really must have time to collect my thoughts.

The King smiled kindly upon me; he understood the degree of my agitation, and to calm me he began to explain the plan of things, and while he talked I contrived to gather my scattered wits, began to grasp the whole proposition, to see my way more clearly, to quietly weigh the difficulties, to gather my strength.

'Yes I would go – and I would do my best. It was a mission I could undertake, I felt capable of doing so, I was not nervous or afraid. I would like to do it. But did he think I could go first to Jassy? Jassy was waiting for me; I had promised to go back for a few days. Good old Jassy felt so forsaken without us; might I go?'

Yes, I might go to Jassy; besides, the foreign journey had to be organized: travelling was still very difficult; there were not yet any regular trains, the routes were still uncertain, as were the frontiers, and when a queen travels . . . Yes, there was still time.

So with my two elder daughters, I returned for a week to Jassy, dear town of our exile, and Jassy received us with emotion, opened its arms to us, who for two fear-filled years had shared its every hope, its every danger, its every want. Jassy, that town which had been so uncomfortably overcrowded and now was silent, empty and forsaken.

What memories crushed in upon us! Every turn of the streets, every house, every stone was familiar, down to the distressing bumps of the atrocious pavement, some of the holes of which had been precariously filled for our reception, Jassy having done its best to put on a festive face. But new bunting was not to be found; the poor old flags waving in the wind were pale and colourless, which made their effort to look bright and festive rather pathetic.

Hardly had I reached my house than, according to old habit, my room was overrun by all those needing advice, sympathy, help. The town, which had once rather resented our invasion, was today feeling abandoned, lonely, even a little slighted. Its citizens had got accustomed to having us in their midst, to counting on our aid, our encouragement, so that today their welcome was not free from complaint and lamentation.

I had to call upon all my strength and every ounce of my tact to meet all their needs and to allay the resentment that Jassy was no longer the centre of our world.

I revisited all the hospitals, schools, alms-houses, and all the different institutions which were being run as efficiently as possible. The Metropolitan Pimen,[9] General Petala,[10] Olga Sturdza were working hand in hand, upholding with energy those charities still so needed in these days of want. I was not allowed a moment's breathing space and my girls bravely did their share; they too were overwhelmed by the memory of all that had been.

A touching and noisy farewell at the station, many blessings and good wishes – many regrets, many promises, words of encouragement – and our train relentlessly carried us away again, away from Jassy and its poignant souvenirs.

THREE

The Peace Conference

Now we had to get ready for our journey to Paris and London. Effervescent excitement, questions to settle, complicated arrangements to make; the journey itself was difficult to organize as trains were still irregular, their routes unsettled and not always safe, and frontiers having shifted it was difficult to decide today which land belonged to whom! The new sizes and shapes of countries were being settled in Paris round 'the green table', where the so-called big men of the world had gathered together to discuss problems too deep and too complicated for even the most intelligent brains, and to Paris I was to go!

It was not without uneasiness that I parted from the King. I knew he was overwhelmed by problems. He had efficient and devoted helpers, but his task was arduous and I was the one with whom he could most unrestrainedly discuss every question; with me he had no need to be careful or tactful. I sometimes annoyed him, but I was safe, difficulties did not appal me; besides, I had an unending supply of good humour and was fundamentally buoyant, a quality not to be despised in times of perplexity and stress. He would be lonely without me and the children. Nevertheless he was eager to see me start upon the mission for which I had been chosen. He believed in me and thought, as others did, that I could do good work and that Romania might profit from the popularity which had come to me during the war years.

The world had not yet settled down to hard, unemotional indifference, there was still enthusiasm in the air, and, with it, hopeful expectation.

In most lives there comes a moment when a person has the opportunity to live up to the top of his capacities – when it is, so to

21

speak, his day. Now it was my day and I must not miss it, but live up to the best there was in me; the chance might not be given me again.

It is not very easy to conjure up anew this particular period of my life, nor to describe the glad impetuosity which carried me right into the heart of things. It was overfull, so teeming with possibilities that the excitement of it was like wine running through my veins. It is difficult to resist the pride and joy of being popular and I was no exception to this rule; I liked being liked! My enormous vitality answered the call made upon it; it was not in vain that I was born vigorous and full of health. The *joie de vivre* of my youth had been gradually transformed into a strong desire to live up to the peak of my possibilities, an urge not to waste an ounce of my strength while my country needed it. As never before, I felt eager to give my best in every way, to face and overcome the most difficult problems, to stand firm in my belief in myself and humanity.

It is a grand thing to feel overwhelmingly alive and to be carried forward on the wings of your enthusiasm so that others are swept along with you. I also carried joy within me, and joy is irresistible; few have the courage to surrender to joy; they are generally too diffident, too self-conscious, too afraid of criticism, of ridicule, but, with an impetuosity belonging generally only to the young, I allowed joy and confidence to take complete possession of my whole being, setting aside my doubts and even my grief. There was work to do and I felt I could do it, so I just rushed forward with my great desire to win, without reserve, trusting to my instinct; and the love of all things and all men shone like a light in my heart.

All this is a long time ago, but looking back on it from my retreat of today, I seem to see myself standing very upright in glaring sunshine, and what is more, enjoying it to the full, and I confess I am glad I was allowed to live through that time, when I believed in myself and in others. It was worthwhile, it brought me into contact with interesting people, and it permitted me to use my wits, to give every ounce of my energy. The long school of suppression lay behind me, those endless years of fear when I was never allowed to discover my own capacities; also the dreadful shadow of war lay behind me, and now for the first time I strode forth right into the glare of the world, to hold my own as best I could. Being courageous, I liked to face things squarely, to look all men in the eye, perhaps rather dangerously indifferent to strict conventions, but sure of my convictions, and bravely ready to confess my colours and to stick to my guns.

Yes, I enjoyed it, without undue vanity or special ambition, but as a good fighter who revels in the fray!

Finally, everything settled, we started off for Paris in a special train, with no end of uniformed followers, and when our frontiers (they too somewhat unsettled) were crossed, a guard of French soldiers was given us under the command of Captain Perrain, an aviator who had been cited 'à l'ordre du jour' seven times for bravery, a very nice man with whom we made great friends.

We had a tremendous send-off at the station: everybody had crowded together to bid us farewell and to wish us good luck – the government, foreign ministers and officers, diplomats, generals, eager ladies with flowers and a knowing look in their eyes because they guessed I was being sent abroad on a 'mission' and this filled them with pleasurable excitement. I was considered a sort of 'mascot'; once more my people looked upon me as their brightest hope, so I departed, carrying with me my country's blessing and good will.

Tired out as I was physically, the journey was a great rest. Progress was slow; everywhere there was a shortage of coal, in parts floods due to melted snow.

We never knew exactly which country we were travelling through, as the new frontiers had not yet been fixed. Everything was exciting, interesting, new and rather strange. Where were we? Who did this country belong to today? There was a feeling of spring in the air and when we reached Fiume the fruit-trees were in blossom, white and pale pink against a blue-washed sky. My heart sang within me; beautiful, blessed sight! Leaning far out of the window, I inhaled the keen sea air, my lungs expanding rapturously, and here too, a French guard of honour! We got out of our train to be greeted by many officers, including a very nice English general, Scott. Accustomed to making gifts, I had with me provisions of tobacco, so with my daughters I walked down the ranks giving cigarettes to the smart-looking, blue-coated soldiers peering at us from under little helmets – everywhere an exhilarating atmosphere of expectation and mutual good will.

During the long hours between the receptions, I lay on my bed, luxuriously enjoying the unwonted rest, reading, thinking, chatting with my children – they, too, enchanted with everything, Ileana looking at me with enormous, expectant blue eyes. Travelling was new to her and everything was wonderful, waiting to be explored, full of hidden possibilities.

Before we arrived in Paris, Collette Willie, the well-known writer of so many charming and witty books, came onto our train to interview me. In her hands she held a bouquet of gorgeous orchids! Their exotic beauty burst upon me like a revelation. They were a sort of message that the war was over, that there were places where such pleasant things as hot-houses still existed – places of luxury and plenty! After the long dearth of the war years, these delicate orchids were something of a miracle.

I liked Collette Willie. She was a wonderful talker, her language was eloquent, her words full of subtle homage and praise – she was a sort of forerunner of what was to come.

Then at last our train ran into the Paris station – and here I feel that to quote from some pages of my diary would give a real picture of those days so incredibly full of events and people.

PARIS, WEDNESDAY, 5 MARCH 1919

Paris! Yes, we have actually reached Paris, today, so to speak, the centre of the world. I can hardly believe that we are really here!

Our train ran into the station punctually at 8.45 a.m. Unaccustomed to fast trains, we all felt somewhat bewildered and tremendously shaken about. I was given an unforeseen reception, although I'm not here officially; there was a dense and confusing crowd. All my Romanians were there of course, and endless French dignitaries, generals, officers, many personal friends and so many flowers that I did not know how to cope with them. The public cheered and the photographers persecuted me like a swarm of mosquitoes. From the moment I set foot on the ground I was seized by a wild rush I shall never be able to describe!

Faces, faces, and flowers in such gorgeous masses that I was almost buried beneath them, and everybody talking, chattering, each man wanting to tell me his news, to impart his special information, each, according to his or her personal point of view, and during these conversations the door was continually opening and ever more flowers were brought, whole woods of lilacs, roses, calla, orchids, irises, daffodils, freesias, violets, as though to make up for the several years' flower fast. My room has become a real flower-show, I can hardly turn round. I am beautifully installed in the state apartments of the Ritz. Everybody fusses about me, I am treated as a sort of heroine and must try to fit into this unexpected role which is thrust upon me. All the journalists of the globe seem to be circling round me, they buzz like swarms of bees, waylay me, dogging my every step. It is a modern conception of things I am unaccustomed to; everything has become so different! I smilingly pass through the rush, noise, confusion, doing my best to remain calm and not to lose my head.

Everything and everybody presses in upon me at once. Brătianu came for a long talk to give me a picture of the political situation, to explain whom I must see, how I must behave, in what way I can be helpful. But goodness, it is confusing; everything rushed in upon me at once before I had even been able to take off my hat or wash my hands!

And, waiting for me outside, is Paris – great humming, distracting, entrancing Paris – which I hardly know at all, just now overflowing with English and Americans and goodness knows what other nationalities. Old friends keep pouring in, doctors and officers who have been in Romania, their faces all beaming with welcome – then there are all those I met in 1913 when I was in Paris for the first time: artists, authors, dukes, marquises before that war, once comfortable people, and what not else, and all the time, in every corner, hungrily, expectant journalists, ever on the lookout to catch me. A nightmare!

I am interviewed, photographed, pressed, honoured, invited here, there, everywhere, and all this is so-called unofficial.

The atmosphere, so I was told, was not favourable to Romania, but it certainly is favourable to me! If only they do not suffocate me with their attentions, and if I can make use of my evident popularity to help my country, then all will be well. I will not say that it is disagreeable to be made such a fuss of, but it is overpowering, and one day is not long enough, and one head and brain do not suffice for all that is offered me. Besides, I'm so far from home, communication is slow and difficult, and I've left many who depend upon me, for whom my departure means a blank. No one must be forgotten; also I must get into touch with Nicky at Eton . . . I can hardly believe I am so near my Nicky-boy!

After lunch, taken in the company of Elise Brătianu[1] and the Antonescus (our minister here), I tried to get off for a walk with my daughters who were stamping with impatience to get out, but I was not able to escape until Antonescu[2] had, in his turn, tried to initiate me into all the work I am expected to do. Finally, however, I got off and we trotted down the Rue de la Paix, but were so terribly mobbed that we had to take our motor and drive to another place; there we again got out and walked. Bought a beautiful book for Nando, for Carol; the shops are entrancing!

Wherever I go, the public runs after me. They even run out of the shops, the *vendeuses* pursue me and flowers are continually pressed into my hands. The weather is beautiful; I was much too hot in my coat and had to take it off. We met two amiable officers who volunteered to carry it back for me to the hotel. Elisabetha[3] and Mignon[4] were delighted, but in these crowded conditions shopping is difficult, nor are we any longer accustomed to seeing such a magnificent spread of goods! We are like country bumpkins.

Returned for tea to the Ritz. Henriette Vendôme[5] and husband came to greet me, such a lot to tell each other, so much sadness also. Nando's younger brother Carlo has just succumbed to the Spanish flu, Josephine is a widow and their castle on the Rhine is in the parts occupied by the English! A confusing state of things. But I was so pleased to see Henriette.

At six a big reception of the Romanian colony, and until bed-time a steady flow of people coming to see me. French, English, Americans, Russians, endless war acquaintances, exclamations of joy, talk, talk, talk – oh dear, my poor head! And this in only the beginning, tomorrow it will be worse!

PARIS, THURSDAY, 6 MARCH 1919

I shall never be able to describe the rush and excitement I am living in. What ought to be done in two weeks is being crushed into a few short, hurried days. I had foreseen something of the kind, but was not prepared for this!

I cannot defend myself against the flood, I must just cope with it as best I can and call upon my unquenchable energy and power of resistance to give me courage and insight. But it needs patience to see everybody, listen to everybody, answer everybody. To cap it all, my wardrobe is in an awful state, my dresses are five years old and almost comic in this centre of fashion. But how to find time to see dressmakers, choose hats, cloaks, shoes, linen and stockings, if I am called to interview ministers and politicians from eight o'clock onwards? Then there is Ballif, there is Simky[6] and Irene,[7] my ladies, also my children and, to cap it all, I was not able to bring my maids with me as they are Germans, so I am served by Mme Pantazi (my hat-maker) and her daughter. They are ardently devoted, but do not know the everyday routine. This complicates matters and makes dressing and getting ready in a hurry very difficult. My room is overrun by dressmakers, hat-makers, shoemakers who fill it with cardboard boxes. They are as bad as the reporters and photographers! They press and tempt me and try to persuade me that I need everything they want to sell. And I do not like the fashions! Horrid short skimpy dresses, tight, sleeveless and the evening dresses as nearly naked as possible, made of separate pieces of material which hardly hold together, leaving arms and back completely bare, if possible also the legs! Preposterous gowns for a queen, to which I will not submit for all the coercing of dressmakers with big names, who try to make me feel small and out of fashion.

27

But I remain firm and will not be rushed into ordering things unsuitable for my age, size and dignity! But all this takes time and I am never left a moment's breathing space. Besides I have a natural craving to see something of Paris, to be occasionally allowed a single little hour when I can do what I want, not only what others want.

This day seems to have been chiefly sacrificed to the Press. All the journalists of the universe seem to crop up like swarms of fleas, and my advisers insisted that I must receive them, so I submitted. But just imagine a door opening and being ushered into a cage, peopled by forty real live journalists, and forty of them hanging over you asking you every imaginable sort of question. I did my very best, looked them straight in the eye and spoke up bravely for my country. But now, even in sleep, they continue to haunt me! There were even Poles and Japanese and what not else . . .! These were received last; first came French, English, Italians, Americans; and when I thought I was done with them, it all began again in a big room downstairs. I only hope I really kept my wits about me and that my French was not too English!

Besides the Press, I held a big reception for all manner of people, old friends and new acquaintances. One stumbles upon all sorts of unexpected people like quaint old General Verblumasky, with whom I had worked at Jassy, and Jack Chamberlain, an American boy I had known years ago in Romania. But all the same I did get out for a short hour and bought Ileana a watch she was longing to possess. 'Oh! Mama I did see such a lovely watch in town!' Paris of course being the town! So I had to find that special watch!

Flowers kept pouring in stupendous masses. Tomorrow I'm to see the great Clemenceau. I saw Anna de Noailles[8] and enjoyed her beyond words, and thus it went on all day without a pause. Even when I was in bed people still came to see me! It is certainly hard work, but I must carry it through!

PARIS, FRIDAY, 7 MARCH 1919

A lovely sunny day, but I was never allowed even to dress in peace. Everyone wants to be the first to get at me in the morning; I cannot even quietly take my bath. To cap it all, the whole of Paris seems to crowd into my room with dresses, hats and every imaginable kind of clothes, which I am supposed to need. How on earth they get there I cannot imagine – and every creature, down to the *portière*, seems to have his or her protégée from whom I am expected to buy. But I am firm when it comes to buying, I will not allow myself to be coerced into ridiculous expense. Besides, at this moment, when my country is still suffering so, I cannot spend big sums on myself. Also, I've quite lost the habit of gorgeous attire, so I can, without temptation, look upon all the treasures being endlessly dangled before my eyes. The truth is, I have so entirely become 'the first servant of my country' that it entirely dominates me. All vanities of yore have for the moment been set aside for a sterner reality; nor after the dreadful war years can I reaccustom myself to plenty. I do not feel justified in spending money on myself, although I am being so bewilderingly glorified. But the atmosphere of Paris is so saturated with 'fashion' that it is a regular struggle to stick to my ideas as my ladies, my maids, and all those around me have succumbed to the Paris craze for clothes!

But how I am being flattered and lionized! I am simply being lifted up to the skies. It is lucky I am 43 or I might really imagine I am irresistible; as it is, I feel what a degree of natural magnetism I have, and this is independent of age. Besides, the French know how to appreciate a woman.

Having with the usual difficulty struggled into my clothes, I found Brătianu and Mişu already waiting for me in my 'salon', especially eager, as today I am to encounter the 'Tigre'. Brătianu, who was evidently somewhat nervous, was lengthy and my head ached. But I patiently imbibed all the wisdom with which my two politicians felt they must fill me, and promised to do my best with the formidable old gentleman I was to encounter. While we were talking, Victor Antonescu rushed in, full of excitement, overjoyed at the way the Press comments upon my yesterday's interview.

Being our minister here he has the pleasurable feeling that he has something to do with my success, and I am only too delighted he should have his share; he is so eager, and loves his country. As to his wife, my little Lise or Mme Butterfly, as I call her, she is an angel. I'm glad the Press is nice about me, it's something gained for Romania! All honour shown to me is shown to my country – so if Paris goes off its head a bit about me, all the better: it opens the way for the work I have to do.

The principal event today was my interview with Clemenceau.

Paris was golden with sunshine and the smell of spring was in the air as Antonescu, Ballif and Simky accompanied me. I was received with military honours, and our national anthem was played beautifully, like a solemn hymn. The old gentleman came running down the stairs to meet me as though he were quite a young man. What struck me as queer was that he wore gloves. We went upstairs together, followed by numerous officers, then he took me into his bureau alone, for a tête-à-tête.

I always imagined I would like Clemenceau,[9] and I did. He looks the old man he is, but otherwise there is nothing old about him, and not the smallest little corner of his brain is old or stiff. There is the directness of a soldier about him, but he is certainly stubborn. He has some grievances against Romania to which he sticks like a leech, and at several moments we glared at each other like two fighters. I quite enjoyed it, but he certainly had no intention of being convinced. He attacked me 'de front' about Romania having treated for peace, and when I explained what had led up to this, and why it had come about, he looked me ferociously in the eye: '*Ne me racontez pas ces histoires là, vous étiez pour la résistance, vous!*' [Don't tell me those stories – you yourself were for the resistance!] This was a knock-out, but I bravely confessed that being a woman, I had a passionate 'point du vue', and being at that time so near to events, I had had no 'recule' from which to see the situation as a whole. I believed in the Allied victory so I was ready to hang on by the skin of my teeth, but whether this had been a wise attitude is for others to judge. I had not come to speak about myself but to modify his attitude towards Romania, and this I meant to fight, as I had fought my battles during our tragic war years. Unfortunately I cannot write down all our conversation; I am too pressed for time. I cannot say how far I convinced him, but I know I did not bore him, because when once I half-rose to leave, so as not to steal his precious time, he impatiently waved me back to my seat 'I have plenty of time for you; you do not whine, you speak up, I like that!' If I touched his passionate old heart or not, that I cannot know, but my face brought him a pleasanter picture of Romania, my smile was more convincing than tiresome political debates. The feeling I had that he liked me was confirmed by what he afterwards said to Antonescu: *'Une reine telle que la vôtre on ne peut la recevoir qu'avec honneurs militaires, le Maréchal Foch en tête!'* [A Queen like yours can only be received with military honours, with Marshal Foch at the head!] I left to the sound of the Marseillaise, the air filled with golden dust.

For lunch I had the company of the English ambassador Lord Derby and his wife. We got on splendidly together. I had also invited the Brătianus, and Mişu. Brătianu was very excited to know how I had got on with the 'Tigre', who does not like Brătianu, declaring that he has a 'lamenting voice' – *'et je n'aime pas ça!'* I don't like that!

After lunch, endless audiences and a surprise visit from Sandro,[10] Xenia's[11] husband, we talked about Russia's awful disaster. Then Eulalia of Spain[12] appeared, looking incredibly young, full of talk and very funny, but hardly a good word for anybody; her eye is watchful and she has no love for her neighbour.

Particularly warm was my meeting with Albert Thomas, who asked to see me. In his joy 'du revoir' he almost embraced me, remembering every detail of his visit to Romania. He talked and laughed, and laughed and talked and was altogether too delightful. He declared he loved Romania and would stick up for her with all his might, and approved of my having come unofficially, declaring that that was the right way to come, that thus the 'peuple' could enjoy me more, and that I must go about among them as much as possible, to get the human touch, Paris was delighted to see me, etc. . . . etc. . . . He was in bursting good humour, *'et rigolait tout le temps'* [and laughed continuously], and perspired as freely in the cold season as in the warm; it seems to be one of his particularities. I think it is because he talks so much and about so many subjects at once. St Aulaire, who came afterwards, severely aristocratic, was his

31

direct antipode. He too has remained our warm friend and bravely defends us. Having lived through all our tragedy with us, his word has weight.

But this did not end my activities, I still had to go to a reception given by Brătianu for many interesting people. I saw many friends and had a long talk with Paleologue, former French ambassador at Petersburg, who is most interesting. There I also found the Ruspolis, Leo Kennedy, Baron Beyens, and our friend Nicolai who had been in Romania.

There is neither space nor time to enumerate everybody I saw, but I must still mention General Thomson, Mme de Gauney and above all Anna de Noailles, who was making my daughters laugh in a corner of the salon, her very short dress pulled right up over her knees, and her flow of talk equal to Albert Thomas's, though quite another style!

I still had to go to the opera. I dressed all in white, but I have no jewels.[13] The Bolsheviks have got them all – but although my dress had nothing to do with the fashion of the day, I did my best to do honour to the reception given me, which was semi-official, and our national anthem was played with special fervour; they have a particular way of playing it here which makes it very beautiful. The house was three-quarters full of American uniforms. Endless people came into our box during the entractes; there was an atmosphere of tense emotion – my daughters were enjoying themselves; this is a very exciting time for them.

After all this, bed was not unwelcome, but astonishing as it may sound, I was not really tired!

The six days I spent in Paris were every one of them as breathlessly overfilled as the two cited from my diary; in fact the pace increased. It was all I could do to hold my ground and meet every demand. It was all too much, but just had to be endured. It was probably my enthusiasm which carried me through and also that immense desire to serve my country to the utmost. When asked why I had come to Paris, I answered: 'To give Romania a face – she needs a face, so I have come to give her mine.' And this I succeeded in doing. At that hour I was Romania – I say so proudly because I feel I have a right to say it. There are few I then worked with still alive to confirm this statement, but if they could rise from their graves they would not gainsay me!

Immense sympathy was shown to me everywhere, my ever-growing popularity carried me as if on the crest of a wave, and the exhilaration was such that I seemed to feel no fatigue, and when tried to the verge of desperation, my sense of humour was always there to smooth down any irritation.

Probably I shall be criticized for speaking thus about myself, but it would not be my true story if I did not tell things as they were. There was no selfishness in my behaviour, but I would not have been the full-blooded human being I am if I had not enjoyed feeling my force. But it was an effort not to be occasionally confused and overwhelmed by the situation.

My days began regularly with a visit from Brătianu and Antonescu, and often also Mişu. They would appear punctually at nine so as to coach me for my day's work. I listened devoutly to their wise exhortations, but with each passing day their faith in me grew. They understood that I had better be given a loose rein. I did not always strictly obey their advice; I had my own ways and means which were often more efficacious than theirs, if somewhat less conventional. It was a case of 'rushing in to win'. My anxious gentlemen began to feel as though they had placed their money on a winning horse, so by degrees they eased off, encouraging me to go my own way, at my own pace.

But time was my enemy; it was like a flood continually threatening to drown me. Everybody seemed to want to be received, or to receive me. It needed a great deal of attention not to fix three things for the same hour – not to become hopelessly confused by the excess of demands, the excess of petitioners, it needed more than my untrained brain to keep each case separate.

On the day following my interview with Clemenceau I was quasi-officially received at the Elysée; a whole battalion several thick was lined up all round the inner square, and I was received like a king. Before leaving, an honour was done me, never yet done to a queen:

I was asked to review the troops. This is just the sort of thing I can do in best style without any embarrassment, so I marched down the ranks looking the soldiers straight in the eye while the most invigorating salute was played upon gay-sounding bugles, whose sound I love. My Romanians wept with joy and my own heart was beating with quite justifiable pride. My people understood that this was a special tribute paid to the woman who had so staunchly upheld their country's honour.

It was the first time I had been at the Elysée. Poincaré[14] received me most graciously; he was friend of Romania but had no great ease of manner: I felt there was an underlying shyness about him which seemed to restrain him. His speech was abrupt and a little dry, but he was ready to discuss with me things concerning my country.

As to Mme Poincaré, perhaps she also was shy, but she certainly lacked the usual French amiability. She wore an entrancing little orange velvet cape, which satisfied my colour-loving eye. On my left sat Mr Pichon,[15] minister of foreign affairs, a talkative and friendly gentleman. Conversation ran generally upon the same subjects and all things were full of intense interest, but I got a bit confused about all the important old gentlemen I met, which of course ought not to have been the case!

A most select company sat round the exquisitely laid table, we ate wonderful food on old china in a perfect setting, and after the meal was over I was able to talk to several pleasant interesting people such as Maréchal Foch, the celebrated painter Bonnat, and others.

That same afternoon there was a solemn 'séance à l'Académie des Beaux Arts' where I was admitted as the only woman amidst the most doct company of very old and important gentlemen. This was also a very special honour; I felt deeply flattered, but not being 'une intellectuelle', only normally intelligent, I felt somewhat bewildered about all the fuss they made of my talents etc. . . . I was not entirely convinced that I deserved these conspicuous honours, whilst I had accepted the military tribute paid to me without a blush.

I was pompously ushered to a chair in the celebrated old room of 'l'Institut' and had to listen to a very flattering speech of welcome by

Mr Charles Vidor,[16] to which I answered in a few simple, unprepared words. When deeply moved I can luckily always express myself, but emotion generally makes my English accent more conspicuous. Anyhow, my amiable old colleagues were more than enchanted with me and we said extraordinarily sweet things to each other, and then I and my daughters were conducted to a second building where we listened to some exquisite music and conversed with innumerable elderly gentlemen with famous names recognized all over the world, among whom were Henri Bergson, the great philosopher, and François Fleming.

I was soon to leave Paris to go to England, where I had been invited to Buckingham Palace – but with the plan of returning afterwards to France's gay and overcrowded capital to keep many flattering engagements forced upon me, almost against my will.

Each day was a greater rush than the last, and those who came to see me were as a river in flood. I was in touch with so many different countries, and Paris just then seemed to be a meeting place of countless nationalities. All manner of men crowded my rooms eating up the hours of the day; it was vastly interesting and not a little confusing: French, English, Romanians, Americans, Italians, Russians, Serbs, Greeks, even Japanese. And each man or woman who came had in their wake a trail of followers and friends, all eager to make my acquaintance, to express their feelings, to offer their services, their advice, who came to give or to receive. A dozen languages were talked at my table – voices, voices, voices. I was eternally switching my attention from one question to another; the press, hurry, rush and diversity of it all was enough to loosen the screws of brains better regulated than mine.

Closing my eyes, I pass in review many of those who came to me then: Briand, Deshanel, Jules Cambon, Dubox, Paleologue, House, Hoover, Davison, head of the American Red Cross, Venizelos and many more.

Briand[17] was a great friend of Romania, he was helpful to Brătianu and lent a patient ear to our needs. Deshanel was polite, elegant and especially attentive, his language, even for a Frenchman, was beautifully laden with delicately flattering words. Colonel House at that moment was representing the President[18] during his absence in England, I think, and Belgium. Our interview was short and I had no time to become well acquainted. For Mr Davison I felt immediate sympathy, and spontaneously, then and there, he became my friend and helper.

Mr Venizelos, at that time a much-trumpeted favourite, was well to the fore: wisdom was supposed to flow from his ready tongue and even the Great Powers were inclined to lend him an ear. Very sure of his own charm, his voice was soft, his manner ingratiating, his smile was as the smile of a professional beauty who had a place to gain in the world . . . one felt he was out to seduce.

Mr Hoover was his direct opposite: he had no desire to charm! Sparing of words, dry, reserved, frowning a little, his attitude was not particularly congenial, but my old friend Colonel Boyle, who had worked for some time with him in Belgium, held him in high esteem and made me promise to see him as he was sure Mr Hoover could, if he wanted, be of great help to my country; so we met and talked earnestly, as I had heard of his great competence, and I had just cause for which to plead.

Mr Hoover had no sentimentality about the countries he was helping and had no special sympathy for Romania and her queen, but as his magnificently organized units were spreading over many distressed areas, his desire for equity made him extend his work also among our poor and starving population; for this I shall be everlastingly grateful. Later, during our campaign against the Bolsheviks in Hungary, he took sides against us, a difference of opinion which led to an exchange of letters in which we agreed to disagree!

At that time all conversations were weighty, important, charged with interest, full of possibilities, hopes and fears; some were even like skating on thin ice! I was sailing ahead, bravely fighting for my country's interests, with an immense desire that our side of the question should be understood. Patriotic ardour made me doubt of nothing; my convictions were so strong that every courage was mine. I never paused to consider how others might judge or criticize or even ridicule my attitude, and Romania believed in her envoy!

There was still enthusiasm in the air, a show of fraternity, of mutual good will; outstretched hands still desired to be generous, some still believed in the friendship they offered . . . and around a large green table, important gentlemen were piecing together a new Europe, and talking of justice and peace.

Having quit the world's arena, today, and looking back on that time, I marvel somewhat sadly at the uncrushable enthusiasm which lent me faith and gave me wings. There was no doubt something quixotic about it, but my belief in the quasi-sanctity of the fight I was fighting excuses my exaggeration of feeling.

Almost twenty years ago! Yet sometimes it seems but yesterday. From the half-shade of my retreat today, I look out upon others fighting the eternal battle and wish I did not feel quite so wise, for 'in wisdom is much grief . . .'. We overcome the years to be finally overcome by time. There is a certain peace in realizing that 'All is vanity and vexation of spirit', but we must not realize it too soon, or we would lay down our arms before we should. The world needs believers, fighters, enthusiasts. I was a believer in those days; the thought that my efforts might be futile never entered my head. I never doubted they would bear fruit; I did my share, without counting the cost; I was a glad fighter, convinced I was right, and this is what made it worthwhile.

Younger hands bear today the lighted torch – I do not always appreciate their methods or understand their creed, but it is their turn now to rush in and win. With heart and soul, I wish them good luck!

It was at a lunch given for me by Mr Balfour that I met Mr Lloyd George.[19] We were a small party including Lord and Lady Derby, Sir Robert Cecil[20] and a few others, so conversation at table was general and flowed pleasantly, touching upon many varied subjects. Mr Lloyd George loved talking, company stimulated him. He was full of fun and wit, thoroughly enjoying his own jokes. I let myself be carried away by his undeniable charm, while wondering how much he really understood about Europe outside the British Empire. I never dared forget, however pleasant their company might be, that these important gentlemen were concocting a new world, and like the mother of a very large and exceedingly distressed family, I wondered if they would understand, or even be interested, in my country's needs. I had to gather all my wits about me to be continually on the alert, ready, at the right moment, to slip in a word here and there which allowed me, unostentatiously, to lead up to my own subject. This was a pleasant luncheon party, not a political meeting and must not be rendered uncongenial with heavy talk.

My conversation had to run along and fit in with theirs, but occasionally, while amusing them with some quaint anecdote, lightly told, I could catch their interest and lead the conversation towards those things nearest my heart. It was no easy task and needed some tact. Brătianu had warned me that Mr Balfour[21] was not very kindly inclined towards Romania, and being so very suave and charming, combined with a certain absent-mindedness, it was not easy to discover a chink in his armour.

I realized only too well that these busy, big men could hardly be expected to understand the intricate hopes, desires, ambitions, preventions, nor the feuds or even the geography of that group of small countries 'in the Near East'. Romania, Serbia, Greece, Bulgaria, Turkey – we were all classed together in their minds as 'troublesome little states always too ready to flare up and become a nuisance at inconvenient moments'. But during the Great War, we had done our share, some of us had been useful, if only to play off one against the other. We had suddenly come to the front and could no longer be totally ignored, and patiently or otherwise, we had to be given a hearing.

Having myself been born in a 'Great Country', I could only too well comprehend their mentality, but through long years of uneasy learning, I had also come to understand the mentality of the 'small' ones, and was today even the defender of one of those. The situation was not without humour, and I smiled inwardly, while retaining the attitude expected of me. I sat there among them, letting all Brătianu's pressing instructions filter through my brain, remembering every one of his arguments why we had more rights to Transylvania, which our neighbours (Hungary) also claimed, and in spite of my ardent Romanian patriotism, there was a second 'me', nothing to do with the mission, that was thoroughly amused. I had an uncomfortably clear perception of how indifferent they really were to the anxious hopes of 'those Balkan' countries, which is certainly the name they gave us when we were not in the room! I almost felt their thoughts and surmised something of their irritation and impatience when our rights and claims came under discussion.

In their pleasant, easy company, where I felt so much at home, I was dangerously tempted to take a rest from 'patriotism' and allow what I like to call 'my all-round brain' to have full sway and to talk with them 'beyond the limits of frontiers and nationalities'. I could so easily, with the purely 'thinking' part of myself, slip over into their attitude, familiar to me from birth. It was like floating comfortably along with the tide, but I also divined that a task had been set before them beyond the competence of even the cleverest brain. We small countries were but pawns in their great game, but we were living pawns; we too had our pride, our aspirations, our hopes, our rights, our sufferings, and today fate had placed me among the 'small'. Their cause was mine, so I must shut away all temptation to understand too well their side of the question. To walk in the middle of the road could not be indulged in, unless everybody was ready to do the same!

Sometimes one must put on blinkers; we have not yet reached the happy stage when we are able to stand 'au delà de la mêlée'.

Before leaving Paris for London I wished to carry the beautiful flowers brought to me in such vast quantities to the graves on the battlefields, so under the guidance of a French officer, Colonel Nodet, I set off for the whole day accompanied by Mignon, Ballif, our minister Victor Antonescu and our military attaché. The impression received of what I saw is best quoted from my diary:

A strenuous day visiting by motor the French battlefields, the churchyards, the devastated towns and villages; a pitiable and terrible sight. We went to Noyon, passing by Courcy, le Château Chauny, Antreville, coming back by Lassigny, Montdidier. No words can adequately describe what cruel devastation we have seen; we seemed to be wandering through some unimaginable terrible dream. Nothing has remained standing; all is ruin and destruction. The towns and villages have been entirely obliterated, they exist no more, are a thing of the past, can never be brought to life again; nothing can ever rise again out of those heaps of stone, mortar and brick. The land spreading around is a vast waste from out of which the spectres of decapitated, lacerated, charred trees stand like sickening apparitions, belonging to nothing that has any name upon earth. And everywhere the ground is torn to pieces by large round cavities filled with water. Out of this horror-filled chaos, dead villages with their skeleton churches rise like expiring martyrs crying out their agony to the indifferent heavens. It is terrible – '*l'irréparable*'.

The castle of Courcy was perhaps the most heart-breaking sight of all. It is said that this was voluntary destruction. It was one of the most celebrated beautiful castles, dating from the Middle Ages, with its tremendous basements and prodigious round towers. Not even a silhouette is left; it is not even a beautiful ruin; it simply exists no longer!

Destruction – utter, complete, irretrievable. A monstrous event has happened in these regions, an event that decades, perhaps centuries cannot repair. Along all the roads, row upon row of fruit trees have been brutally cut down so that they can never again bloom or burst into leaf. Dead, everything dead, and graves everywhere, poor, humble little crosses like those I have seen by the hundred in the hills and plains of Romania.

We drove for twelve whole hours and lunched in a corner of a devastated house in Noyon where literally not a single building remains intact. We climbed over the ruins, talking to a few stray inhabitants who had crept back to what were once their homes, and visited the skeleton cathedral whose gaunt remains look sadly on what was once a flourishing little town.

Wherever I saw graves I covered them with roses, lilacs, carnations, violets, orchids and mimosa, all the precious blooms brought to me by great and small. Today my vases are empty!

On my return I was asked to receive General Pénélon, who, in the name of the president, brought me the Grand Cordon de la Légion d'Honneur.

Next day I drove to the Elysée to thank Mr Poincaré for the honour done me. We had a long talk and he was most pleasant and very kindly inclined towards our country. He told me that Clemenceau had much changed towards us since 'I had given Romania a face'. The fifty engines I had so insistently pleaded for have been granted and are being immediately sent off; we were urgently in need of these as our railway equipment is completely ruined. I did not know how much I had been able to achieve materially, but of one thing I was pleasantly aware: I had created another atmosphere for Romania, and this, in particular, had been my mission. I had certainly done my best, straining every nerve, every faculty, to be worthy of the confidence my country had placed in me, and in leaving for London I promised to come back, as Paris still desired to honour me in several ways. These ten short days had been too much of a rush.

FOUR

England

Paris gave me a tremendous send-off: Mr Poincaré, his wife, and endless officials came to the station, friends of all nationalities, and I had solemnly to promise that I would come back.

Elisabetha asked to remain in Paris: she did not want to tear herself away from many French friends, so I left her under the care of Elise Brătianu and was accompanied only by Mignon and Ileana,[1] both of them in a fever of excitement to go to Mama's beloved England.

The journey seemed very short after the endless, meandering way we had travelled between Romania and Paris.

Everywhere generals, mayors, officials of every sort with magnificent flowers and a wonderful flow of beautifully expressed wishes of welcome mingled with flattering words of praise. It had become the fashion to receive me as a heroine, 'la Grande Amie de la France'; it was certainly very pleasant and stimulating, and as all honour done to me was also being done to my country, I rejoiced and my daughters were beside themselves with delight. So many pleasurable events after the sad war years was almost too good to be true.

We took the boat at Boulogne, then still entirely run by the English. Everywhere English uniforms, English faces, English language, also the boat was crammed with khaki – crowds of soldiers and officers, everyone strapped into life-belts for fear of floating mines. An animated, jostling, good-natured crowd, a sea of smiling faces, each man interested in his neighbour, ready to make friends, for this was a time of general good feeling and the atmosphere of comradeship created during the war still held good. We received a tremendous tossing, which gradually silenced many voices and paled many a face.

42

Tied into my chair, this being the only way to resist the rolling, and half drenched in spite of being wrapped in oilskins, I sat much amused, contemplating the lively medley, rather dazed by the 'too much' which had lately been poured over me. My family and I are good sailors, but my ladies and servants paid their uncomfortable tribute to Neptune. Ileana immediately made friends with the captain, and Mignon, although more loquacious than her younger sister, enjoyed chatting with the soldiers and officers, mixing with the crowd in that simple way particular to her. Mignon was at home everywhere, she was the most unselfconscious girl I ever met.

We reached Folkestone as night fell, so I could hardly perceive the beloved English coast, the sight of which never leaves me unmoved.

Sir Charles Cust, an old naval friend from my dear Malta days, had been sent to meet us, having been attached to me during my stay at Buckingham Palace. His delightful ruddy face was all smiles, but we felt giddy and confused by the rush and noise and the many different impressions.

England in uniform! It was an unusual sight. But this was only armistice: peace had not yet been signed and it was not easy to pass over from four years of war to a demobilized order of things. Besides, it must not be forgotten that the world was still heaving from the past fearful effort, from all the ghastly experiences, was giddy from loss of blood. A difficult time of transition, full of upheaval and social convulsions. The old order of things had been upset; the new was not yet established. Dangerous socialistic movements were anticipated: I noticed everywhere a great uneasiness, a fear of what Russia's blood-curdling example might instigate in quiet, steady England. Everybody seemed to tread lightly, carefully, so as not to awaken sleeping forces which would be difficult to channel. I was even rather shocked at the way the king[2] was obliged, because of public opinion, to treat his own relations: no grand duke was welcome, and the sovereign, being strictly constitutional, never even tried to impose his will, or to allow his personal sympathies to colour his actions. More passionate, less disciplined, also less responsible, this seemed to me a very cold attitude to adopt, and I often resented the fact that those who had come out on top did not more readily stretch out a hand to the defeated and overthrown. For a King, I suppose, the reasons of State must always overrule sentiment; but it saddened me and inwardly I vowed that I would stand up for the fallen whenever I could. It had already been a great distress to me that, on leaving Romania, I had not been allowed to take Marie Putiatin with me, because she was a born grand duchess. I was to have many such shocks as time went on, but personally I never resigned myself to what I considered this cowardly attitude of the great, this denying of their own kith and kin. I had too clearly before my eyes the words: 'Do unto others as you would they should do unto you.' Everything had been such a horrible game of chance, we, the winners of today, might just as well have been the losers. I could never forget this, and marvelled at how easily others did – but then I was never careful or calculating and was often over-impulsive and therefore probably unwise.

It was a tremendous emotion to arrive in London and to be greeted at the station by George[2] and Mary [May],[3] with a crowd of officials and many, many friends. As in a dream I saw familiar faces smiling at me, faces from out of the past and faces belonging to the near present – my war friends: good old Boyle, General Ballard, General Greenly, Locker Lampson and my Welsh friend Evans Griffith, both of the 'armoured cars', Lady Barclay, and then also, tall and brilliant, was Sybil Chrissoveloni, with tears of joy in her eyes, and many others, until my heart felt like bursting with joy. They were all there, faithful, welcoming, glad to greet me on this homecoming to the Old Country, after years of stress.

It was late; we arrived at Buckingham Palace in time for supper. At the front door stood David[4] (prince of Wales), Bertie,[5] Mary,[6] – my young cousins; we were strangers to each other but soon made friends, especially David. I find in my diary this description of him: 'David is the most attractive boy I have ever seen; he is a real little beauty with still a child's face, an adorable short nose and hair the colour of ripe corn, and he is so nice and has an enchanting smile. To me he is irresistible.'

My two daughters quickly made friends with their cousins after the first shyness had worn off, and Ileana became the great favourite of old and young; her quiet, unaffected self-assurance enormously amused her uncle and aunt. They loved to hear her relate her experiences during the war, and she spoke quite simply about all our past misery and dangers as though they were everyday events each child lives through. She was treated with extraordinary kindness, and the weeks spent at Buckingham Palace remain for her an unforgettable memory, to be treasured for the rest of her life.

Mignon was at a more awkward age, but fell so much in love with England that when we went back to Romania she pleaded with me to be left in England so as to be able to go to an English school.

The important event of our first day in England was to go to see Nicky at Eton. Nicky as an Eton boy in his absurd top hat! Long and lanky, he was as ever full of fun, talk, and nonsense, already quite at home in his new surroundings. Fond of everybody and everybody fond of him. It was both incongruous and delightful to see him here, in this celebrated old centre of British tradition. He, the untamed, unconventional little scamp who had run loose at Jassy and who had been my constant companion in hospitals, among the poor or with the troops at the front . . . Indeed a strange contrast: after turmoil and disarray, absolute peace and order.

Dr Alington, the headmaster, received us at his house, where he gave us luncheon. He was a charming, quiet, good-looking man and lived in beautiful rooms. I shall never forget the harmonious colour scheme of his long, narrow sitting-room: bright green Chinese paper on the walls, gay with flowers, trees and birds; dark wooden furniture and pleasant coloured chintzes to match the walls; on the piano and tables green Chinese bowls with slim golden daffodils, logs burning cheerfully on the hearth. I felt strangely at peace in that long quiet room with its unique English cosiness.

Nicky lived in the house of Mr Brinton, a kindly, intelligent married man, sparing of words, but with a pleasant twinkle in his eye, who seemed to understand Nicky's quicksilver personality. My boy was treated kindly and not made to feel an outsider; of course he amused everybody with his originality and quickness of wit. It was difficult to label Nicky as a species: he could become anything,

45

there was both good and bad in his nature. I hope the good predominated, but he was difficult to control as he always had the laugh on his side. This often gave him an unfair advantage over others, more worthy, but less quick.

Brinton's house had all the simple charm of an English home, I seemed to breathe it in with satisfaction and I felt strongly that vague but persistent feeling of 'Heimweh' with which everything essentially English fills me. Nothing can be quite compared to the atmosphere of Eton, with its quiet peace and regulated life, so shut away from all the turmoil and fluctuations of the striving, quarrelling outside world.

How far off seemed those two tragic years in famished Jassy: our overcrowded miserable hospitals, our tatlered suffering soldiers, the Russian troops turned Bolshevik, clattering in their devilish motor-trucks over our bumpy pavements, singing revolutionary songs and waving their odious red flags. How far also the eternal straining effort to keep off final disaster, to stand firm amidst ever-increasing misfortune!

All these pictures rose before my eyes as I sauntered with my companions through eternal Eton. We visited the old buildings, the library, the chapel. Peace, order, quiet, discipline, tradition, unchanging amidst the overwhelming upheavals which were convulsing our old world . . . And Nicky was here, secure, anchored for a while in a safe port. He was being offered a blessed and precious opportunity.

In a part of Windsor lived old Green, formerly the children's nurse, the friend and ally of my lonely youth, of my early, storm-shaken years in Romania, now pensioned and possessing a villa christened after 'Mignon', her last 'baby'. We paid her a surprise visit: she nearly fainted with joy; she had not expected us. As profuse of words as in the olden days, she wept, laughed and exclaimed, blessing and scolding us in turns. She had endless questions to ask, tales to tell, souvenirs to dig up. It all poured forth in a comic jumble of 'H'-less words, to the great amusement of Mary and Sir Charles Cust, who had accompanied us on our wanderings. Mignon, after whom the house had been named, came in for the lion's share of hugging and kissing. Of course we had to accept a cup of tea and sat down in a small parlour, the walls of which were lined with royal family photographs, representing all of us at different stages of our lives, our faces, expressions and clothes changing with the different dates. It was no easy matter to tear ourselves away from her loquacious hospitality . . . Dear old Green!

My life in Buckingham Palace with George and Mary was very different to my hectic days at the Ritz in Paris. Here I was hemmed in by traditions: I was a royal guest and had to be very careful not to overstep any of the established conventions. Although so closely related, we had in fact never been much together, fate having taken me at the early age of seventeen away from my old home and surroundings. We had grown up differently. My life had been all struggle and adaptation among a foreign people, in a family I had not known as a child. I had become a stranger to the familiar circle once my own. Besides, the war years had brought me face to face with a reality which had been spared my cousins. I seemed to know too much of the outside world, and I did not want to disturb their peaceful conceptions with my cruel experiences. They were full of kindness and sympathy, but I felt I must measure my words, dampen the independence of my personality and opinions, so as not to shock their royal standards which had not changed with the years.

I loved this beautiful stately setting, the dignified round of their everyday life – it was wonderful to be again suddenly part of this life I had once known so well; but I was still too throbbing with eagerness to help my suffering people to be able to give myself up to perfect peace and restful contentment.

I felt they were watching me, a little anxious as to what surprises I might bring into their well-ordered existence. My freedom of expression was unusual; no conventionality hemmed me in, and one day, after I felt I had shocked him, I gently laid my hand on George's arm and pleaded: 'Try not to be shocked at me, try to enjoy me as I am, in spite of the strange atmosphere I have brought into dignified Buckingham Palace. Forgive me if I am different from what you think a queen ought to be. You see I have not been a comfortable queen, my life has not been easy, but I have lived as bravely as I could, far from all to which I had been accustomed. I did not have people to do things for me – I had to do them myself . . .'

Yes, that was the exact truth: I had had to do things myself. In the face of pressing necessity I could not pause to consider if I was overstepping royal conventions; I simply had to act, to speak on my own authority, to shoulder according to the need of the moment my own responsibilities. So of course I had become accustomed to somewhat ignoring the smaller niceties of language and behaviour, and the only way to disarm my relations was by being absolutely candid.

George looked somewhat startled, I certainly was a rather disturbing element, a being who stirred up thoughts and ideas which did not fit in with his preconceived notions of what was fitting for a queen. But being sincerely fond of me, he was ready to be indulgent, even if he could not entirely understand this somewhat perturbing cousin who had lived her life outside 'the family fortress'. So he laughed his jolly laugh, which wrinkled up his nose, and listened patiently to what I had to say. Mary listened also, and her feminine instinct let her guess that my bed had not always been a bed of roses, and as the day passed and they both became better acquainted with the real 'me', we began to take confidence in each other and to entirely enjoy being together. By degrees, also, our conversation became much more hearty and unguarded. Some of the family meals were full of laughter and fun.

In spite of the joy of being with my cousins, I did not however dare to give myself up entirely to happy contentment. I had been sent abroad to speak up for my country, to put its problems before those who, today, were remodelling the map of Europe, and I was well aware that Romania was in a delicate position and that her case needed to be rightly understood. We had been so isolated, cut off from all contact with our great Allies, that we had often been maligned and our sufferings had been little known. Today so many diplomats and politicians were having their say that it was difficult to get a hearing. It needed an exceptional ambassador to plead for a country which did not enjoy special popularity. Here also, as in

France, Romania needed to be given my face, so as to draw sympathy towards her.

I do not wish this to sound as though I believed I could perform miracles, where others, cleverer and better prepared than I, failed. This was in no wise my attitude, but I knew that, fatigued by too many ardent, complaining bearded emissaries of small countries, all arguing and quarrelling together, each one convinced of the superior justice of his demands, the arbiter would find a woman's voice, a woman's face, a pleasant change, and be more ready to lend a kindly ear, especially if the pleader was the Queen herself.

So with the courage of the innocent and of those who believe in their moral right, I threw myself into the fray, never pausing to consider how my action might be criticized by onlookers. I was so sure that my cause was just that I felt no hesitation, convinced that the right arguments with which to move those who held our fate in their hands would come to me at the hour of need. I knew that truth sounded from every word I said.

But living in a royal palace, I was less free to come and go, or to receive all manner of people; I had to observe the outward etiquette, so my work was slower. I had, however, many devoted helpers and they, in sympathy with my efforts, brought me together with important people who could expose our cause, and stand up for us when necessary.

Thus with each day that passed, the pace increased and it became difficult to cope with all I had to do, or was asked to do. But I met with more kindness and understanding as time advanced; I felt I was making headway and this was encouraging. I was beginning to imprint another picture of my country upon the minds of those who could help us. Statesmen, politicians, diplomats, soldiers and sailors, important men of business, oil magnates and big industrialists came to see me, and with never-flagging enthusiasm I demonstrated that what we needed was immediate help, as we had our backs to the wall!

Our population was starving, decimated by poverty and sickness, our transports were entirely disorganized, our bridges and railways had been destroyed, our riches torn from us, our stores and reserves looted, our oil-fields blown up by our own allies who did not wish our wealth to fall into enemy hands. Everything had to be begun anew without help or the equipment needed, and being so far off, it was cruelly hard to get a hearing, to receive sympathetic attention or even common justice.

Although I had no official mission, both the King and the government had confidence in me, believed I could accomplish more than the most erudite emissaries. There are moments when the accents of the heart are more efficient than those of cold reason, when the words of one who has suffered with the suffering and prayed with the desperate carry more weight then the cold argument of common sense and logic.

When the fire of conviction moves a woman, she can find accents not at the disposal of tired and sometimes even bored statesmen, arguing with stodgy old gentlemen seated round a green table.

It was interesting but very exhausting work, and hardly left me a moment to live for myself or to enjoy my sumptuous surroundings, which seemed so marvellous after our years of dearth and misery. But now and again I spared an hour for myself when I could gather friends and acquaintances around me, and also the younger members of the family, who liked to assemble in my room for big teas. I would then throw off all cares and could be gay among the gayest, and these tea parties, often headed by golden-haired David, were great fun.

David was allowed to go out with me, and together we went to several dinner parties, among others to the Astors and to the Duchess of Rutland, where we met and talked to all sorts of interesting people, including artists, writers and musicians.

Sir Charles Cust, specially attached to me and chosen by King George V, because he had been a friend of the dear old Malta days and had served under my father on the flagship HMS *Alexandra*, was at first inclined to be critical about my ways of independence. He was ready to consider me more unconventional than was in keeping with a crowned head, and showed signs of anxiety about what I might do next.

Knowing, however, that he had kindly feelings towards the former little Marie of Edinburgh, daughter of his one-time admiral, I decided to have it out with him in a heart-to-heart talk. I was devastatingly frank with him, looking him straight in the eye and explaining my somewhat exceptional position and why I was obliged to go ahead on my own lines. I spoke up bravely, I knew I had a friend before me whom I must win over. And I did finally win him over. Although he was somewhat surprised at my fearless outspokenness, we finally shook hands like two comrades and I begged him to be quite open with me and never to hesitate in giving me good advice, as I was only too glad to be steered by one who knew all the ins and outs of court life and its restrictions, which occasionally, in my ardour, I could overstep. This was a pact to which we faithfully adhered during my stay in Buckingham Palace and, by degrees, Sir Charles began to take an interest in my mission and loyally stood by me whenever he could.

Because many of my personal friends were busy all day, or were hardworking men bound to regular hours, and as I always lunched 'en famille', to King George's intense amusement, I used to give breakfast parties, about which he liked to tease me, endlessly. Punctually at nine o'clock, I assembled at a huge round table all those who could not put in an appearance later in the day: naval and military friends, politicians, MPs, businessmen, which did not exclude children and a sprinkling of Russian refugees. Lord Astor,[7] Colonel Boyle and Colin Kepel were the 'habitués', each bringing with them anyone they considered it useful for me to meet. There were also, of course, old friends of my childhood whom I was delighted to meet again, and friends also of later date.

The old 'page' attached to my personal service during my stay at Buckingham Palace, and who looked after me like a kindly and indulgent parent, entered whole-heartedly into the spirit of these unconventional meals, and saw to it that there should be a generous spread of excellent food, which added greatly to the general good cheer.

The kindly old man had quite taken me under his wing. I think he found me stimulating; he became confidential, giving many a useful hint about the 'rules of the house'. Having been in the royal service for several decades, and having also served under Grand Mama

Queen,[8] he knew exactly what could or could not be done, and ended by being a real stand-by. For all his magnificent punctiliousness and royal dignity, he did not seem out of sympathy with my unconventionality and spirit of fun, following in fact with intelligent interest my every move, marvelling at the amount of activity I could cram into a single day. He too, like Sir Charles Cust, became an amused and convinced ally, helping me in his own small way to save time and trouble.

Occasionally, when perplexed, I would ask his advice. During the war we had run out of every kind of provision and I did not want to go home empty-handed. My stately liveried mentor was profuse in addresses: he seemed to have a cousin in every trade, and these would be only too 'honoured' if Her Majesty would give them her orders in person. They would immediately appear from Scotland, Ireland, Wales, no matter where, to attend to the royal command, delighted to have a word with the former Princess Marie of Edinburgh. H.M. Queen Mary approved of these particular houses, and beloved Queen Mary was a great authority upon all things practical as well as artistic.

I was especially very much in need of tea! Romania had quite run out of tea since there was no more communication with Russia, whence it was formerly imported. 'Oh! Twining is the best man for tea.' So early one morning Mr Twining or his chief representative was ushered into my presence and I explained that I wanted a tea which tasted neither of smoke, scent nor hay, upon which clever Mr Twining promptly answered: 'It is Darjeeling tea Your Majesty wants. May I send samples? There are three special mixtures.' 'Yes, that would be perfect!' But the difficulty was, how to find time to imbibe three separate cups of tea in close enough succession to properly distinguish their different aromas? My old 'page' came to the rescue with a practical solution, having well grasped the importance of not losing any time. He would keep three separate tea-pots all ready prepared, which he would bring in turns between my several audiences, 'Besides, Her Majesty will be all the better for an occasional cup of tea, as she seems to be having a strenuous time!' Strenuous indeed! I laughed heartily and the arrangements proved both satisfactory and refreshing. Between the different audiences, my old friend would peer in through the door, with a neat tray in hand, tea ready brewing, and I finally found the mixture of which I dreamed, which tasted neither of hay, smoke nor scent: Darjeeling tea!

Thus in turn did 'cousins' from Wales, Scotland and Ireland also present samples of biscuits, jam, soap, and no end of other useful local products, of which I acquired large provisions, the cases I was to take back with me accumulating in a way which made severe General Ballif sigh and shake his head.

Beautiful Queen Alexandra[9] had aged at last and her deafness had increased. We met with the old warm feeling of sympathy. In a way she clung to me because I was a link with unfortunate Russia. Aunt Alix was suffering intensely because of the long and painful separation from her favourite sister, Empress Marie, still in a dangerously precarious situation in the Crimea, cut off from everything and surrounded by Bolshevik danger. As I was harassed by the same sort of anxiety about Ducky, who was still in Finland, we understood each other perfectly.

When I went to visit her at Marlborough House, she showed me, heaped up on her writing table, all her beloved sister's letters, and, her arm linked within mine, she led me through her different rooms, showing me all her Russian souvenirs and treasures, full of grief over all the terrible happenings which had swept away the old order of things. She spoke much of my mother and both our eyes were full of tears.

She gave us a large lunch, inviting also my girls – Ileana as usual holding her own, interesting and entertaining everybody with all she had to relate. She did this with the charm of a child neither shy nor forward, but whose large blue eyes had seen sights they would never forget.

Many familiar faces, not seen for years, were assembled round Aunt Alix's table, such as Queen Amélie[10] of Portugal and Soveral (the Blue Monkey), and also all those who had grown old in the queen's service, Charlotte Knoles, Sir Dighten Probin and others;

I was touched to see again how faithfully she clung to all these, upon whom Time was laying an ever heavier hand.

I also visited Uncle Arthur,[11] who lived now in our dear old Clarence House, Aunts Louise, Helena and Beatrice, and the different cousins of my own generation. I took a special liking to Irine,[12] Drino's tall and handsome wife, whom I saw for the first time. We felt instinctively drawn towards each other.

All my relations were patronizing different institutions and charitable war works; I thus had occasion to visit several marvellously run organizations and everywhere I was given the warmest welcome.

With Queen Mary, I visited one of the large hospitals for wounded soldiers, run upon grand lines with every possible modern innovation and nothing left undone that could ease pain and suffering. I could not repress a certain feeling of envy when I compared this superb order and comfort with the want and misery of the hospitals I had tried to help at home.

The men were flatteringly glad to see me; I had brought many flowers and conversation flowed easily between us. It was such a joy to be able to converse in my own tongue; nearly every invalid was eager to talk and have his say.

A sad sight were those who had been wounded in the spine, so-called hopeless cases. They lay on their backs in the high comfortable beds and most of them were busy with some kind of work. I went from bed to bed, admiring their different productions, taking an interest in their artistic efforts which seemed to give them great pleasure. Several years later I received a letter from Canada, which begun thus: 'You will be sure to remember me; I am the wounded soldier who lay in the bed beside the man who was plaiting baskets. You spoke to me so kindly that I would like you to know I am back home again and really able to move about', etc. This letter, so simply confidential, touched me very much.

While visiting a hospital run by the YMCA in some distant London slum district I heard the matron who was showing me round whispering to a nurse: 'He would so like to see her'. 'No, no', answered the matron. 'It is impossible; we cannot ask it of her', followed by more whispering. Laying my hand on the matron's arm I enquired what could not be asked of me. With some hesitation the matron explained that one of their wounded was dying – he knew I was here, and longed to see me. 'But he is very bad', added the matron. 'He cannot last much longer'. 'But of course I shall go to see him', I exclaimed. 'For two years I have done little else but go to those "who cannot last much longer".'

So they took me to him, and having just been offered a wonderful bunch of red roses, I laid them between the trembling fingers of the dying man, and to this day I have not forgotten the look of gratitude he gave me.

All communication was slow and difficult, but letters from home finally reached me, and the news was upsetting. Under the leadership of Bela Kun, Hungary had turned Bolshevik, voting for Russia and communism. A wave of revolution was sweeping the country: towns and properties had been ransacked, and intentions towards Romania were anything but peaceful. As Hungary was our next-door neighbour this could mean great trouble and danger for us and there was the question of our not yet demobilized troops being marched over the frontiers to re-establish order. Rumours of all kinds were afloat; nothing could be absolutely verified, which made them them all the more perturbing. I longed to be at home to carry my share of anxiety, but I knew that, for the moment, I was more useful here.

Brătianu came over from Paris and I managed to arrange it with George that he should be invited for a private lunch. Brătianu displayed all his charm, but George was no longer very fluent in French, so I had to do a lot of translating to keep the conversation afloat, which was a handicap to our eloquent statesmen.

Brătianu approved of my work in England and begged me to follow closely the line I had taken, making as good an atmosphere as possible for Romania, because weighty discussions in Paris were imminent, and I could do much to modify England's none too favourable attitude towards our country.

I certainly remarked that my coming to England had already created a change in public opinion, and *Punch* published a cartoon in which Romania was represented in the shape of a woman in peasant dress who, with haggard face and hungry eyes, sees whole transports of foodstuffs being carted to enemy lands, while she, the ally, is allowed to starve.

From Russia also the news was heart-breaking: the French, no longer able to hold out against the Reds, were evacuating Odessa, which meant an added danger for us from the further side.

By some miracle a year-old letter from Ducky[13] reached me from Finland where they were still quasi-prisoners and unable to get away. They have lost absolutely everything: nothing now remains for them, not even hope. They are completely destitute. They too are suffering from hunger, and for the moment there is absolutely no possibility of escaping from Borgo. More than two years of fear and horror, not knowing what the next day might bring: death, starvation or relief.

I immediately set about with May's help to plan how I could send her provisions, and May deputed one of her ladies to help me to select and buy those things most nourishing and best for lengthy transport, adding all sorts of biscuits and jams as delicacies to the more solid foodstuffs. I also included soap and scents and other small luxuries, not seen for years. Both George and May guaranteed that these precious goods would reach her safely.

Much later I heard that she did receive them and that their arrival was a mighty event in their desolate corner of exile.

My days were getting fuller and fuller. I had made headway – and felt waves of sympathy mounting towards me on all sides. My pleading had not been in vain. In my heart of hearts I knew that my people had not put their trust in me to no purpose. I knew how to talk of and for them – how to 'put them on the map'!

It would take too long to enumerate all those who came forward to help me. So as to leave no one out, I shall mention no particular names, but if there are any still living today who did their best for me, rendering my difficult task easier, may they read in these pages my deep-felt thanks.

Today others have taken my place, I can only look back, not forward, but within my soul rests the feeling that I did my best.

Reading through my diary of those days it all comes back to me, the magnificent enthusiasm and that almost sacred desire to help, to serve . . . Was it in vain? Perhaps not, but we each have our day and it is not for us to decide its length.

Why this digression? Perhaps because I am sad. One cannot help being sad sometimes, and as I said before, these are only 'chapters out of my life', not quite the whole tale as I could tell it, with its inner conflicts, pains and disappointments; 'disillusion' is a word I will not allow myself to use!

But back to London! Although it is not habitual for the Lord Mayor of London to give an official lunch to a Queen travelling without her King, and although my visit was not an official one, the City desired to receive me as an English princess who had done honour to her British birth by doing her best for the country of her adoption, and this under exceedingly difficult circumstances. For wherever I went today I was received as something of a heroine, which was both flattering and embarrassing, but good for our Romanian cause. So I accepted the gracious invitation as a compliment to King and Country as well as to myself, and was ceremoniously received with all the quaint and stately pageantry inherent to receptions given in the Mansion House, which I was visiting for the first time.

A solemn procession into lunch – the insignias of the City carried before us, golden plate on the table, flowers, address of honour, etc . . . Husbands and wives going in arm in arm.

I bore up bravely: having nearly entirely overcome shyness, I can today hold my own almost anywhere by being as simple and human as possible, fired by the desire to put others at their ease, responding warmly to all manifestations of sympathy. Paris had already been good training and here in England, for me, everything was easier as I could speak my own language. To have eternally to speak a language not one's own is like labouring uphill!

But in my heart of hearts, I could not help marvelling how all this glorifying of my person had come about. It did not seem so very long ago that I had been but a much-reproved little princess who was supposed to possess but few virtues and was entirely subjugated by an old king with an iron will. Now every sort of honour was being paid me as though I myself had been a King. Such are the changes in life, but I humbly accepted all the kindness offered me as a marvellous recompense, beyond my deserts. I cannot say it did not fill me with a certain feeling of elation, but I never got accustomed to consider it quite natural to be made such a fuss of.

Among the several receptions given in my honour was a tremendous tea party offered by the Canadians at the Ritz. From the first, under the enthusiastic leadership of my faithful friend Colonel Boyle, the Canadians had been eager to help Romania through her Queen.

Boyle had been able to paint a vivid picture of our country's distress and my efforts to help my people. This had fired their imagination and they came forward in more ways than one, among others offering me enormous provisions out of their Red Cross depots.

A great crowd of eager friendly faces, but all of them strangers to me. A show of jovial good will, the shaking of many hands, smiles, promises, a little propaganda talk on my side, and 'Uncle Joe', like a kindly father, beaming down upon us all.

I also had to receive the foreign ambassadors and ministers en bloc, always a challenging proceeding, but I came through it with flying colours, and in this case was inclined to put myself on the back because it is the most difficult circle to deal with. Representatives of all the countries of the world lined up in a row and to have to find something, not too idiotic, to say to each in turn, while the last spoken to can always hear what I am saying to his neighbour! All crowned heads know what an ordeal this can be!

I remember that I especially liked Mr Davis, the American ambassador, whom I also met at several dinner parties. We felt decided sympathy for each other and he urged me to come to America, declaring that the United States would give me a tremendous reception.

There was also a visit to the House of Commons arranged by Locker Lampson, where I listened to a debate from the gallery and made the acquaintance of several interesting men, Sir Edward Carson being one of those I found most striking; besides, he was intelligently interested in Romania. Locker Lampson was indefatigable in his effort to help me in every possible way.

Lord Curzon, then secretary for foreign affairs, offered me a big official dinner. His house was beautiful, filled with art treasures; we ate at several round tables of green marble decorated with rare and exquisite flowers and all the guests were specially chosen so that I could plead my Romanian cause before those who could be most helpful. I did so with an eloquence which I did not realize I possessed, sweeping my audience along with me, until each man promised to do what he could for my suffering country. Winston Churchill[14] was one of those who listened with the most intelligent sympathy. I thought his wife perfectly beautiful. Lord Curzon himself was too ceremonious to inspire any feeling of warmth. His attentions were like a ritual, perfectly staged. His politeness was as exquisite as his house, but I was too much of a throbbing human being to feel at ease in such a superbly regulated temperature.

Every day some new kindness or attention was paid to me. Lord Landsdown, accompanied by several other important gentlemen, came to Buckingham Palace to offer me the order of 'St John's of Jerusalem', which made of me a 'Lady of Justice', a quaint and charming title! Also Aunt Alix, as head of the British Red Cross, gave me officially, but with her inimitable grace in the presence of others, a special golden medal of honour in recognition of my war work. I was more than touched.

There was also a satisfactory interview with General Baden-Powell, to further our Boy Scouts movement in Romania,[15] where it had already taken firm root, giving excellent results during the war.

Every day was filled to bursting: my every nerve was strained to the utmost because, besides all my work, there was also family life and endless social entertainments, and the receiving of precious friends, such as Mrs Hamilton and Pauline Spender Clay.[16]

On the day before my departure a last difficult ordeal lay before me: the receiving of the Press and this on a day when I had never been allowed a second's breathing space.

There were always endless discussions about whether it was seemly or not for a queen to speak to the Press. Some were for, some against it. My different mentors, including Sir Charles Cust, were consulted and finally it was Mr Mişu, our minister in London, who won the day: although this was a modern, post-war innovation, as H.M.'s mission was quasi-official, her work would not be complete unless she spoke to the Press.

So I submitted, but as the meeting could not take place in the palace, I went to our Legation and once more held my own among those important gentlemen who, in our restless days, sway public opinion for good or evil. There were some exceedingly agreeable and interesting men among them, but today their faces are hazy to me and I cannot remember their names – and Mr Mişu who introduced me to them is dead.

My saving on these embarrassing occasions was the way I could always feel a warm and lively interest in people and things. My want of conventionality gave me an impetuousity which royal persons generally suppress; besides, a sort of desperate fearlessness had come to me because of the way I had, by force of circumstances, been pushed to the fore. One step led to another, there was no going back. Even if I were to drop by the wayside, I had to accept burdens seldom laid upon queenly shoulders, no shirking was today permissible. '*Je devais avoir tous les courages*' [I must bolster up my courage]. So once more I spoke up bravely, going into all the details of our sufferings, needs, hopes and aspirations.

When strongly convinced I can be eloquent, and I always allow humour to lighten my seriousness. There are many ways of saying things, and although my mission was almost a man's mission, my way of pleading was a woman's way. During that strenuous post-war period no situation baffled me: I was in a fighting mood; the spirit of patriotism upheld me; I gave my best without counting the cost.

Today, with folded hands, I look back. My services have been forgotten, most of my collaborators are dead. I was much younger than they were, but they had recognized a force in me which they meant to exploit. No record, except that of my diary, has been kept of that brave campaign I sustained for my country, putting all doubt, all physical fatigue, all moral apprehension aside, to work heart, soul and brain for my people. I relate it all very simply, because it belongs in 'the story of my life' to its later chapters. All those who believe in their work know how to pull others along with them; I did this in my time. *Mais tout passe* . . . For all is vanity and vexation of spirit . . .

The day of departure came.

In Paris, many were clamouring for my return. No end of functions, of which the dates were fixed a long while ahead, were awaiting me.

It was hard indeed to tear myself away from my kind hosts and from my many friends, foremost among whom were the Astors, in whose house I had been several times, always to meet pleasant or interesting people. Nancy,[17] of whom I was becoming more and more fond, was a wonderful hostess and would unite at her table guests of most diverse opinions and standing, linking them all together with her never-ceasing flow of talk and inimitable sense of humour, added to her quick, sometimes over-caustic, American wit. It was in their house that I first met Thomas, then a rising man.

David[18] liked to come with me, and with special delight I watched his charm and ease amongst every sort of people.

Seldom have I felt such an instinctive affection as I felt for David. To me he was irresistible: I loved his mild face, his voice, his adorable golden hair. My diary is full of praise for him. He showed me both affection and confidence, and was absolutely sweet with Ileana, who fascinated him as she did the older generation. She was at a delightful age and had become a universal favourite with old and young, high and low.

Though still quite a small child, without being old-fashioned, she was perfectly self-possessed and even when I was lunching or dining elsewhere, she was always invited to Their Majesties' table, where she would take part in every conversation, feasting the while, to George's great amusement, on endless quantities of excellent fruit, a luxury which for long had not come our way.

With each passing day the intercourse with my cousins had become warmer and happier. My stay had been long enough that we were able to become well acquainted and understand each other. Both the king and queen had given us the kindest sort of hospitality, realizing in some measure the dreadful ordeal we had been through and the good this visit was doing us.

Their hospitality was, however, to be extended further, as Ileana, the very day of our departure, went down with a sort of influenza. This was a terrible dilemma for me. Was she going to be very ill? Everything had been packed, engagements had been made on the other side of the Channel, special trains has been put at my disposal, the tickets were booked for the boat, people were coming to the station to see us off. How could I cancel everything at the eleventh hour?

Consultations took place with the royal doctor, with Their Majesties, with my own followers, with Mr Mişu, and it was finally decided, as the precious child was not seriously ill, that George and May would have her looked after at Buckingham Palace, while I must leave as planned so as to keep my engagements, and 'Uncle Joe', always ready in an emergency, would, when she had recovered, bring her over to me in Paris. Old Woodfield, her nurse, would remain with her.

George also kindly promised to keep an eye on Nicky, deputing Mr Hansell,[19] the former tutor to his own sons, to be the boy's English mentor while at Eton and during those holidays which he could not spend at home. Nicky seemed absolutely happy at school, which made the wrench of separation less cruel.

So finally I left. George and May took me to the station, where many members of the family, crowds of friends and officials had gathered to wish me good speed.

A good-bye full of regret, many dear faces smiling at me – handshakes, reiterated promises that our cause would be upheld, murmured blessings, misty eyes. Good-bye . . .

At Dover we parted with Sir Charles Cust, having become firm friends.

Hand in hand with Mignon, I watched the retreating cliffs of Dover – both of us had been happy in the old home country which cannot be compared to anything else upon earth.

Queen Marie of Romania.
(*Diana Mandache Collection*)

King Ferdinand of Romania. (*Diana Mandache Collection*)

The Cotroceni Palace, Bucharest. (Reprinted from Constantin Gonta, *Aero-topografia.*
Ridicarea de planuri şi hărţi prin fotografii aeriene, Bucureşti, Atelierele grafice Socec & Co,
1927)

The Golden Salon at Cotroceni Palace. (*Diana Mandache Collection*)

Queen Marie and Prince Mircea, Bucharest, *c.* 1915. (*Diana Mandache Collection*)

Queen Marie and the British Military mission (together with Mignon, Elisabetha, Nicolae and Ileana), Jassy, 1918. (*Diana Mandache Collection*)

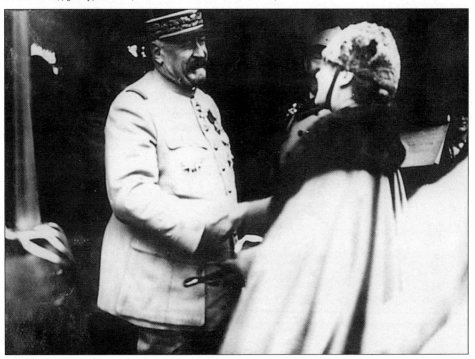

General Henri Berthelot and Queen Marie, December 1918, Bucharest. (*Diana Mandache Collection*)

The Romanian delegation at the Peace Conference, 1919, Paris. From left to right: Grigore Danielopol, Constantin Diamandi, General Constantin Coandă, Ion Brătianu, Emil Pangrati, General Arthur Văitoianu. (*Diana Mandache Collection*)

The Inter-Allied Commission Conference, Budapest, November 1919. (*Diana Mandache Collection*)

David Lloyd George. (*Diana Mandache Collection*)

Queen Marie in London, 1919. (*Diana Mandache Collection*)

King Albert of Belgium, who met Marie in Paris in the spring of 1919, was first cousin of King Ferdinand of Romania; Albert's mother was the sister of Prince Leopold of Hohenzollern and King Carol I of Romania; Albert was also related to Queen Marie through the paternal Coburg line. (*Diana Mandache Collection*)

Queen Marie at the Paris Peace Conference before the meeting with George Clemenceau, 7 March 1919. (*Romanian National Archives, Regina Maria, III/116*)

Left: Pelesh Castle in Sinaia, in the Transylvanian Alps, was the royal summer residence built by Carol I in the style of the Hohenzollern castles of Southern Germany. (*Diana Mandache Collection*) *Right:* Princess Marie (Mignon) of Romania. (*Diana Mandache Collection*)

Left: Princess Ileana of Romania. (*Diana Mandache Collection*) *Right:* Princess Elisabetha of Romania. (*Diana Mandache Collection*)

FIVE

Back Again to Paris

We were back in Paris on 30 March and I was left just twenty-four hours' peace before the rush began again, daily increasing like a swelling flood, finally threatening to drown me. The Ritz was a real Tower of Babel, and somehow I was claimed by every nationality. There seemed no limits anywhere, everything and everybody pressed in upon me at the same time, and I often sighed for the stately protection of Buckingham Palace, where occasionally there had been hours of blissful family seclusion when the pandemonium ended.

Every living soul wanted to get into touch with me, it was a real craze, and each new acquaintance had a troop of other people at his or her heels, who for one pretext or another had to see the Queen of Romania. I had become uncomfortably popular and there were times when I could have wept from sheer exhaustion.

There seemed to be no means to protect myself from this extraordinary inflow, because I considered it my duty to receive all those who presented themselves under the pretext of wanting to help our cause. There were some really important, influential people among the daily avalanche, but many came merely to make my acquaintance, and though most of them were agreeable, often even interesting, they were nevertheless robbers of my precious time. My enthusiasm lent me almost superhuman strength. Today, only to think of it all makes me giddy; besides, almost twenty years lie between! Even then I thought it almost too much, as this sentence, found in my diary, demonstrates: 'I am obliged to live three times the life of an ordinary mortal; everybody comes to me with a different question. I am expected to listen to and comprehend everything, whether it comes within my competence or not. Even

63

business and military questions are brought before me as though I had a universal brain!'

Humorous! But the fact remains: I was being treated as though I had 'a universal brain'. Politicians, statesman, diplomats, generals, men of science, oil magnates, inventors, doctors, writers, artists and altruists – they all came, and my 'universal brain' had to switch from one subject to another as though it were a shunting-machine. To cap it all, each separate interlocutor would awaken my interest so vividly that I quite forgot to be tired. That keen, alive interest I took in everything had much, I think, to do with my popularity. I never looked bored or resigned, as many royal persons do. Time was my only enemy: the hours slipped too quickly through my fingers; exert myself as I would, time could not to be found for everything.

A great satisfaction to me was Brătianu's admission that lately both Clemenceau and Lloyd George had modified their attitude towards Romania, and at last he was making a little headway. He continued to come and see me nearly every morning. Also Mr Mişu told me that the work I had done in England was of immense value to our cause, which had become much more sympathetic to public opinion, since I had myself pleaded for it. To give Romania my face had not been a bad idea!

I kept as closely in touch with Mr Mişu as possible; he was, although infinitely modest, a remarkable man. Quite extraordinarily intelligent and learned, speaking fourteen languages. He never, however, put himself forward and was the most selfless man I ever met. Being a philosopher, he was above party passion, neither did he care for personal honours or recompense, hardly even for recognition. Only, knowing life and humanity too well, there was a streak of cynicism in him which occasionally distressed me. But his heart was in the right place and our consideration for each other was daily growing stronger.

It was not only among the highbrows that I had become popular: the Paris population had also taken me to its heart. My motor (driven by a 'poilu' in blue uniform and helmet), with its little Romanian flag in front, fluttering gaily in the wind, was well known. I was often mobbed, and men, women and children crowded round it crying 'Vive la Reine!', even occasionally 'Vive notre Reine!', all wanting to have a word with me and often pressing humble flowers into my hands, while peering with curiosity into my face.

Once, after a very long 'matinée' at the grand opera, I found a huge crowd assembled at the entrance, and when I moved off, the crowd moved with me, and at one moment my heavy, closed-in car was actually lifted off the ground by the enthusiastic population, which was cheering, screaming and clapping. Indeed, the crush finally became dangerous so that I was in continual fear that someone might get hurt. Letting my windows down, I smiled at them for all I was worth, imploring them to look out for their feet! My every word awoke fresh frantic cheers, and the moment I looked one way, impatient taps on the opposite side induced me turn my head in the other direction. I did my best to deal out my smiles equally! Finally, when, with much difficulty, I had reached my destination, a workman strode up to me with a huge, outstretched hand: *'Je veux vous serrer la main car vous êtes une brave personne'* [I want to shake your hand because you are a good person] – a compliment I much appreciated.

Our military situation in Romania was becoming very precarious, with Bolshevism on both sides and our army in sore need of armaments and equipment. I received urgent telegrams from the King imploring me to redouble my efforts so as to obtain as quickly as possible what was so pressingly needed by our troops.

So with the courage of the desperate, I found means of interviewing the most influential military authorities, including Marshal Foch[1] who, because my patriotic ardour moved him, lent me a kindly ear; besides, in those days friendship still counted, and sentiment could still be called upon. I drew their attention to the geographical and strategic situation of Romania, emphasizing the fact that we were the outpost against Bolshevism in the Near East, a barrier against Russia's pernicious propaganda to which our people had shown themselves immune. Whilst other armies could no longer be mobilized, ours was still patiently ready to march again without protest, but our reserve supplies had entirely run out. We were in sore need of military equipment, with which the French depots were overflowing. Now was not a time to haggle and barter; the danger was too real, not only to us but to the whole of Europe. France, I well knew, would not send out a single man to help us, however great the alarm might be. We had the men, let France send us the equipment! But it must be done without loss of time, immediately, or the worst could come to pass. I pleaded with shining eyes, full of the ardour of a battle I had to win; I explained, coerced, waxed eloquent, until my breath gave out.

Thus I had also long military interviews with Generals Henri and Diaz, and Colonel Pétain,[2] who was being sent out to Romania. With each in turn I used the same argument: by helping us, you are helping yourselves, but be quick, lose no time!

I also considered it important to keep in touch with the Poles, who were also up against the Bolsheviks. They were making overtures to me, as they needed Romania because of common frontiers. General Henri was being sent to Poland; we must all work together.

To my great joy Albert of Belgium[3] came to see me. When I was a bride at Sigmaringen,[4] I had already felt instinctively drawn to him. We had, from the first, been friends, and each time we met, this sympathy held good. We discussed my problems. He encouraged me to go on working bravely for my people. We also compared our war impressions, our different experiences. We were gay and serious by turn. Albert, beneath his quiet, almost professor-like exterior, could be exceedingly funny. His wit was dry and often sarcastic, his speech was slow, somewhat monotonous and he would look at you from his great height with a kindly, brotherly, humorous twinkle in his very blue eyes, incompletely masked by glasses.

The difficulty was to ascertain if any of my pleading and interventions had brought about results. Was I making headway? What had I obtained? Were the promises received becoming facts? Was help forthcoming? Besides all my propaganda work, I also had a royal lady's part to play: I was being made much of and being lavishly entertained both officially and privately. Also the altruist in me was being claimed by hospitals, sanatoria, private, state, war and Red Cross works. Every day I had to put in an appearance somewhere – and wherever I went, there was the same enthusiasm, the same incense burnt before my so-called virtues, mercilessly rubbed into me, in speeches, addresses, poems and so on.

In spite of all the audiences I had to give and the man's work expected of me, I had to accept dinners, lunches, huge receptions, theatres, concerts. At the end of an exhausting day I had, without being allowed the necessary time, to robe myself in smart dresses which I hated, because I was against the actual fashions, considering them hideous and undignified, although the materials were superb. I even had comic scenes and discussions with my ladies about this, as they reproached me for going about in evening gowns which did not all correspond with what was being worn by 'tout Paris'.

However, I vehemently declared that, in spite of 'tout Paris', I had no intention of making a sight of myself in golden rags which barely covered my knees and from which, for no apparent reason, skimpy little pieces of tulle trailed to the ground at unexpected angles – a temptation for every man to tread on, or for the servants to tear while helping me out of the motor. For one of my generous proportions, this attire was absurd and unbecoming; besides, it robbed me of my self-assurance as I felt out of harmony with my ridiculous dress. Neither could I give any brilliant finishing touches to my apparel as all my jewels were in the hands of the Soviets, having been sent, during the tsar's reign, for safe keeping to Moscow!

The first real proof I had that my pleadings had borne fruit was when I met with General Gassoin, head of the French transports. I had a long and satisfactory interview with him in which he assured me that a hundred engines were leaving for Romania, with many carriages filled with the food and equipment for which we were clamouring. He even authorized me to send the King a telegram announcing this good news. It can well be imagined with what joyful alacrity that telegram was dispatched! General Gassoin also assured me that I should have the promised carriages, which were to be attached to my own train when I left, so that I could take home with me all the precious provisions given for my poor by the Allied Red Cross and by the various private depots which were still stocked with priceless goods that would mean salvation to the destitute in Romania. Fired by Colonel Boyle's interest in my country and its troubles, the Canadians were exceedingly generous. Also the Americans came forward from all sides. I was rapidly gaining great popularity among them. They came to me in droves and were all eager to help and especially eager to make contact with me, whom they had singled out as 'an outstanding figure among the women of today'. General Olds of the American Red Cross became a special benefactor; I liked him exceedingly and he promised he would fill fifteen wagons for me to take home, if I could secure the rolling stock!

All my energies were directed towards bringing my collected treasures back with me on my own special train when I finally left, and General Ballif was bravely seconding me in this none too easy enterprise, though occasionally he shook his head and smiled at my insistence. But I meant to leave nothing to chance and firmly intended to puff back into Romania dragging behind me, on my own train, all my honestly gained loot from different lands!

It became more and more difficult to cope with all my invitations, with all the different festivities given in my honour and the official ceremonies in which I was asked to take part. They cannot all be mentioned here; nor can I recall the names of all those who, during that period of hectic excitement and sentimental glorification, were helping to lionize the 'Queen of Romania'. Besides, it is all so long ago; it already belongs almost to history. Every single name and detail, however, many of them humorous, is religiously preserved in my copious, faithfully kept diary.

There was an official reception at the 'Hôtel de Ville', when the city of Paris wanted to express its admiration for 'la Grande Amie de la France', as they liked to call me. Magnificently worded speeches were pronounced, to which I answered with becoming modesty and as fluently as my French allowed. The public assembled on the square outside the Town Hall giving me an exuberant reception when I came down the stone stairs and drove away.

I was also officially received 'à la Sorbonne' by Poincaré, who addressed me in a vibrant speech, and I had to take a seat among all the great men of France. At the 'Institut', Mr Vidor, composer and organist, treated us to wonderful music, playing the organ himself and afterwards presenting many interesting people – among others Bergson, with whom I had a long, but not long enough, talk.

An enormous mass was also celebrated in Notre Dame, in memory of artists and writers fallen in the war, at which Mr Vidor played the organ. I had hoped to slip in unseen with my daughters to hear him play, but I was discovered and ushered with embarrassing fuss to a seat within the altar rails, where, in solitary grandeur, I knelt opposite the representative of the President of the Republic, with the eyes of 'tout Paris' glued to my back.

Being a Protestant, I was in mortal fear of not behaving exactly as I should in a Catholic church, or neglecting to do anything that was expected of me.

Receptions were arranged at all the different charitable institutions which assisted the wounded, the blind, the widows, the orphans. Occasionally I was even expected to answer the speeches addressed to me. At one of these institutions, half run by the Americans, I first met Mrs Wilson and old Mr Nelson Cromwell,[5] with whom in later days I remained in close contact.

There were lunches and dinners at different embassies, also a big lunch given to me at the Quai d'Orsay by Mr Pichon, then minister of foreign affairs, where of course we visited the celebrated room in which the Peace Conference was sitting. Dear old Madame Pichon, a quiet, unshowy, elderly lady suddenly became confidential and confessed that 'she adored me' but had been much too shy to express this today; however, '*parce que vous êtes si humaine*' (because you are so human), she had picked up courage enough to give vent to her feelings.

At the British Embassy I sat between Lord Derby, who was smilingly jolly and full of fatherly benevolence, and Sir Walter Long, a steady, unemotional gentleman, but who made me flush with pleasure by declaring that I had done wonderfully good work for Romania in England, and that he was astounded at how cleverly I had put our cause before the British public, not sentimentally, but practically.

Propaganda, he said, was a most delicate art, countries spent thousands of pounds on propaganda, with, very often, poor results. I was the most astonishing propagandist he had ever met. This appreciation from one who did not in the least seem to be a ladies' man gave me quite special pleasure. I tried so hard to do my best, this unexpected praise from a sober Englishman was most gratifying.

More worldly, but none the less formal, were great gatherings at the Interallié and Jockey Clubs, select entertainments when Paris elegance could be demonstrated in full. Comte Jean de Castellane and his charming wife had become close friends, and the count, being a real Parisian, wished me to see something of 'smart Paris', for which I never seemed to have the time.

I also got a taste of Paris elegance at lunches, dinners and soirées given for me and my daughters by the Duke and Duchess of Camastra, the Duchesses of Uzès and Rohan, Mme de Gannay, Prince and Princess Joachim Murat, old Prince Bonaparte (a very intellectual entertainment), le comte de Beaumont (very artistic), who had been in Jassy during the war, helping with my private ambulances, Anna de Noailles, Hélène Soutzo (now Madame Paul Morand) and countless others. Besides all this, as it was not physically possible to give separate private audiences to everybody who asked, I had enormous gatherings at the Ritz, bringing together all those who had asked to see me. This meant vast 'cercles' among hundreds of people of every standing and nationality, all jumbled together. It was very interesting and sometimes touching, but exceedingly fatiguing, as having to speak in many languages, to recognize people sometimes only met once before in a crowd, called upon the maximum of brain-elasticity. It also meant trying not to get confused, not to make mistakes, not to overlook anyone, not to mistake one person for another. Let me add that these embarrassing gatherings generally took place at the end of an exhausting day, and were often followed by some other evening entertainment.

'Sufficient unto the day was the energy thereof!'

My meeting with President Wilson was, to me, an interesting episode. He was then at the zenith of his spectacular career. The world had selected him as the great Arbiter of Peace. Wherever he went, he was being received as a sort of Messiah; the fuss made about him was enough to turn a god's head. This extreme adulation, this elevation of an outsider to first position in the seething Europe of that day, belongs, in my view, to the special 'war neurosis' of the time.

Humanity was searching for a superman who would be able to quell the evil spirits let loose by four years of appalling war, so it fastened its hope and illusions upon the long-faced, sober-looking man from beyond the seas. President Wilson, whose language was so wise, was he not the one indicated to lead the way, to blaze a trail others could follow, a man whose advice would be worth listening to, who, because not a European, would be a perfectly unbiased umpire, judging all questions impartially and without passion?

The world has an instinctive need of idols. It likes to set them up and bow down to them, without pausing to enquire if perchance they may have feet of clay. And even if at first the idol of the day is somewhat bewildered by this sudden uplifting to giddy heights, he gradually begins to agree with those proclaiming his superior position; for praise and adulation are difficult to resist. Finally he believes in his superior perfection and enjoys the part he has been told to play, fitting comfortably into the niche selected for him.

But humans are fickle, and are as ready to pull down as to set up. They even do this with a certain, it seems to me, incomprehensible gusto, as though avenging themselves upon the unfortunate idol for their own mistaken enthusiasm. The fall of the idol is often as cruel as it is unfair. At the outset the chosen one is perhaps instinctively aware of his own limitations, but having been lifted up to the highest crest of popularity, he is quite unprepared for this sudden and blasting change of wind. Thus it was with Wilson, whose fall was, I think, as unjustified as his sudden elevation had been. I dislike unfairness in any form; but then I am no lion-hunter; nor am I ever inclined to howl with the wolves. I like to hear of great men being recognized and getting their due, but I am wary of too explosive hero-worship, and can never understand why man must be so excessive, in both adoration and hatred.

71

Anyhow, when I came to Paris, Wilson was the man of the day. His name was in every mouth; there was something a little sickening about the way he was being glorified and set up on a pedestal which could not but make him giddy.

So much indeed had his head been turned by all the fuss made of him that he wondered if, as great representer of democracy, it was not beneath his dignity to pay a visit to the Queen of Romania – a mere queen! But as everybody was doing so, he thought he would cleverly escape this politeness expected of him by letting me know that he would be delighted to pay his respects, but, being a very busy man, he had no time at his disposal after nine a.m.

With perfect amiability I sent answer that, myself an early riser, I would be glad to receive him even at seven in the morning, if this were agreeable to him. The wind having thus been taken out of his sails, he compromised and came to see me with Mrs Wilson at half past eight.

So they came, both he and she, accompanied by an admiral who was doing duty as ADC and who took part in the audience, which to us seemed unusual, as our military or naval attendants generally wait in another room.

The President was exactly like his pictures; tall, lean, with a very long face and benign smile, his whole appearance very much that of a sleek and rather puritanical clergyman.

So as to be quite precise about my impressions I think it perhaps not uninteresting to quote from my diary of that date.

10 APRIL 1919

President Wilson came early to see me this morning with his wife and the smile he has in his photographs. I received him with my usual simplicity and directness, so that conversation never lagged, although our time was sadly limited. We talked about many things 'à l'ordre du jour', also touching upon the subject of Bolshevism, ever uppermost in my mind, and I could give him a few savoury details about what Bolsheviks really were, which he did not know.

I also expounded upon the hopes of smaller countries, for which he had set up a defender, and this led us on to the League of

Nations,[6] and he began proclaiming the excellence of his pet idea, and how it would be especially the smaller countries that would benefit from the League. All in admiring the beauty of the thought, I could not, however, abstain from drawing his attention to the way great ideas were often marred by future followers and partisans who gradually corrupted the initial thought, finally making something quite different out of a great ideal. It was thus with most religions, and today Christ would probably weep over what man had made out of His teaching. What horrors had not been perpetrated in the name of religion? Our modern world was sadly mercenary and commercial, nor had I noticed any turn to the better after all this tragic upheaval of war. Still, the hope always existed that a new and happier solidarity might arise out of the actual chaos. 'But,' I added, 'let us not treat our fallen enemies too mercilessly. Hatred is a bad counsellor, and leads to more trouble!'

On the next day we lunched with Mr and Mrs Wilson, and I continued to study the great man with interest.

11 APRIL 1919

Lunched with the President, accompanied by my sister,[7] daughters and suite. A small party and a most pleasant meal.

Being profoundly interested in the old gentleman's ideas and ideals, I encouraged him to expound his theories, which he was very willing to do, and was, I think, pleased with the attention with which I listened. He spoke much and well.

President Wilson is exactly as he has been described. He is a born preacher and might be a highly cultivated clergyman. Very convinced of always being right, there is something slighty patronizing about him, but at the same time he is quite *homme du monde*, polite, amiable, even somewhat ceremonious. Very ready to argue, he is, however, owing to his superior, detached attitude, '*qui le fait planer au-dessus du commun des mortels*' [which raises him above the common run of mortals], certain that he will always have the last word. Although not unsympathetic, he nevertheless awakes that certain feeling of antagonism particular to those who, because of their aloofness, are convinced of their indisputable superiority. It makes one wonder if they are absolutely genuine. I can only hope that Wilson is genuine, so as to justify the extraordinary confidence Europe has in his arbitration. Many of his own compatriots look upon him as a fraud, and there is a large party in the United States eagerly awaiting his downfall; for such is the world.

We had one clash. He very sanctimoniously preached to me about how we should treat our minorities, demonstrating how very important this was and expanded at great length upon this topic, becoming exceedingly unctuous and moral as he warmed to his subject, treating me the while as a rather ignorant beginner who could profit from his advice. No doubt I could, but he struck me as being rather too fond of the sound of his own voice, so finally, when he paused to take breath, I mildly suggested that he was evidently well acquainted with these difficulties because of the Japanese question in the United States.

Upon this he bared his rather long teeth in a polite smile, drew up his eyebrows and declared he was not aware that there was a Japanese question in America! Not being a preacher, and as I was his guest, I merely shrugged my shoulders and dropped the subject.

Before leaving, I got him to promise he would call Brătianu so as to give him a chance to lay our situation before him. But I had the feeling that if there had been time, I could do much more with the president than our prime minister, who spoke no English; besides, I always rather enjoy a skirmish.

Thus far my diary.

Mrs Wilson was an attractive lady, and much better-looking from near than far. Built upon generous lines, she had a lovely complexion and charming grey-blue Irish eyes. She was kindly and amiable. The first time I saw her, she was wearing a wonderful bunch of orchids. I shall always remember her thus, with those lovely lilac orchids close up against her smiling face.

I feel I ought soon to be leaving Paris so as not to linger too long in one place, but there are still just a few things I would like to mention, among others a flying visit to Reims.

A moving sight, indeed, that mighty cathedral rising like a ghost of unimaginable beauty from a grey mass of formless ruins. Because of its many wounds, its lines and angels have become blurred, softened as though seen through a veil; its glassless windows paint a tracery of lace against the sky, and, like so many decapitated martyrs, its statues seem frozen with pain. Yet there the great building stands invincible, having defied the modern means of destruction and with them the spirit of hate. A vision of another age, of a stronger faith, ascending above the surrounding chaos, more sacred than ever because of its mutilation, more supremely stately because all around it has been laid low, and today the sky is its only vault.

Such it appeared to me that early spring day, when we stood, mute, gazing up at its perfect majesty. Somehow one became speechless or spoke only in whispers.

We wandered about among the ruins of the city until we were quite exhausted, and then, to lighten the distress of all the sad sights we had seen, Marquis and Marquise de Polignac gave us a lunch in their several-mile-long champagne cellars which had defied every bombardment. The guests were pleasant, there were flowers on the table, and my daughters and I were quite unworthy of the quality of the champagne set before us. I suddenly thought of old Sir George Barclay,[8] who, during our exile at Jassy, had so pined for a bottle of good champagne – and I wished he could have been here with us today to enjoy, as I could not, this famous wine.

As I sat there under-ground, the precious drink sparkling in the glass before me, I closed my eyes for a moment and it was as though I felt the great cathedral rising above my head from the dead ruins of the crumbled city, and I wondered why I was sitting here, supposedly drinking champagne while the gay voices laughing and talking in the large vaulted cellar seemed to have forgotten all about war.

But there must be some who can forget . . .

A great emotion accompanied the arrival of my sister Beatrice,[9] Infanta of Spain, Baby, as she was called in the family. She had come from Zurich to see me; we had not met for five years, and she was the first of my family I met again.

75

So cruelly much, seemingly a whole lifetime, lay between our last parting at Tegernesee and today. Then she had been a gay, well-rounded young mother with a quite small baby in her arms, and here she was, thin to emaciation, with a very small, very attractive, but rather care-worn face. Her attire was simple but exceedingly chic. Her hands had become long and pale, her movements remarkably graceful. Whilst her wit was as quick as ever, beneath the sparkle of her conversation she seemed to be hiding much suffering, and the memory of various experiences which would probably never be entirely revealed to me; for war has a cruel way of making the nearest and dearest almost strangers when first they meet again.

We had to feel our way towards each other gradually, by small 'étapes'. I had become nervous of every question I wanted to ask, for fear of stirring up secret sources of grief.

Little by little, however, we were able to talk more easily and I gleaned her side of the news – home news which I almost feared to hear. About Mama,[10] especially about Mama, I wanted to hear, and yet just this was the news I most dreaded, because I knew that, for Mama, the whole world had crumbled. How had Mama stood all the dreadful events? It was six months since I had had no news from her.

And strangely enough, a few days later a letter from Mama actually found me in Paris – I know not by what route it was sent.

I was just dressing for some great reception; a new dress had been specially made for the occasion, of some golden, shining tissue . . . and suddenly an envelope was laid in my hand . . . Mama!

With trembling fingers I tore open the envelope and read . . . a letter, terrible in its grief. Every word was a fiery dart of pain, every sentence a cry of smothered anguish. Everything had fallen to pieces: first her beloved Russia, then Germany, the country of her adoption, become dear to her heart. Nearly her entire family had been murdered, she herself was ruined and had to live poorly in a country which had gone 'red' and had upset the old order of things. She had lost everything at once: not only her fortune, but all her old beliefs, traditions, ideas and ideals had been shattered, desecrated. A new world had grown up around her in which she could find no footing, in which the grand old autocrat she was no longer had a place. She could not fit in; she would never be able to fit in. Wherever she turned, she saw nothing but change and destruction, and everything she heard augmented her pain. She dared not even look back and remember, for in remembering lay the greatest agony of all.

There I sat reading those terrible pages, and the thin sheets of paper seemed to burn my fingers with their tragic pain. And what was I doing here, in a golden dress, ready to go among a crowd of people who were making a fuss of me, treating me as though I were a heroine? I felt like tearing off my festive gown, of sending to say that I could not come this evening; that I was tired; that I was ill.

But a queen cannot suddenly refuse to go to a reception given officially in her honour; she cannot cry aloud her pain, so that everyone should understand why her eyes are red. For all the glitter among which she moves, there are hours when she is like a smart horse in harness, whose bearing-rein has been tightly drawn so as to oblige her to told her head very high. There is no way of explaining her absence to the expectant crowd.

So I went to my festive party, I smiled, I even laughed; I was overwhelmed with honours, compliments, adulation, I pretended to be light-hearted, even gay; but to me that evening, the world was terribly like a masquerade!

There was something else which made my heart heavy, but this will probably be understood by few.

As in the darkest days in Jassy, when I read the abominable peace conditions Germany was trying to impose upon us, so was I today reading the conditions imposed upon the Germans. The wheel had turned full circle, but I shuddered, remembering the overwhelming indignation and hatred which had then filled my heart, and I knew how poisonous hate can be. I had gone through it.

But I am not of a revengeful nature; another's suffering, even if well deserved, fills me with torturing pity. If I am not exactly for 'offering the other cheek', I am certainly not of those who demand 'an eye for an eye'. Besides, reading through one clause after another, I felt that the conditions were not practicable, they were exaggerated, inhuman. A country could not submit to such excessive demands. The foe had been overthrown, brought to his knees, but he had been brave, it had needed nearly the entire world banded together to beat him; was it fair or even politic to want to strangle him altogether?

I thought of the hideous suffering which would follow, of the seething hatred which would make many million hearts fester with an undying desire for future revenge. Besides these conditions being merciless, I could not help feeling that it was unwise to go so far – too far . . . In my diary of those days, I speak again and again about the uneasy and miserable feelings which assailed me in reading those peace conditions, and goodness knows I had enough reason to resent the way the Germans had treated us! But beneath my quite human passions and indignations slumbered a sort of instinctive sense of equity – something which saw beneath the surface, which seemed to grasp and fathom a deeper sense of things – God's law – which is often not the same as man's.

But I shall not enter deeper into these speculations; too few will follow me along this line of thought. Besides with me, I confess, they are more instinctive than reasoned.

As can be seen, my so-called 'success' did not prevent me from feeling the underlying sadness which lay beneath all things today. The mask of tragedy stalked ever at the heels of those other masks: triumph, joy and success.

One day, I quite suddenly met tragedy in the hall of the Ritz, an upsetting encounter with the past. I was coming in briskly from a walk, chatting with my daughters, my hands full of flowers which had been given me in the street, my cheeks flushed by pleasant exercise, my eyes bright from agreeable sights, and there, before me – a face . . . I hesitated a moment; could it really be? . . . Izvolsky!

He came towards me, seemingly from a great distance, for he was like a ghost – a ghost of ancient might, glory, ambition, I could even say ruthlessness. Izvolsky, who in my earlier days I used to meet at Tegernsee, and who, thinking that there might come a time when I could be useful, would talk politics to me, cleverly trying to lure me towards 'his side of the question'. We had also met in Russia when he was very powerful, and although few in those days saw much importance in me, he had gone out of his way to be amiable, treating me as a future force in the Near East, with which one day one would perhaps have to reckon.

And now . . . this mask of tragedy, this old, broken man, with a look of poverty, of decline, of humiliation about him. It was as though the dust caused by the failure of his country, of the ancient regime, which had been his *raison d'être*, clung about him, rendering him hazy, indistinct, no more quite among the living.

He came to me through that haze of ruin and clasped my hands, while slow tears coursed down his pale, hollow cheeks: '*Madame! Un tel revoir, qui aurait pu penser – notre pauvre Russie!*' [Madam! Such a meeting, who would have thought – my poor Russia!]

A choking feeling rose in my throat – my eyes became dim. I seemed to be gazing down a long passage full of terror, fear and pain. I could find no words, and can only hope that the touch of my hands expressed what my tongue could not utter. A thought written with fiery letters all over him was the cruel word: *Vorbe, vorbe . . .* [in Romanian: 'words, words'].

Here I must mention someone who came into my life during that time, to stay there until death closed her eyes in 1928 – my old friend Loie Fuller.[11] Much has been said about our friendship; mostly it has been scoffed at and misunderstood.

We can so seldom see ourselves from outside, with the eyes of others. Most things, while we live them, seem simple enough; event follows upon event, and they come to us, we do not look for, or invent them, and thus it is also with the people we meet. One day they suddenly appear; and some of them remain.

Loie Fuller came to me quite simply, quite naturally, because she was an artist, because she was an altruist, and because her heart was overflowing with love and a desire to help.

I attracted her like a light. In my youth it was she who had dazzled me with her luminous dances, and magic colour lighting with which her name will always remain associated. She had come to Bucharest to demonstrate her art. Carried away by my enthusiasm, though in those days I was still timid with artists, I had written to her: 'Your dances are a dream come true; I never believed I would see my visions of beauty realized here upon earth.' I was also then, by chance, able to help her out of a difficulty. We were both young in those days – and lived in countries far apart. Nor did we meet again until much later; but beauty had for each of us the same meaning.

Then came the Great War; there was a tremendous shuffling of cards and events took all sorts of shapes. Loie danced no more and most of her time, though she also ran a school for dancing, was given over to good works. She had a passionate desire to help all those in need. Knowing the distress of my country, she began ardently to espouse our cause. Although she had countless friends and patrons, I was the chosen one of her heart. In me she saw the reason for everything. I was the culminating experience of her life. In her last delirium, many years later, she called out to those around her, 'Open wide all doors, my Queen is coming to me', and in this faith she died; but it was not before the world had tried to break both our hearts, and tear asunder our friendship.

In spite of her deep knowledge of many things, Loie was a simple soul. Like me, she was born to be deceived and betrayed, because, like me also, there was no guile in her: *'elle a été toujours de bonne foi'* [she was always sincere]. All through my Paris days she came to me constantly, at all hours of the day, bringing to me all those she thought could be useful to me. She was an enthusiast, had a charming voice, lovely hands, and a marvellous power of persuasion; but sometimes she was taken in.

Thus did she one day bring me together with that strange and romantic old gentleman, Samuel Hill,[12] of whom there is no end of stones, for he was indeed a picturesque figure, but it would lead me too far from my actual subject, were I to begin to tell all about him. In these Paris days he swore me eternal friendship; nor did he ever break his oath. Through long years he remained my devoted champion, and in this case also, it was only death that severed the friendship.

Dear old Samuel Hill was a visionary. He saw everything over life-size, was always ruminating over some gigantic project and had extraordinary and mysterious connections with other countries, particularly with Japan, where he had often been. He loved Japan and the Japanese, and spoke their language fluently. Amongst other activities, he built wonderful roads, but especially he dreamed. Some of his dreams occasionally came true, but some were so fantastic that they had to remain dreams. He mixed sentiment with everything he did, and this was his great link with Loie.

Loie was very small and round with a face exactly like Shirley Temple's; beside Samuel Hill, with his huge bulk and leonine head, covered with a mass of white hair, she looked tiny. Small Loie, however, had tamed this enormous and somewhat uncouth pioneer, and he would follow her about like a great Newfoundland dog, and his rather fierce blue eyes became mild and gentle when he looked at her. This great big man had a strangely soft voice, little in keeping with his immense stature, and though he was certainly no drawing-room hero, he could be politely ceremonious in a quaint, old-fashioned way. He was certainly an unusual figure, and always had so much to relate that I never had a clear picture of all he really did, or meant to do. Veil-draped Loie and her giant follower were a queer couple one could not expect everybody to understand. I understood them with my heart – that is the only explanation I can give. I understood them, even though they missed their target; but this belongs again to that queer little twist in my nature which allows me to see the spirit beneath outward absurdities.

Besides his love for me, Samuel Hill had a fervent adoration for Albert of Belgium, with whom he had scaled mountains somewhere in America when Albert was still almost a boy. Of all the sovereigns of Europe, it was the King of the Belgians and the Queen of Romania that this dear old original had singled out as those most worthy to be served and helped.

This queer old gentleman has now passed over into another world and sometimes, in looking back, it is hard to believe that he really existed, so unlike was he to anyone else.

It was also Loie who persuaded me to go to Aix les Bains to visit the American YMCA camp of rest for American soldiers. So taking

Mignon, my sister and a friend, Yone Kennedy, with me, we spent a day among the American 'boys', who gave us a tremendous reception.

General Pershing had sent one of his generals to me, asking if I would come and visit the American headquarters, but this had been too complicated to arrange, so I went to Aix instead. I was becoming more and more popular among the Americans and wanted to show some appreciation of all the attention paid me and also to express my gratitude for the generous way the American Red Cross and the Hoover organization were helping my poor in Romania.

This was a quaint, cheerful entertainment and a great success all round, the soldiers becoming more and more excited and delighted as we went about among them, watched their games and took an active part in their entertainments; there was a happy atmosphere of simple-hearted good will on both sides.

In the end I was asked to speak to the men and to tell them about my country and what my people had suffered during the war. This I finally consented to do, the men grouping themselves around me in an enormous circle. I also gave a lengthy account of the difference between Democracy and Bolshevism, which some were inclined to believe was a wonderful new creed which was to bring about a better and fairer world, based upon a marvellous liberty, which would mean happiness and prosperity among men. With extraordinary ardour I demonstrated how ghastly was, in reality, what was going on in tortured Russia, how brother had risen against brother – a dreadful tale of suffering, cruelty, wholesale destruction and death, the entire vast country soaked in blood. I waxed eloquent, because this was a subject upon which I felt strongly, having seen from too near what Bolshevism really meant. All faces were upturned towards me and I was consumed by thousands of eager eyes. Americans are fond of being talked to, there is something child-like about them, which is very sympathetic.

Before we left they began to dance, and my sister, daughter and friend joined in with the fun, eagerly snatched from one arm to another, for there were far too few ladies to go round!

Thoroughly exhausted, that same night we travelled back to Paris.

Among the many movements at that time was also a strong 'feminist' movement. As women had bravely done their share of work during the war, it was no longer possible to ignore their voice or set them aside. They had become a force.

Lady Aberdeen, who was the principal fighter for women's rights, came to me to ask if I would put myself at the head of the movement and go with them before the League of Nations. She declared that I had all the qualities of a pioneer and that it would be the greatest honour for them to march under my leadership; that I would be a wonderful flag for their cause, if they could persuade me to do this. I was much flattered to be selected as the one most for such a part, but explained that I could not put myself forward in this way unless it was sanctioned by all the other queens of Europe. I could not take it upon myself to stand out alone in this, in such a conspicuous way, unless those of my caste agreed.

The dear old lady understood my point of view and did not insist further, while regretting that she had not been able to persuade me.

Thus one thing happened to me after another in such a varied way, that life, although impossibly exhausting, was also intensely interesting.

The only hours I could reserve for my friends were the evening hours when I did not go out. Then I would assemble a gay little party at my round table, where at the end of a tiring day I was able to let my poor brain rest and join in the fun with others.

New and old friends joined these parties, my own and my daughters' acquaintances, people of every nationality, of all ages, royal, titled or humble, I jumbled them all together, and among them were many who had helped us during the cruel days at Jassy – doctors, officers, nurses; French, English, Americans.

Kind Colonel Anderson of the American Red Cross reappeared, full of touching loyalty and devotion, ready to continue to help suffering Romania; Colonel Boyle, bringing now and again a useful Canadian, friends from London, from home. There was an extraordinary atmosphere of friendship and good will, with an undercurrent of excitement which made everyone very talkative, occasionally even a little boisterous, as here officialdom was at an end, this was relaxation after the day's rush. I like to look back and see all those faces again; let me name a few: Lady Astor with her eldest boy Billy, then at Eton, my godson, who considered he had a special right to me, such a delightful, affectionate little fellow; the Castellanes, Poliniacs, Mme de Sansay, Nicolai and Rochefort, Pierre Reindre, Drs Devaux, Championière, Vaudescal, Lelaurier etc. Billy Astor is today a Member of Parliament. There was also Marie Putiatin, Yone Kennedy and others . . . Today we are all dispersed and some are no longer of this world.

The time was approaching for my departure. Mignon, who had developed a passion for England, was possessed by an ardent desire to go to an English finishing school. So, considering that this might be really good for her, especially as conditions in Romania were so very unsettled, I got Nando to telegraph his consent. Queen Mary was very kind about helping us find the right school and promised to keep an eye upon my child herself, so, although the wrench was great, especially as communications were still so irregular and uncertain, I had the courage to separate from her. Also Lisabetha was not to return with me, as she wished to remain for a while in Paris to follow up a course in an art school. I left her in charge of the Brătianus, who were still in Paris because of the Peace Conference. This meant separation from three of my children, Ileana alone remaining with me. Accustomed to being surrounded by a whole flock, this made me feel suddenly very empty. But there were so many problems to face and the children's education was one of the most perplexing, and I was obliged to take weighty decisions, doing my best to act wisely on my own responsibility.

One of my last activities in Paris was a lunch given for me and my daughters by Paderewski,[13] then Polish Prime Minister, surrounded by endless other important Poles with names echoing Polish history.

It was strange to see the great musician metamorphosed into a statesman and talking politics instead of art. His fine, keen face, crowned with a mass of hair, did not deny his past. He was a charming host, genial, eloquent, full of fiery enthusiasm, and he seemed exceedingly keen to gain me as an ally. He considered our interests identical and urged on me that Romania and Poland should work as closely together as possible.

In those days, when everything was in a state of exuberance, politicians and diplomats of many countries talked to me as though I was one of them. Their interest in me was heightened by the fact that I was a woman: I was a stimulant to their overstrained minds, a pleasant and invigorating change from the solemn and often quarrelsome equals with whom they had generally to debate. Besides, it had become the fashion to glorify me; the tide of change had carried me high up on the wave of popularity. I had become a favourite with all classes and my presence was supposed to give greater glamour to a meeting, a banquet, a festivity. I will not deny that this was pleasant, flattering. Luckily I did not lose my head, nor imagine that I was a competent judge of situations with which even the most initiated found it difficult to cope. But I kept my eyes and ears wide open; I listened and watched, trying to plumb the different currents whirling about this new Europe arisen from flames and ashes. I was intensely interested, my brain seemed keenly on edge, but I had had no real training, my attitude was entirely spontaneous and unconventional. I never deluded myself into believing I was a great intelligence, but I could learn to understand, to see my way, to grasp many problems which hitherto had left me indifferent.

I had no small polite tricks, I never played a part nor pretended, but I had a naturally elastic brain: I seized things quickly, understood people easily and could rapidly grasp the other's point of view. On all occasions I was unaffectedly myself, a queen and a woman, and my absolute naturalness was refreshing to those many men wading through endless nets of intrigue.

Anyhow, that Polish lunch was brilliant and a great success: enthusiasm ran high and many an amiable and flattering word was uttered. To hear my hosts talk, it was as though the future welfare of Europe depended on the queen of Romania's collaboration!

Their tongues were smooth, their compliments well turned, there was no want of 'charme slave' about the Poles. However, that ever-bubbling sense of humour, my most precious standby through life, yet again prevented my success from going to my head. Instinctively I felt that this was a period of general excitement. People were off their balance, were searching for new values; almost anything seemed possible to those who had realized their dreams of independence. They were drunk with success, and hope stood before them like a dazzling doorway. Their hands were eagerly extended toward new friendships, new pacts. They suddenly felt rich and were sending out feelers in every direction. The future seemed full of promise and a thousand new ways were opening out.

Thus it was in that giddy, breathless year of 1919. I speak of my share in it, because it was like a light thrown across my path, and it added just then to life's glamour; I too belonged to the searchers, my hands were also eagerly ready to build. Greater Romania was my dream and I ardently wished to place it upon a firm basis.

Nigh upon two decades have since elapsed. Many a deception, many a disillusion has overthrown the feverish enthusiasm of newly won victories. Reality was stern, ugly, difficult; the rainbow hopes faded one by one. Humanity did not live up to its best possibilities; the warm generosity of those early days melted into the mud of selfishness and cupidity.

The victors forgot to be generous, also they wasted precious time in quarrelling among themselves instead of building, building strongly, economically, their eye upon time, profiting by the hour when luck was on their side. Today, therefore, we stand in the uneasy chaos of a world that has squandered its possibilities; most problems are still unsolved; there is no real peace or assurance anywhere; friendships have been betrayed, and with disillusioned eyes Europe sees ink-black clouds rising on every horizon, while humanity has tried to wipe God out of its conceptions . . . But God is waiting . . . He cannot be denied for long.

The hour of departure from Paris finally sounded. I was nearly at the end of my tether, and eager to turn my face towards home again, though I was well aware that home stood for more effort, more struggle, more fatigue.

Paris gave me a tremendous send-off: from President Poincaré and Marshal Foch downwards, everybody was at the station to bid me farewell. I had made many friends, had gained sympathy in many quarters, had given every ounce of my strength to carry out the mission entrusted to me. I was tired, but I felt I had done my best, bravely, relying entirely on my own intuition. I had shunned no effort, had allowed no doubt or discouragement to sap my energies, I had endeavoured to grasp situations, to face difficulties, occasionally, even, hostility, intent upon lessening any prejudice entertained against Romania. I had brought forward the needs and aspirations of my people. I had pleaded, explained, had broken endless lances in their defence. I had given my country a living face, and many had understood and aided my efforts, understanding the enthusiasm that sustained my strength.

It was not without emotion that I took leave of Paris,[14] which had taken me into its heart. It had been a great experience, although the strain had been such that I could not have kept it up much longer, so I had to make an end. In spite of prayers that I should remain longer, I had to tear myself away from too much personal success, too much admiration, adulation, adoration: enough is as good as a feast, and I wisely remembered Nietzsche's words: *Man muss die Kraft haben Abschied zu nehmen, wenn es am besten schmeckt!* [One must have the strength to say goodbye when it seems best!]

So away puffed my train out of the gay city's station to the sound of two national anthems, to the sound of 'Vive la Reine!', 'Vive la Roumanie!'. The eager faces gazing up at my window began to grow smaller, to dwindle into the distance until they finally became indistinct, fading entirely away. Along the line many voices were still calling: 'Vive la Reine!'. It was over, I felt tears burn in my eyes. Finished, the end of a chapter; a new page must be turned.

Among the many faces that had gazed longingly up to my window, I especially remembered Mignon's, her round cheeks wet with tears. She had chosen to remain behind, but at the moment of parting her courage had almost failed; Mignon had a loving heart.

SIX

Home

True to my word, I was bringing back several carriages with provisions for the sick and needy – all the precious gifts collected while abroad. These carriages had been attached to my train because I knew how precarious transport was just then, and I meant to leave nothing to chance; only thus, attached to my own special train, did they run no risk.

The actual journey was for me a rest: in the train my energies could not be called upon and the enforced inactivity was a blessed and well-merited relaxation. It was a slow journey full of interruptions, and it lasted longer than planned. The lands we passed through were still under military occupation and their security was doubtful, especially as we advanced further east. Everywhere there was unrest, tinged with a tendency towards Bolshevism which could break out anywhere at any moment. Added to this there were early spring floods which blocked our way. Finally at Semlin we were obliged to leave my train for a boat on the Danube. Here for the first time I met my future son-in-law, at that time crown prince and regent of Serbia, his father being still living.

He came to greet me, accompanied by Admiral Trowbridge and Mr Alfred Stead, whom I had met before. Alexander[1] was very shy, but we exchanged amiabilities and both hoped that disagreement about frontiers in the Banat would not prevent neighbourly feelings being established between our countries.

I loved the journey down the Danube. It was early spring: the air was balmy, the fruit-trees and lilacs in flower, nightingales singing everywhere; besides it was Easter, and although I could not go to church I felt Resurrection in every breath I drew.

Last year, desperate and outwardly beaten, I had moved among our troops at Oneşti,[2] had gone to the 'Înviere'[3] with them, had taken part in their Easter feast, breaking eggs with them according to Romanian tradition, endeavouring with the last shreds of my energy to keep hope alight in their hearts.

Today Greater Romania was a fact, but hard battles of another kind still lay ahead. I had no illusions as to this, and every hour of rest was employed in bracing myself for new effort, and in bringing my thoughts to order. I had experienced so much in so short a period, had met so many people, had been tossed on so many different currents, it needed a little 'recule' to see clearly in the 'too much' that my mind and heart had absorbed. The Paris excitement was still rushing through my memory; my body was having a rest, but my brain was keenly at work.

Our journey lasted four days, and at last on 21 April I reached Bucharest and was given an overwhelming reception. From the moment I reached Turnu Severin, there was no more rest: at every station were huge crowds and tumultuous shows of welcome. The news had spread that the Queen had been sent on a special mission, and had gone to speak for Romania, bravely espousing her cause before the Allies with success, so my journey home had about it something of a triumphant advance.

As the days when one meets the full measure of success are few, I here copy out an article written on my return to our capital. It expresses what my people felt for me then. This may be considered vanity, but life has taught me since that memory is short and gratitude a luxury often dispensed with, so it is only fair that this appreciation of my activities should have a place in the 'Later Chapters of My Life'.

In the days of my enthusiasm this recognition of my efforts to help my country made my heart warm with pride and joy. Today? Well, today, I smile sadly and the words which often ring like an echo through my pages best express what I feel: Tout passé . . .

It was pleasant to be home again. The king was pleased to have me back. It was springtime, everything was in bloom and timely rains seemed to bless our fields with the promise of a fine harvest.

A few days' rest to put my house in order and to unpack the glorious provisions I had brought back for my poor, and then, like an avalanche, all my different duties fell on me again and it meant work and exhausting effort from morning to night. These were the Jassy days in another form. It was no longer war, but the chaos it had created and the results of two years' occupation were heart-breaking. All things had to begin anew; everywhere I turned I was met by destruction, disorder, disorganization. Besides, this was a new world. Never again would the old times come back, everything was changed. War had created an enormous precipice between yesterday and today.

Incalculable social upheavals were taking place: one had to readjust one's mind to new ideas and try to understand them, and face them bravely, but this could not be done all in a day. My royal mentality was anchored in beloved traditions, which now were being flouted and denied. Concessions to the 'Zeitgeist' had to be made, for it was hurling us along as on a tide which could not be stemmed; but certain treasured beliefs had to be saved, certain destructive tendencies withstood. If change must be, it must not come about too destructively: bridges had to be built from the old to the new and everything could not be focused at once; difficulties loomed too large.

The most immediate necessity was to set about relieving some of the distress ravaging our different districts, and two valuable American organizations were helping us most efficiently: the American Red Cross and the Hoover organization. They were immensely generous, but inclined to be rivals. Both, however, immediately recognized me as a smiling force that added prestige and glamour to their undertaking. So I kept in continual close touch with both sides, trying with my never-diminishing wealth of good will, and with that royal patience acquired through long years of training, to smooth over difficulties, avoid offences and show the necessary appreciation so as to keep their enthusiasm alive. Also I was for ever smoothing over differences with our local authorities who did not always understand American methods.

I became a great favourite among these many selfless workers who had been recruited from the four corners of the United States. I thus learnt more American geography than out of lesson-books, and often united at my table men and women from the north, south, east and west of that surprising continent, so full of young force and unlimited possibilities.

There are, however, some fundamental differences between Americans and Europeans, and occasionally the New World's point of view, its methods and manners baffled me. These people from beyond the seas were so astonishingly efficient and yet so disconcertingly childlike and artless, confident, self-assured. They liked to see and to enquire into everything and loved to be talked to and 'told things'. Their attitude towards royalty was disconcerting. They evidently liked to have to do with 'a real live queen'; but I always felt that they looked upon royalty as a strange species, remnants of other times, now outlived – a sort of decorative luxury without which their 'enlightened' democracy could do perfectly well, and yet their ardent desire to investigate all things made them eager to approach me and to probe of what stuff I was made. This both amused and stimulated me, though occasionally their curiosity was somewhat galling. Here again my sense of humour saved me from ever taking offence, when I understood that no offence was meant and their politeness was always above reproach, although their questions were sometimes embarrassing. We in old Europe had started so much sooner than they had; their younger efficiency was more vigorous, but there is a poetry, a mellowness about our old civilization which will never be theirs; nor can their newer minds ever quite fathom wherein lies the charm of those old, almost worn-out prejudices and habits to which we cling and which they feel, without understanding.

They interested me, and I interested them, and though we were in certain conceptions miles apart, our mutual outspokenness and our great desire to help and do good was a strong link between us. Also there was a largeness about their possibilities which refreshened our tired ranks.

There was especially Colonel Anderson, head of the Red Cross Mission, my old friend of Jassy days, and on the other side there was energetic Colonel Amant of the Hoover organization, a man from Texas to whom nothing seemed impossible, who wore his uniform with the 'chic' of a cowboy, who knew no fatigue and delighted in my power of resistance.

To him no distribution in the villages or feeding of hungry children was completely satisfactory unless I came to smile upon his work. He had the feeling that our joint energies could bring blessings down upon the country, no matter how insurmountable were the difficulties. In fact difficulties were Amant's chief stimulant; he actually thrived on them. Although his restless activities occasionally made me gasp, Colonel Amant was a most refreshing personality, even if I did not always understand his Yankee twang.

I have a vivid and amused memory of how one day, on one of our wanderings amidst far-off villages, we stopped to drink our tea at a quiet convent hidden among the hills. This sleepy place of rustic beauty, inhabited by a community of black-veiled women who did little else but ring the church bells and pray at odd hours of both night and day, was absolutely incomprehensible to him. His principal object in life was to push forward, get there, to accomplish things; was it possible that there should exist human beings with such an impractical, time-wasting conception of life? His young indignation vastly tickled my sense of humour – and we had a good laugh.

But the place was lovely, so incredibly still, peaceful, lost to the world – and when the evening bells suddenly began to sound I could not help being glad that all things on earth were not as relentlessly 'driving' as Amant's Texas energy.

There were many other Americans who devoted themselves to our villages, hospitals and suffering people. Among them was Dr Bayne,[4] who did wonderful work and was adored by the rural population. No impediments cooled his ardour, he had almost become a Romanian, so keenly did he espouse the suffering of our peasants, so passionately did he combat poverty, sickness and want in our villages. There were still many others, both men and women. As I write, their different faces rise before me and over time and distances I send them one and all the thanks of a heart which has never forgotten the precious aid they gave us in those difficult days of reconstruction.

Thinking back on those many excursions we made among our villages, a strange little incident comes back to my mind.

Somewhere near Curtea de Argeş, Colonel Anderson had asked if Ileana and I would come and help distribute the provisions they were dividing among the peasants.

Clad in their picturesque costumes, men, women and children crowded around us in dense ranks. Their expressions were strained and anxious; their eyes had become over-large in their emaciated wax-pale faces. It was easy to see that want and misery had been their constant companions, but, accustomed to suffering, they accepted without protest or surprise the unexplained events which swept through their frugal existence. The coming of the Queen was, however, a happy event and they crushed in upon me in such numbers that the authorities wanted to drive them back. I begged, however, that they should be allowed to approach me as they wanted, so as to show their love and devotion in their own simple way. They wanted to kiss my hands, to touch, if possible, my sleeve, the hem of my skirt, or to look into my face. I knew their ways and felt at home among them; all through the war had not our soldiers crushed in upon me in much the same way?

I soon noticed a woman who never left my side, although a certain shifting of the crowd occasionally separated her from me. She always worked her way back through the human surge which threatened to engulf her. She was grey-haired but probably younger than she looked; her features were calm and austere, with something noble about them. A white cloth round her sorrow-ravaged face made her the most perfect type of Mater Dolorosa I had ever seen. She looked at me with large sunken eyes, in which all the world's pain seemed to be centred; her gaze never left me, but at the same time I felt she was staring beyond my face at a vision which haunted her.

Peasant-wise, she kept one hand pressed to her mouth, a gesture which seems to try instinctively to conceal every emotion. Her profoundly sorrowful eyes fascinated me: it was like looking down into a well and wondering what was hidden in its depths . . .

As hundreds had flocked together, the distribution lasted hours, and finally a high-backed chair was found somewhere so that I was able to sit down. The strange woman did not budge from my side, but stood like a statue with one hand laid possessively on my shoulder, her eyes fixed upon the distance in an unblinking stare. There was unconscious possessive dignity in her attitude, but also something rather odd.

Several times those accompanying me tried to coax her away, and I could not help noticing a certain disquiet in their efforts, but when I protested against her being removed, someone made the descriptive gesture of tapping his fingers against his forehead, and all at once I understood: the woman was out of her mind!

'Ever since war . . .' whispered the village priest, 'it was her only son, but she is quite harmless . . .'

I pleaded that she should be left in peace. If it could comfort her to stand beside me, why send her away? I took her hand in mine and she looked at me with her deep, uncanny eyes, but she said nothing, only closed her fingers over mine in a possessive gesture.

Suddenly she moved away, but returned almost immediately with a bundle in her arms. Her movements were slow and full of that dignity often adopted by the mad; she had the air of an offended and beggared queen. She stood for a moment, the precious bundle clasped to her heart, and then, with a tragic gesture, as though giving all she had, she dropped it into my lap.

I understood that she, too, although in rags, had a gift to give; but her gift was for the Queen!

What could it be? Carefully I untied the ragged strips of cotton which held the packet together, and out tumbled an old military tunic with rusty buttons, a shabby cap, a worn pair of boots, a tarnished medal, some soiled underwear . . .

Simple as was this silent scene, there was something extraordinarily dramatic about it, which imprinted itself for once and for all upon my memory. The crazy peasant mother offering to the Queen, who had come as a giver, the only treasure she possessed: the uniform in which her son had been killed.

It is hardly surprising, is it, that I never forgot that woman whose eyes were like a bottomless well? The village Mater Dolorosa who had a gift to offer the Queen!

94

Queen Elisabeth (Carmen Sylva) and Crown Princess Marie attending a charity event at 'Leagănul Sf. Ecaterina', Bucharest, 1904. (*Diana Mandache Collection*)

Marie and Ferdinand in Turda (Transylvania),
27 May 1919. (*Diana Mandache Collection*)

Queen Marie with Iuliu Maniu, attending a peasant reception at Baia Mare (Transylvania),
26 May 1919. (*Diana Mandache Collection*)

The King and Queen observe the 2nd Division of the Romanian Army crossing the Tisa, 13 August 1919. (*Diana Mandache Collection*)

Queen Marie with Romanian soldiers at the 'Carpaţi' Sanatorium. (*Diana Mandache Collection*)

Marie and Prince Mircea, *c.* 1913, shown on a postcard sold for the benefit of the Society Prince Mircea in 1919. (*Diana Mandache Collection*)

Queen Marie, 'the mother-in-law' of the Balkans. (*Romanian National Archives, Regina Maria III/147*)

Queen Elisabetha of Greece, once a princess of Romania, in 1923. (*Romanian National Archives, Regina Maria III/145*)

Queen Marie of Yugoslavia, once a princess of Romania, 1923. (*Romanian National Archives, Regina Maria III/137*)

Queen Marie with Prince Michael, January 1923. (*Romanian National Archives, Regina Maria III/148*)

The wedding of the Crown Prince Carol of Romania with Princess Helen of Greece, with Ileana of Romania and Catherine of Greece, Athens, 10 March 1921. (*Romanian National Archives, Regina Maria III/127*)

Queen Marie and her borzois, 1922. (*Diana Mandache Collection*)

Left to right: George II of Greece with Elisabetha, Ferdinand of Romania, Alexander of Yugoslavia with Mignon, and Marie of Romania with Ileana, Sinaia, 1922. (*Diana Mandache Collection*)

Before the coronation at Alba-Iulia on 15 October 1922. First row: King Ferdinand, Queen Marie; second row: Crown Princess Helen. Miron Cristea the Patriarch and Crown Prince Carol. (*Diana Mandache Collection*)

The Coronation, 15 October 1922. Beneath the canopy in front of the cathedral at Alba-Iulia, Mihail Pherekyde, President of the Senate, reads the Coronation message to the Nation. (*Diana Mandache Collection*)

Queen Elisabetha of Greece, Queen Marie of Romania, Queen Marie of Yugoslavia and Beatrice Infanta of Spain, 16 October 1922. (*Diana Mandache Collection*)

At the Coronation parade, King Ferdinand and Queen Marie, with, behind them on the left in the second row, Bertie, Duke of York, later King George VI, Alba-Iulia, 15 October 1922. (*Romanian National Archives, Regina Maria, III/136*)

Queen Marie with Crown Princess Helen, on horseback, 10 May 1925. (*Diana Mandache Collection*)

Moving thus from place to place, I could see for myself where help was most needed. For a while, politics was set aside so that I could give all my energy to relieving the poor. I was well aware that what we were able to accomplish was but a drop in the ocean, but all the same I toiled, worked, encouraged, organized, called upon everyone's good will, strained every faculty to the utmost degree.

This also is long ago; others have today shouldered my work, but the memory of the great effort we then made still surges through my veins like a river in flood. It was tiring, it needed every ounce of my strength, especially as never-ending conflicts, jealousies and prejudices made doubly fatiguing every victory we won.

But as long as such belief was put in me, I had to go on and on: faith moved mountains. In those days my people had absolute faith in me, and this belief lent me patience, strength and enthusiasm, and much was achieved.

SEVEN

Transylvania

The great day came when it was decided that the King and I should make our first round through Transylvania[1] to visit our liberated people. This was the supreme moment; it was to be the seal set upon our victory, the ultimate realization of the great dream for which so many had striven, for which so many had died.

Future generations will tell of this journey as of a triumphant *tournée*; they will relate how the King and Queen moved from one town to another, from one village to another, in an atmosphere of continental enthusiasm, of how they were everywhere hailed as deliverers. It will be remembered how the people knelt down before them, kissing their hands, their feet, the very ground on which they trod, how the old women wept for joy and how small children were laid in their arms so that, as symbolic father and mother of their delivered people, we should bless the little ones by our touch. And thus it really was an unforgettable journey, a trance-like advance from one place to another, a never-ending pageant of wonderful peasant processions unrolling before us in a fantastic display of colour; a glorious, gorgeous fulfilment of the Dream of Dreams: the uniting of all Romanians under one sceptre, and this had become reality under our reign!

Yes, it really was thus; outwardly it was brilliant, wonderful, never to be forgotten, and yet . . .

As this is, to a certain degree, a Queen's confessions, the story of her inner as well as of her outer life, to make it quite a true story I must go deeper than that outward picture, and try to reveal my own feelings. I must try to make others understand exactly what I felt, while, a smile on my lips, I lived those days of triumph at my husband's side.

96

There was first of all that great grief which had, last autumn, while we were in the ultimate throes of the Great War, torn our inner happiness to pieces, and which was still pouring through our lives, sapping all joy at its very foundations, making of each day a new anxiety, darkening every picture, every hope for the future. There had been heart-rending hours just before our departure, when I had moved heaven and earth trying to save one of my own who seemed to be drowning, and who wilfully turned away from my outstretched hand. Love each other as we did, we had reached a tragic turning, when another conception of honour and duty confronted us, a tragic misunderstanding which erected an inseparable barrier between us, and we stood one on each side of it, broken-hearted, but absolutely unable to come to an understanding or even to a truce.

There was also that other sad knowledge which had come to me, that if you are a thinking, conscious human being, joy can never, alas, be complete. Words I wrote in my diary just after we had passed the old frontier of Predeal,[2] no longer a frontier today, express so perfectly what I felt and still feel that I shall quote them here.

All the peasants are frantic with joy. For them it is deliverance after centuries of dependence and oppression, and Nando and I, with our army, are acclaimed as their liberators. It is a wonderful thought, one which ought to fill me with nothing but glorious, bubbling joy, but life is too much of a struggle to ever allow one's greatest hours to be complete and perfect joy. Besides, all the world over, one man's happiness too often means another man's grief. It is one of the great, disconcerting problems which sway the world. There is no real happiness for anyone, because of the too many conflicting passions which tear life to pieces. One man desires one thing, and another desires just the contrary, so that no wish can be fulfilled without someone suffering. It is the same with countries, and all things, until one's brain aches at the very thought. To liberate our people, another people had to be beaten, another country had to fall to pieces, so on one side rejoicing, on the other gnashing of teeth, and unlike the victors of old, I cannot rejoice over the fall of my enemy!!

Thus I felt then, and never at any hour of my life could I get rid of the other man's pain; it haunts my joy like the ghost at a feast, it treads on my heels, follows me even in my sleep.

But this is inner history, the reverse of the medal. Let us return, as is fitting, to the outward picture of joy.

Oradea Mare, Bichis Czaba, Careii Mari, Baia Mare, Jibou, Dej, Bistriţa, Gherla, Cluj, Turda, Câmpeni, Abrud, Ţebea, Alba Iulia, Blaj, Copşa, Sibiu, Sălişte, Făgăraş, Braşov, were the towns and hamlets we visited, going from one place to another, and received everywhere with frantic manifestations of joy by the Romanian population.

Everywhere indescribably picturesque receptions, the peasants flocking together in thousands, the most distant villages having sent deputations to greet us. A never-ending pageant of wonderful costumes varying according to the districts, for Romania, like Yugoslavia, is a land of costumes. The different processions were sometimes quite fantastic in their quaint variety, some of the women's dresses and head-dresses strangely reminiscent of the Middle Ages and of the coifs, wimples and hoods of our ancestors.

There were also grand parades of carts drawn by magnificent white, wide-horned oxen, brightly decorated with garlands and floating streamers, the carts hung with carpets of many colours and packed with singing, shouting, cheering peasants old and young. Whole bridal processions also passed before us in festive array, with music played at the head and heralded by troops of youngsters on horseback waving banners like great wings over their heads.

The Saxon outriders had a quaint way of attaching bright silk kerchiefs all over their costumes. These floated in the wind in fantastic colours, a never-ending rainbow of every possible tint. These same gaudy, printed silks were also carried as flags. The effect was dazzling and a delight to the eye.

By hundreds and thousands they came, no matter from what distance, old and young, men, women and children. Wrinkled crones and handsome maidens, dignified matrons clasping their last-born in their arms, their elder children trotting along beside them, wearing exactly the same dress as their elders, miniature little men and women with huge eyes full of astonishment, but already stoically patient, unemotional, uncomplaining, as is characteristic of their long-suffering race. Stalwart tillers of the land, marching proudly in their superb coats, embroidered in many colours, green or blue upon brown, red or orange upon white leather, crowned with huge fur bonnets, and at their side the ancients of the village, their long, uncut, grey hair hanging from beneath wide-brimmed felt hats. Leaning upon their sticks or crutches they came, they too, eager once in their lives to look upon the faces of their 'deliverers', although some were so bent that they could scarcely raise their heads. Many carried gifts in their hands; the women would often step out of the ranks to lay delicate embroideries, coloured eggs, local pottery or carving at my feet. Some even brought whole costumes resembling those they wore themselves. Distance was no obstacle to them, nor did they care where they slept nor what they ate. A religious fervour moved every heart.

In certain places there were troops of young riders who strangely resembled the wild *haiducs* and *pandurs* of our national legends. They scampered past on their small shaggy horses, dressed in rough fur mantles and enormous fur bonnets, waving their banners above their heads, uttering strange cries, or singing in chorus songs in which there was still an echo of the war-songs of old. The musical instruments on which they played resembled nothing ever seen in tamer countries and it would have been difficult to give them a name.

Brides played a prominent part in these village displays; theirs were always the brightest costumes and their head-dresses took fantastic forms and dimensions. In one hamlet these hopeful maidens wore enormous wreaths of woollen flowers interwoven with gaudy ribbons, whilst their hair, at the back, was plaited into a sort of net which must have taken hours to do.

In other places their heavy wreaths were crowned with peacock's feathers spreading like a halo at the back of their heads. Others wore close-fitting helmet-like caps which also covered the nape of the neck, composed of a mass of old silver coins sewn closely together, which made them resemble the carapace of an armadillo, and endless rows of these heavy coins hid the upper part of their richly embroidered shifts. Among the Saxon matrons were coifs almost exactly similar to the close-fitting head-dress worn by Mary Stuart in her different portraits. In several villages the girls paraded top-boots of red leather over which their pleated skirts swelled like crinolines, revealing a wealth of starched petticoats beneath. It would be impossible to describe the endless variety of these national dresses, jealously preserved through the ages, unchangeable even in our times of change.

It would be hard to say which receptions were the most touching, where the people were most enthusiastic; wherever we went we were met with bubbling manifestations of loyalty and clamorous outbursts of joy.

Three-quarters of the rural population was Romanian, whilst certain towns were still quite Hungarian, and when we drove through them, in spite of the loud rejoicing of the peasants who had crowded to receive us, many tight-shut windows in the principal street were like cold shoulders turned upon those who were looked upon by many as intruders, and these hostile, tight-shut windows saddened me. I would have liked to penetrate behind them with outstretched hands, which probably both conqueror and vanquished would have criticized and misunderstood; but even at this hour, outwardly so glorious, I could never forget those who wept while we rejoiced. Irresistibly my gaze was drawn to those barred shutters, wondering what resentment or grief lay hidden away behind them in the dark!

The situation was further complicated because at that time our army was fighting Bela Kun's Bolsheviks, so that in many places the Hungarians looked upon us as deliverers, come in time to save them from the red terror, and more than one Hungarian deputation came to offer their thanks to the King. On the large central squares characteristic of Transylvanian towns, Nando reviewed his troops who marched proudly past with conquering tread. I watched them with pride, my heart full of conflicting emotions, and I kept pondering, more than would have been considered fitting, had my thoughts been known, the vicissitudes of Fate. I could never even at the hour of victory, give myself up in blind surrender joy of triumph.

I deeply loved many of the landscapes of our newly gained territories; there were, especially, certain mountain villages between Turda and Câmpeni which entranced me. This was the home of the 'Motzi', a very poor but specially heroic population, hill-dwellers, who, in spite of centuries of oppression and persecution, had remained staunchly, even pugnaciously Romanian. Their cottages had exaggeratedly high roofs whose thatch, continually exposed to sun, wind and rain, had acquired the colour of moleskin and looked like giant fur bonnets, completely squashing the rest of the house and giving them the shape children delight in. To cap it all, these grey-brown roofs were thickly padded with intensely green moss and overhung small wooden galleries whose arches were often roughly but artistically carved with quaint designs. Seen from afar, half hidden behind a mass of blooming fruit-trees, they resembled giant ant-hills. To this must be added the brightly embroidered costumes of the inhabitants, who came out in masses to greet us, headed by their priests, the tolling of bells, the squeaking of bagpipes and other strange instruments, shouting riders on fidgety little horses, brandishing flags above their heads – delightful pictures such as more sophisticated and tamer countries cannot offer us.

Our motor rolled through exquisite valleys succulent in their early spring verdure, meadows full of cowslips, of which the women and children threw great bunches into my lap as I passed. Small gurgling streams along which the willows stood in green feathery bunches against a background of hazy blue hills. We flew for hours over hill and dale, passing through vast, undulating landscapes to plunge into the shade of huge beech forests where the trees arched like cathedrals over our heads. Nothing is more soul-satisfying than a beech-wood in early leaf! I quite especially recollect one of these enchanted forests on the way between Abrud and Alba-Iulia, which was a fairy world indeed. Our motor swept down into a deep valley while the trees rose, like giants, on both sides of the road, their upright grey trunks crowded and noisy demonstrations that these long drives through beautiful and ever-changing scenery were a blessed rest.

In the small mountain towns, distant from every railway, where there was neither our train or official dwelling to live in, we became the guests of kindly people who took us into their comfortable houses, surrounding us with touching care. Among these were the Ciceo Popps, a cheerful family, of which every member was big, round, well fed, comfortably opulent without ostentation. Theirs was a house where the food was cooked by the ladies of the family, where there were spring flowers in early Victorian vases, sprays of lavender strewn among the linen, and enlarged photographs of broadly honourable relations hung on every wall.

These home-like dwellings were pervaded by a simple atmosphere of good will, not mingled with the anxiety of housing such exalted guests. The food was super-abundant: cakes, tarts and puddings played a predominant part, so that it was a regular problem to live up to what was expected of us in the way of appetite.

But even if too copious to be digestively comfortable, these friendly family meals were a blessed relief after the numerous banquets we had to submit to in the larger towns. I confess that these endless, slowly served banquets thrust upon us, on top of all the other fatigues, were the last straws which broke the camel's back. They lasted for hours, with long pauses between each course, the flowers on the table faded, conversation wilted and deadly fatigue set in.

Indeed, those banquets were the 'drop too much' and did not fill me with the Christian feeling of good will towards all men they were supposed to promote. The King stood them with more resignation than I did. As to me, a slow exasperation would gradually filter through every drop of my blood, until I could actually have wept, and any smile which still stuck to my lips was a heroic effort which, when I think of it, still today overwhelms me with a feeling of unforgiving weariness!

The Transylvanians who accompanied us during our entire journey were Iuliu Maniu, Ciceo Popp and Goldiş. Old Mr Pherekyde[3] was with us as provisional prime minister, Brătianu being still at the Peace Conference, and also my friend Jean Duca,[4] who was always a specially excellent companion and so extraordinarily appreciative of every detail and every incident that came his way. He also enjoyed talking things over with me, occasionally somewhat modified by the Russian blood which ran alongside the English in my veins. But unfortunately Jean Duca was never my neighbour during the long banquets; his spritely conversation and brilliant wit might have made them less tedious!

Of all our receptions, the one at Turda was perhaps the most impressive. On the spot where Romania's favourite hero, Michael the Brave, had lost his life, thousands of peasants from all the surrounding villages had flocked together to give us a tremendous welcome.

Upon a vast field they had all assembled, a picturesque and motley crowd, and there, beneath God's blue vault, an impressive requiem was sung in memory of the one who, several centuries ago, had for a short while united all the Romanians under his sceptre. The requiem was followed by a Te Deum of thanksgiving. Standing upon a heightened platform, the priests in their dazzling, gold-woven vestments, painted a colourful picture against the sky, partially veiled by clouds of fragrant incense mounting in spirals from their silver censers. The sun shone down upon the kneeling multitude whose voices occasionally joined in with the priest's exultant fervour.

After having laid an armful of flowers upon the spot where the hero of yore fell in 1601, but where his body lies no longer, the King and I wandered about on foot among our peoples, who crowded around us, a living sea of fervent hustling, enthusiastic humanity, each man, woman or child pressing in upon us, eager to embrace our hands, our feet, calling blessing down upon our heads, crossing themselves, often throwing themselves down on the ground to kiss even our footprints. A wave of irresistible, almost sacred, emotion had taken possession of every heart. As in a dream I moved through this surging flood of adoration, marvelling that such an hour should be granted me on earth.

Though my soul was not free from sorrowful anxiety, I can only humbly thank God that such a wonderful experience was granted us. That visit to Transylvania, at that season of Nature's awakening, when early flowers are abloom and human hearts full of gratitude, remains a unique event which I often, when life is sad and perplexing, look back upon, repeating the words of the poet: 'Not even God can undo this hour'.

No matter what followed; no matter that man is inferior to his generous aspirations, that brotherly love is less easy to live than to imagine; no matter that selfishness, personal ambition and animosity undermine the most gallant intentions, that the ideal retreats before the too human grasp of our hands, that disenchantment follows too closely on the heels of exultation – no matter; we did live through that great hour with our people, and so as to keep it for ever unspoiled in my heart, I must not allow any later sadness or disillusion to tarnish its memory.

EIGHT

Political Worries

That summer it was very late before we could leave Bucharest for Sinaia.[1] There were mountains to move in every direction, and although the work we had to do was of a different kind, it was almost as arduous as it had been in Jassy.

Both foreign and domestic politics were difficult and had to be handled with infinite tact. Every day new situations arose which needed new planning, new tactics, new deliberations.

Brătianu, although he had done his utmost to serve his country faithfully, was becoming more and more unpopular, and he himself was not satisfied with the results achieved in Paris. The whole world was one great grumble and each country separately became entrenched behind demands which it labelled 'rights'; as in general these demands encroached upon the 'rights' of others, there was little hope for a peaceful understanding.

We, like our neighbours, were ever on the watch for each offence or slight offered us, and I found myself drawn as the protagonist of one cause into a whirlpool of politically conflicting cross-currents out of which there was no escape.

As during the war I had been such a valiant defender of our Romanian cause, it was still considered my duty to be a special front line fighter the moment any new difficulty arose.

But today circumstances were different. War was over, it was no longer enemies who stood before me who had to be beaten if we were to survive, but so-called friends. The militant phase was over, my blood had cooled, so my ingrained faculty of being able to see all sides of a question reasserted itself most forcefully.

In all fairness I have to admit that we had come away with the lion's share, and I was humbly, almost tremblingly, grateful before

105

the magnanimity of Fate, which had allowed us to be among the winners. This extraordinary good luck was always present before my mind, when strife arose about settling our frontiers. I had a strong feeling that winners should not be too arrogant. I longed to inspire others with more generous feelings towards the beaten. But it was almost impossible to argue with those who were drunk with the excitement of success. They quite naturally wanted to exploit to the utmost the great hour of good fortune. The future was not sufficiently considered; nor was it taken into account whether seeds of revenge were being sown in the souls of those defeated. Any voice of reason raised at such a moment was most unwelcome, and I did not wish to play the part of the ghost at the feast of my friends.

But there I stood, alone in my belief: I no longer held a sword in my hand, yet the part of ardent patriot was still mine; I was still the one who had to stand firm against all the odds so as to strengthen and consolidate what had been achieved. Our troops, with whom the King and I had recently been before they crossed the Tisa, had successfully pushed forward against Bela Kun's red hordes and had triumphantly entered proud and beautiful Budapest. Every Romanian heart was filled with exultation. Hungary having been for centuries the classical enemy, there could not have been a more glorious hour for the Romanians than that hour when their army marched victoriously through the streets of the proud Hungarian capital.

At Bucharest the King and I received tremendous demonstrations of joy. Each time we drove out, our motor was almost crushed to pieces by the crowd pressing in upon us, making of us the centre of their jubilation.

Unlike most countries where socialist propaganda was rampant, Romania did not present a fertile ground. The royal family was exceedingly popular; our people were staunchly loyal towards their dynasty, which had shared with them both good and evil days.

But our allies, who had called upon our army, the only one still mobilized, to do their work for them, now sent an inter-allied commission to Budapest, which instead of being grateful to Romania, began to show itself inexplicably hostile towards us, finding fault

106

with everything we did and entirely ignoring the fact that it was our army that had re-established order in this part of the world.

Once again I had to stand up to defend my people; I left no stone unturned, even taking up my pen to vindicate our cause. My sense of justice was outraged and both the King and Brătianu knew that, when I was deeply moved, words would bubble up from the depths of my being that carried with them a force of conviction not to be equalled by the most studied diplomatic language. On those occasions they stood back, allowing me to take up the cudgels, knowing that there was an irresistible ring of truth in all I said.

I therefore wrote to Hoover, who had become one of our strongest opponents, and when the American general Banholz, who headed the inter-allied commission in Pest, came to Romania, I had heated, if not passionate, discussions with him. Strangely enough, we immediately felt an honest liking for each other. As a straightforward soldier, he did not in the least resent my outspokenness, declaring: 'I preferred treating with a queen, of your kind anyhow, because I was immediately given to understand where I stood.'

I also had long arguments and discussions with Sir George Clark, a charming and smooth-tongued diplomat, with a pleasant sense of humour, who had been sent to enquire into the situation.

Never was there any time for rest, hardly even a moment to take breath. The effort was constant: every day renewed troubles and worries came tumbling one on top of the other, and we had constantly to be on the look-out, ready to meet every emergency.

Almost worse than our foreign worries were our own political conflicts. It could not be denied that, for the moment, Brătianu was played out. He had manfully held his own, but a change of government had to be considered; Brătianu felt this himself, but, accustomed to power, he was unwilling to surrender unconditionally. Not having obtained all he had held out for at the Paris Conference gave him the pretext for an honourable retreat. Brătianu knew very well how to stage his retreats. He had only to declare that he must leave to others the signing of a Peace Treaty which, according to him, offended against certain of our sovereign rights and therefore was not in keeping with our national dignity. He was also well aware that he was the strongest in spite of his momentary eclipse. We had always hoped he would form a national coalition government, including all parties and bringing in the Transylvanians; but he and Maniu could come to no understanding, as Brătianu considered Maniu's pretensions too great. According to my humble opinion, Brătianu was making a grave mistake. The country's interests were crying out for a unified effort. And it seems a pity that he did not display a more generous attitude in reconciling the demands of our new elements, but quarrelled with them about the distribution of the different 'porte-feuilles' or 'portfolios'. Had he and Maniu then been able to come to an understanding, much trouble in the future might have been avoided. Working together with Brătianu, Maniu would have become one with old Romania instead of entrenching himself behind a sterile opposition which delayed indefinitely the unity absolutely necessary for our future development and security.

I do not mean to set myself up as a critic, but as the King talked over all his difficulties with me and often called upon my help when perplexed, I had ample occasion for interviews and discussions with our political men and I repeatedly ran up against small and selfish party prejudice, which entirely obscured the larger national interest. Each man considered himself the only one justified to hold power, setting aside the one necessity, the one ideal for which they all should have striven: perfect unity, which would have enabled us to consolidate the advantages gained, and build Great Romania upon strong and secure foundations.

I had endless talks, besides Brătianu and Maniu, with Averescu,[2] Take Ionescu,[3] Argetoianu[4] and others, and in each case I came up against the same, to me, incomprehensible hostility towards 'the other man'.

Brătianu's *bête noire* was Averescu, whom public opinion was at that time lifting up to the clouds. Our great statesman did not trust the general, had never trusted him, even when they had worked together, and each time there was a question of allowing him to come to power, Brătianu violently opposed the plan.

The King and I knew that Averescu was not the very great man public opinion wanted to see in him, but we did not consider him the dangerous intriguer Brătianu thought he was.

Personally I was of the opinion that, as such an undeniable wave of popularity was pushing Averescu to the fore, it would be wise to use him. If he justified the public confidence placed in him, all the better, or if he was not equal to the task, his eclipse would follow quite naturally and the legend of perfection created around him would die a natural death. But of course, although I was often used for negotiations, I was not the one called upon to give the final decision!

Sadly the King and I saw our cherished dream of inducing all sides to unite in a common effort wither before the deadly frost of reality, wilt before the selfishness of our so-called patriots.

One unutterably painful and sad thing I learnt during all those talks and discussions was that fine words and beautifully expressed declarations of patriotism were all too seldom converted into action.

Finally the blessed moment came when we were able to leave Bucharest for Sinaia, and it was a marvellous relief, after the dust and heat of town, to once more fill our lungs with pure mountain air.

The children had arrived in town from abroad, Mignon[5] and Nicky[6] from their English schools, Elisabetha from Paris, Ileana from La Bourgone, where she had been sent for a cure. Gay voices now rang again through the house and each in turn was eager to talk at once about his or her experiences. The joy of having them back seemed to lighten the burden of our various troubles and responsibilities.

At that time I was the proud possessor of twelve fine borzois. Although a somewhat unruly horde, they were a great source of amusement. The sight of this snowy pack drifting in and out of the giant fir trees against the shady background of the forest, a white apparition of swift and graceful beauty, was a feast for the eyes. They became the companions of all my rambles, but also the source of much trouble, because, once let loose, there was no controlling them. Although their beauty was absolute, their manners were those of the steppes! Later, alas, I had to get rid of them. Though each by himself was quite tame and friendly, when chasing in a pack, no power could stop them; their hunting instinct once awakened, they gave no quarter to the game they pursued. Anything fleeing before them had to be caught and disposed of according to the instinct of their kind. Beautiful, wild creatures, I loved them: their grace and swiftness were incomparable, their loveliness made a legend of the Sinaia forest, but no smaller dog was safe in their company, so they had to be given up.

For a while I tried to let them run with muzzles, but this was agony for them, a pain I could not inflict upon their imperial pride and love of freedom! So I had to get rid of them.

The stream of guests received at Sinaia was as numerous as it had been at Cotroceni.[7] They came from all parts; our table was always crowded and I was still going here, there and everywhere among the Americans, working for us, trying to keep a happy balance between the rival organizations by dividing my attentions as equally as possible. Nearly every one of these unselfish helpers, men and women, sat in turns at our table, and I was excellent friends with all of them. The King also received them gladly, and occasionally, giving in to my persuasion, he came to one or another of our distribution sessions, which gave much joy to the population as well as to our American collaborators. Nando was especially great friends with Colonel Amant, whose irrepressible energy much amused him. Amant had no drawing-room manners, but his vitality was such that he simply could neither foresee nor accept failure, and all difficulties were swept aside by his extraordinary spirit of 'push'. In the pages of my diary I find this amusing description of him:

Colonel Amant, although belonging to that category of Americans Colonel Anderson, the Virginian, labels as 'crude', vastly amuses both the King and myself. He is full of 'pep' and has exactly the manners Nature gave him. He asks anything he wants to know, and holds back no information he wishes to impart. He does not realize that people have toes, and rushes in where angels dare not tread, but he is full of uncrushable enthusiasm, and the American nonacceptance of being defeated by difficulties. Everything can and must be overcome – go ahead – quickly! Quicker than quick, if possible, make continual efforts, push, strain, 'do'! For Amant 'can't' does not exist. 'Impossible' is for him a word which has no currency. With a child's artlessness he at all moments invades my cloistered dignity to discuss with me every possible question and to tear decisions from me. He would like to pour American millions into my lap, and dreams of an astounding organization which would save all the country and show the whole of the world what Romania could do through the Americans. But everything must be done immediately, if not before, everything and everywhere at the same time, and of course he, Amant, is going to be my right hand! Yes, decidedly, although Amant, according to Anderson's appreciation, is 'raw and primitive', the King and I think he is bracing, if somewhat unconventional, company.

My faculty for enjoying odd types and absurd or even incongruous situations often eased the tediousness of my royal path. Lurking beneath the seriousness life had stamped upon me was the same old spirit of fun and mischief I had as a child; it was the instinct of self-preservation, preventing 'Billy' from becoming an adult.

We also saw a good deal of our faithful friend Colonel Boyle, who had come again to Romania, heading a Canadian mission; his company was as inspiriting as ever and he took our family worries to heart, and helped us in his characteristically single-minded way. Although his methods were different, he, like Amant, carried through all things he undertook with almost deadly persistence. This Anglo-Saxon way of going so rapidly ahead was foreign to Romanian ideas, and it was not always easy to keep the peace all round.

And ever again I faced the difficulty of conflicting loyalties. All hands were eager to work for me, but the fonder they became of me, the less they liked each other, and jealousies would suddenly flare up in the most unexpected corners.

I tried to be as impersonal as possible, but sometimes I felt like a driver with too many reins in her hands. For a queen, sentimental complications are the most deadly, because there is absolutely no issue.

Occasionally overpowered by the hopeless intricacies of human problems, I would sit alone in my room and weep.

Finally, having received the news from Germany that my mother would probably be able to meet me either in Italy or Switzerland, the King consented to my going abroad, taking Elisabetha with me. So for a while I was able to tear myself away from a situation that was exhausting all my reserves. In spite of our combined efforts, a new government had unfortunately not yet been formed. Was it urgent that I should stay and help the King? I had done my share. With commingled feelings of anxiety and relief, my eldest daughter and I left for Lausanne on 25 September. On 29 September it is her birthday.[8]

NINE

Torn Threads

So I was to meet Mama[1] again – Mama! After five years' separation, five years weighted with such terrible events, wrought through with such overwhelming experience that they could have been twenty years. We were to look into each other's eyes again over a past which was dead, a prosperity which had crumbled and, above all, we were to join hands after having stood in opposite camps.

Torn threads! How to knot them together again, how to find words that would not wound, how to take up the old loving intimacy? What must be said or left unsaid?

How to stand before my mother – I on the winning side and she among the defeated? And gradually defeated: Russia, Germany . . . everything that had been dear to her, everything she had believed in!

Our first destination was Lausanne, where Sister Baby[2] awaited me so that we could discuss where and when Mama could meet me.

Switzerland went out of its way to show me every politeness, and on reaching the frontier I was much astonished to be received by a military guard of honour. Somehow I had so little connected Switzerland with soldiers! I was, however, much touched, because I knew that such attention was only offered to reigning sovereigns. My journey was in no way an official one, so this was quite a spontaneous show of sympathy and all the more precious for that.

It was an infinite joy to be with Baby again. Although she too was harassed by endless troubles and difficulties, she was always delightful and stimulating company, and was quite at home in Switzerland, which she had inhabited a good deal during the war.

Prince Stirbey,[3] who had been for some time abroad with his family, had made contact with my sister before my arrival and 'pourparlers' with my mother were going on, but as all travelling had become difficult and money questions were infinitely complicated, Mama had not yet fixed the date of her arrival. So it was decided, as I preferred Italy to Switzerland, that Elisabetha and I should go to Stresa on the Lago Maggiore until Mama's journey could be arranged.

We spent, however, a pleasant ten days at Lausanne, where I also found my friend Maruka Cantancuzino,[4] who was living in a miniscule villa not far from our hotel. We almost immediately became the centre of a small group of artists, some of whom were Baby's friends, some Maruka's. We arranged most charming little musical evenings in Maruka's house. There was George Enescu,[5] Maruka's devoted admirer Leudicar, a Czech bass singer, a gladly received guest in my mother's house; there was also Maria Freund, the singer, and an excellent Spanish pianist, Itourbi, a quite young man, who was a great friend of Baby's.

They played wonderful music, and Maria Freund delighted us with her lovely singing. Maruka, always deliciously absurd and more erratic than ever, kept us much amused.

She lived entirely according to the moment, having monopolized the right to a freedom and independence she somehow managed to make us accept (goodness knows how) as her special right! Delightfully vague, irresponsible and blissfully indifferent to everything outside herself, she was refreshing company. It was indeed almost a miracle to see anyone so completely detached from unpleasant realities and the many tragic differences lacerating the world at large, living what she called '*en beauté au-delà du bien et du mal*' [in beauty beyond good and evil], creating a fictional existence according to her magnificent belief that all the joys of love and life were hers by divine right. But she was a charming hostess, gay, light-hearted, although at times she pretended to take her impossible principles, theories and self-decreed privileges quite seriously. My sister was most amused by this original friend of mine and much appreciated Enescu's god-like talent which kept us all under his spell, although he himself was the most modest being who ever trod this earth.

At Lausanne I also met the exiled old Queen Olga of Greece,[6] as well as my cousin Ellen[7] and her daughters, at that time exiles in Switzerland. Each encounter was fraught with the weight of experience which had separated our sympathies. Each subject had to be approached with infinite tact and I had to be exceedingly careful not to hurt their feelings. Being the only reigning Queen among them gave me an almost unfair advantage; it made me shy, nearly ashamed of being so differently treated wherever I went. This kept me ever pondering the vicissitudes of fate and the uncertainty of worldly glories: I was received with all the military honours due to a Queen at the Swiss frontier; Mr Ador,[8] the president of the Republic, paid me a visit; everywhere I was flattered and smiled upon, while my relations lived in the shade, banished from their country, an uncertain future spreading out before them, no home of their own.

But worse shocks were to follow.

We spent a fortnight in Stresa, on the Lago Maggiore, an enchanting spot, whose beauties we enjoyed with Prince Stirbey and his family, imbibing that unique, Italian atmosphere in which everything seems to harmonize: light, colour, line, landscape architecture. Then Lisabetha[9] and I moved to Lugano, where we were, at last, to meet Mama.

This was the encounter for which I had most longed, but which I also most dreaded. I foresaw that the emotions would be overpowering, as was indeed the case.

I shall never forget that first sight of my mother after those five tragic years of separation. The last time we had been together at Tegernsee in 1913, she was a masterful, affirmative, energetic and withal kindly lady full of life and activity; the prosperous centre of a large and happily united family which she liked to assemble under her hospitable roof. A cheerful welcoming hostess, dispenser of all the good things of this world, exceedingly astute, occasionally tyrannical, but full of good cheer, managing us all with good-humoured irony, conveniently blind to our foibles when it was wise to be so, yet never taken in. Now she was suddenly metamorphosed into an old lady, hardly recognizable. She seemed to have shrunk;

her plump white hands had become waxen, thin and trembling; they had become anxious hands, which seemed to be gropingly searching for something she had mislaid . . . her face had lost its roundness and ruddy complexion. She moved more quickly than formerly, but her step had about it something uncertain and hesitant, and because she had become so thin, her shoulders bent slightly forward. The dominant look in her eyes, formerly one of her great characteristics, had been tarnished; today they were anxious eyes, almost haunted. Where was the Mama I had known all my life? What had happened to Mama? I tried not to look at her until I could bear the change, and yet kept looking again, and each time pain gripped my heart. She did not complain; nor did she, this I instantly understood, intend to admit how much she had suffered, nor how entirely her life had been ransacked and uprooted. Beneath her changed exterior burned the same proud spirit, unbending, refusing to admit defeat. And worst of all, I felt she was watching me anxiously, with a faint tinge of hostility. We had not met since I had become queen; what had I become? I think she was relieved to find me so simple, so natural, still so impulsive. My change of position, my manifold experiences, the two terrible war years I had lived through, had swept over me, leaving me just the same, her child, her *Missy*[10] of happier days, unspoilt and unpretentious, although she instinctively divined that strength had come to me through trouble; that today I was a woman who was not afraid to act, with a will which had been steeled by many overwhelming experiences.

But there was, above all this, irrevocable sadness: during the war we had been in different camps; and our entering on the side of the Allies had helped to overthrow Germany. This thought was with us both, all the time, underlying our every conversation. Having become unbearably humble, Mama refrained from taunting me, as she would formerly have done, but I knew that what she would have liked to say lay close beside what she actually did say. All her resentment was there beneath her outward composure, and any rash word could have made it burst through, like a torrent, and this had to be avoided as long as possible, until we had learnt to live together again, learnt to accept the new situation. Mama might use harsh, unjust words, which she would afterwards regret; she would excuse herself before me. It was her humbleness today which was to me, her daughter, such excruciating pain.

So this tragic meeting was as cruelly difficult as I had foreseen. There was a feeling as of treading on thin ice, knowing that dangerous depths gaped below. Fortunately, Sister Baby had come with Mama, and Ali,[11] her delightful husband, a very efficient aviator, joined us next day. Their presence helped to ease the strain, and to bridge the gulf which circumstances had opened up between mother and daughter. Being on the winning side, I refrained from speaking about my own experiences, encouraging them to talk of their own, and listening for hours to all they had to relate. Life had gripped each of us with a vengeance, so that remembrance of pre-war happiness, of you, the ease and security are today a vanished vision of unbelievable bliss.

Sister Baby had also serious troubles. King Alfonso,[12] formerly a great friend, was today treating his cousins with inexplicable harshness, preventing their return to Spain, thus rendering them as homeless as those whose countries denied them. This made their situation intolerable. I promised to take up the cudgels for them, as I was in a situation to be able to do so.

As the days passed, the tension between my mother and myself lessened. A heart-to-heart talk, when both of us would have been able to confess our pain, was, however, rendered impossible, as Mama still stuck to her old tradition of separating the generations. Even today she would not speak with me as an equal, an attitude I was never able to break through and which excluded complete confidence.

My sister and her husband had soon to leave us, and after some persuasion, Mama allowed me to carry her off to Florence, a city she had always loved, and very much longed to see again. I believed in the soothing influence of art and beauty, and as Mama knew Florence, and was much better versed in its history than I was, she could to a certain degree become our Cicero, advising us where to go and what to visit, thereby regaining her position of superior and chief authority which was hers by right.

I adored every inch of Florence, Italy having always been my ideal of perfection. Space alone prevents my plunging into enthusiastic descriptions of all I saw, and of the almost ecstatic enchantment with which the city filled me. I also revelled, as only an artist can, in its incomparable surroundings. I shall never forget the exquisite colouring of the golden autumn vines, climbing over and through the grey-green olives and painting their delicate tracery against a sky of translucent blue, with their background of old stone walls. What delight! But my heart ached when I looked at my mother's face.

Though not absolutely cloudless, these were two almost happy weeks, but they came to an end all too soon, as I was being called home where endless work awaited me. I was eternally being torn to pieces by conflicting duties!

At the very last moment, just as I was leaving, Mama's defences broke down and in hurried words she confessed to me something of her grief; she suddenly became soft and motherly, allowing, for once, her oppressed heart to speak. Not many words, as we both feared our emotion, but all the same she said some of those things I longed to hear and for which my soul had been hungering. I was not to go back without some comfort into that other world of mine so separated from hers. She seemed so very frail as I took her, for a last time, in my arms. A strangled feeling gripped my throat and, tearing myself away with a sob, I went down to my motor and drove away. Why was life so sad, and why did it wrench asunder those who belonged together? Why did it dig trenches and raise obstacles between loving hearts, so that they were estranged when they met again? And why was the human tongue so halting, so unable to pronounce those words that would have eased the soul's longing? Poor tormented humanity, would it never find relief in peace? Mama's tear-stained face, with its sunken cheeks and with those eyes out of which all fire had died, kept rising up before me, haunting every hour of my days. It was unbearable to know that I could do nothing for her, and that Fate had so irrevocably parted our ways.

While in Florence, taking Elisabetha with me, I paid a flying visit to the King[13] and Queen of Italy[14] at San Rossoro, quite near Pisa, where the royal couple came to meet us.

I had not been there since the never-to-be-forgotten Moscow coronation[15] where their romance began, when life lay before us all, an unknown journey on which each was setting out in his own way, according to character and destiny. The years which had since passed had not left us unscarred, but the meeting was pleasant and without constraint. Today, Victor Emmanuel had grey hair, his lower jaw jutted out in the same pugnacious way as when he was young, and he had remained just as abrupt of speech and gesture, while Helen was still a very handsome woman, tall and self-assured, exceedingly amiable, full of pleasant and animated talk, almost confidential in fact. I felt immediately quite at home with her, more especially as, for her also, her children were the central interest of her life. She beamed down with motherly pride upon her five offspring, of whom the son and eldest daughter were exceedingly good-looking, slim, tall and upright, with dark hair and brilliant eyes. As to the youngest, little Maria, then about five or six years old, she was all eyes and dark curls, a perfect treasure, almost too good to be true, a real Christmas-card baby one does not expect to meet in reality. Never had I seen eyes so large, round and black; they shone like polished gems, while as a contrast her pouting lips were cherry-red.

The royal couple were very democratic. The king hated all ceremony and pomp and loved to live as simply as possible in the bosom of his family, having given up every right to the magnificent old palaces belonging to the Crown in the different towns, a gesture approved by some but regretted by many. San Rossaro lies on the coast beyond Pisa. Here they had built themselves a simple house amid a forest of pine trees, which spread their moss-green crowns against the turquoise sky. Fishing, shooting, riding, swimming – a healthy, happy family life in a secluded spot where they could be by themselves, living according to their different tastes. We lunched all together, including our 'suites', the children, without any shyness, taking part in the general conversation so that the meal was gay and animated, each one being allowed his say.

In 1919 Italy was still very unsettled; there were communistic movements all over the country, and once, as we motored through the narrow streets of a small town, red flags, carried by an unruly, singing, shouting crowd, were flapped into our faces in an exceedingly rude way. I remember how I laughingly tossed them aside, doing as though the rabble had only wanted me, thus disarming their hostility, changing their frowns into reluctant smiles. But I distinctly felt the ugly humour burning beneath.

Victor Emmanuel knew no doubt the mood of his country and avoided everything that might ignite a fire, which could spread devastatingly. Fortunately, thanks to him, Italy avoided Russia's sad fate and is still the delight of every artist's heart. This was of course before Mussolini[16] had come to the fore as leader of his stricken country.

TEN

The First Parliament in Greater Romania

Unable to unite the different parties, the King had, during my absence, called in a provisional government under the presidency of General Văitoianu,[1] a man in whom both the King and I had confidence. As I had feared, I found Nando as worried as ever, labouring through a tangle of political difficulties which hindered all more constructive work.

Hardly had I crossed our threshold than they all descended on me from every side, and I understood that there was to be no respite. I must bravely take up my burden where I had laid it down a month ago and plunge anew into never-ceasing conflicts. Added to our national external troubles was that cruel family drama which had to be borne in silence. Although it was so closely interwoven with the country's interests, it had to be hidden away in the depths of our hearts, which nearly broke under its weight.

Everything seemed to rush in upon us at once: political strife at home while in Paris things were not going well for us at the Peace Conference, where humiliating concessions were being asked of us which no government would agree to sign. Lately the bitter discussions had reached a dangerous point and our irate allies had sent our government a rude ultimatum summoning us to sign at a few days' notice, or they would break with us once and for all.

Ardent espousers of our cause in Paris, forever on the watch, had sent me an urgent message, imploring me to meet once more in person, even if only for a day, Mr Frank Polk, Wilson's substitute at the Conference who through personal friends of mine had been won over to Romania. According to these people, I was the only really efficient negotiator, being more sympathetic to the world at large than our official deputies, who were worn out. The personal touch was needed. I was indispensable . . .

Unfortunately, although personally quite ready to respond to this call, I could not, having only just returned from abroad, obtain permission to rush off again at a moment's notice. My presence at home was also absolutely necessary, I was undoubtedly recognized as a steadying influence and could not be spared. Torn between conflicting emergencies, it was difficult to decide which was my most pressing duty. Always diffident about giving myself undue importance, I did not finally have the courage to insist, although I felt that my presence on the actual field of battle would have rallied the flagging sympathies of those over ready to slight us on every occasion. All I could do was to write a long and detailed letter to Mr Polk, using all my powers of persuasion. For three days I toiled over this letter (knowing all the while that half an hour's personal talk could have accomplished much more then two pages in script, be they ever so well expressed). Mr Polk was a specially charming man, tall and slim, with beautiful white hair, a cultured, delightful gentleman with whom personal contact was a pleasure. But alas one cannot be in two places at the same time.

On 20 November[2] the King and I opened the first Parliament of Greater Romania. In our country it had not been habitual for the queen to open parliament with the King. But this time my people considered that, as I had played a great part in the realization of our unity, it was my holy right to stand at the King's side during this important ceremony, and I think they were right.

Of course I was eager to look my best; my subjects had always cared for my face, and so it was part of my duty not to disappoint them. A new dress of grey velvet had been made for this occasion and a quite justifiable pride swept through me as I faced this new parliament, assembled for the first time from every part of our enlarged country, and I rejoiced over the tremendous reception given us, especially for the King's sake; he had so often had to bear the brunt of unfair criticism, and so few really understood him.

For a short moment those many men forgot their own petty strife and despicable personal ambitions to hail the sovereigns who had realized the age-old dream. In waves, their cheers surged through the great hall, mounting towards us, a thundering tide of applause. I was deeply touched, but alas I could not be carried away by the spontaneous enthusiasm as I had been in October 1914, when for the first time I faced my people on King Ferdinand's ascension to the throne. Since then I had seen too much. Too many deaths, too many griefs had knocked at the doors of my heart. I had gleaned too many tears, seen too many illusions wither away.

The sun shone down upon us that morning. It was an hour of respite, but I was sadly conscious that my face was not as radiant as it should have been and that my eyes were too sad: 'For in much knowledge there is also much grief.' Today I knew too much. I looked down upon that sea of upturned faces with conflicting feelings, wondering what would come next. What new forces would emerge from the mounting surge of universal voters? Would they understand the obligations and respect involved in this much-longed-for civil privilege, which might endanger?

Hours of enthusiasm are short-lived. What counted was the long-drawn-out, patient, dogged plodding towards a fixed goal. We needed the converging of all our forces, harness every energy so as to build and progress. Were our people sufficiently conscious of this? Would they rise to the heights we expected of them, or would they eternally continue to dissipate their strength in bickering one against the other in petty rivalries, jealousies, betrayals? What would the future bring?

Oh, if I could only blow my spirit into them, uplift them, fill them with the right desire to serve unselfishly, setting aside all hatred, thinking solely of the country, not of themselves! Nearly all of them loved and trusted me; their eyes became good eyes when they met mine. When I talked, a cleaner ideal rose before them, but they are too many; single-handed I was too weak. I was sadly aware the humanity had been exhausted by too much heroism and too much shedding of blood. In our country, as in many others, an era of selfishness was setting in: the desire to get there without effort, to be among the profiteers, to talk, discuss and criticize but not to act. Where would I find collaborators, the right energies to overcome the contagious inertia which was sucking the vitality out of our post-war generation? And Carol my own son, would I be able to save him for his country?[3] Would I be strong enough to carry every man's burden without going to pieces myself?

Thus did many thoughts whirl through my mind on that sun shining morning when my heart ought to have been glad, while the applause of many thousand voices rang through the air. But also at that hour of doubt I swore within my own soul that I for one would struggle on, doing my share (perhaps the lion's share) as patiently as possible, ignoring all discouragement and disappointment, even if I were destined to be beaten in the end.

ELEVEN

Social Reconstruction and Welfare Activities

That winter and spring of 1919–20 was a long, straining effort to cope with the overwhelming amount of work which at times threatened to submerge me. It says much for my magnificent health and steely determination that I never broke down. There were, however, awful moments of acute discouragement engendered by a crushing sense of fatigue of heart, soul and body, so that sometimes I would stand alone in the middle of my room, groaning: 'I am tired, I am tired!' But I fought these hours of weakness with an unrelenting energy which always helped me to win through.

It is not easy to give a picture of that period when everything had to be seen to at the same time (in so many directions): domestic and foreign politics, family complications, social reconstruction involving every branch of activity, charities without end, not to mention the encouragement of art in all its different manifestations. I had to be the living, attentive, inspiriting centre of all these and at the same time not neglect my own house and family. Indeed it was no easy task to be a Queen.

In former days most of our charities were headed by Carmen Sylva,[1] my predecessor. The care of the old, the blind and the sick was her contribution to alleviating suffering. I was quite conscious that in this sphere of activity she had been much more efficient than I was. She had the real spirit of Christian abnegation and although occasionally over-idealistic, she was a wonderful promoter of good works.

Times had moved on since her quieter day; there had been so many fundamental changes, so many social developments brought about by the war that many of the social institutions so useful in normal life were now out of date, inadequate to meet the post-war exigencies. The work which confronted us was one of emergency

125

and of constructive building for the future. Three hundred thousand war orphans, sixty thousand war invalids and forty thousand war widows – hungry mouths waiting for public charity to save them from starvation. On the other hand, throughout the country there were thousands of little babies, growing up under appalling conditions, without clothing, without sugar, without the most basic food. Mothers were overworked by domestic tasks and crushed by dire poverty. And all these problems had to be faced with tired spirits and exhausted public funds.

Fortunately I had some wonderful women who had always worked with me, many of them very much more competent than I, but they needed my constant support as nothing stood firmly on its feet without my patronage. This not only gave them social prestige, but also made available to them the money, the material and the foodstuffs they needed. Their many appeals to different public authorities never received proper attention unless my voice or pen gave the alarm signal.

I had the courage to lay my hand to every plough, even if at times I did not feel equal to it. Having braced myself for tremendous effort, I considered it my royal duty to respond to every cry for help, no matter at what cost. At times the diversity and the exigencies of my duties made my work abnormally exhausting.

I remember endless, harassing meetings. One especially I shall never forget: the first Congress headed by Princess Olga Sturdza[2] of Moldavia and Princess Alexandrina Cantacuzino of Walachia, of nearly three thousand delegates, chiefly women, coming from all parts of the country to discuss the problem of housing and helping the war orphans and widows. It was a stupendous sitting and an assault on my poor tired ears of Romanian fluency at the end of each speech (do not ask how many they were). In the course of three days, I had to submit to having my virtues hurled at me in every variation of tone and dialect: what a refreshing refrain!

To lighten the painful atmosphere, laden with all the present troubles of the bereaved and the apprehension about future generations, I invited this patriotic legion of women to a copious tea at the Calea Victoriei Palace, where I had to smile upon and shake hands with every one of them, while patriotic music played by a

Ferdinand and Marie at the Romanian Legation, Bern, 7 May 1924. (*Romanian National Archives, Regina Maria III/148, p. 45*)

The Romanian and Belgian monarchs at the Town Hall, Brussels, 11 May 1924. (*Romanian National Archives, Regina Maria III/148, p.63*)

Ferdinand and Marie of Romania
with George V and Queen Mary,
Buckingham Palace, 12 May 1924.
(*Diana Mandache Collection*)

King Michael of Romania, ex-King
George II of Greece and Prince Philip
(now Duke of Edinburgh), at the
Romanian shore on the Black Sea, 1928.
(*Diana Mandache Collection*)

Nicolae, the Prince Regent of Romania, 1927. (*Diana Mandache Collection*)

Princess Ileana of Romania, 1928. (*Diana Mandache Collection*)

King Michael as a child and his mother Princess Helen, 1928. (*Diana Mandache Collection*)

Prince Nicolae and King Carol II of Romania, Bucharest, June 1930. (*Diana Mandache Collection*)

Princess Ileana with Anton, Archduke of Habsburg, 1931. (*Diana Mandache Collection*)

Victoria Melita (left) and Queen Marie at Balcic, May 1930. (*Romanian National Archives, Regina Maria III/175*)

Queen Marie at Balcic, 1930. (*Diana Mandache Collection*)

Queen Marie with Carol II, and, behind them, Miron Cristea the Patriarch, Prince Nicolae and Princess Ileana during a procession to the Patriarchal Cathedral, Bucharest, 1 January 1931. (*Diana Mandache Collection*)

Queen Marie in the gardens of the Cotroceni Palace, 1934. (*Diana Mandache Collection*)

Queen Marie of Romania wearing the diamond and sapphire tiara, 1932. Originally, the tiara was commissioned by Tsar Nicholas I for his wife Charlotte of Prussia for the 1825 Coronation. Later it passed on to Marie Alexandrovna, Queen Marie's mother. (*Diana Mandache Collection*)

Queen Marie with her aide-de-camp
General Zwidinek and Dr Stoermer,
1938, shortly before she died. (*Diana
Mandache Collection*)

The caskets in which the Queen's heart
was kept. According to her last wish,
Marie wanted her heart to be removed
and buried separately, as in the medieval
custom. (*Courtesy of the National
History Museum of Romania*)

military band drowned every attempt at conversation. This was, perhaps, useful because it would have been difficult to find something to say to everyone.

I must not minimize the work of these women, which meant so much to the country. They had been labouring ever since the war, with unbroken perseverance, to look after what the French called so graphically 'les pupilles de la nation'. Under their immediate supervision the homeless orphans were housed in rapidly organized asylums – over 300 of them – while the children who had one surviving parent or even close relatives were kept at home and provided with a monthly allowance. Time and again I had secured for these orphanages, grown overnight like mushrooms, bedding and clothing from the American and Canadian Red Cross and the American Relief Administration. I was ever so grateful for the generosity of the manifold friends throughout the world who kept pouring into my private depots cases of goods – foodstuffs, warm blankets, clothing for the poor and the needy. Besides the huge supplies handed out systematically by trained American workers and Romanian volunteers, there were always at hand some clothes and layettes for individual cases, which neither the state not the Bucharest Town Hall could handle through their charitable institutions, and which kept knocking at my door.

I must thank Simky Lahovary, my lady-in-waiting whom – alas – I lost last year, and her brave collaborators: Dr Mamulea and Dr Guilamila who today have also passed on, after struggling for eighteen years to keep our War Invalids' organization afloat, and a host of ladies who did such splendid work, both at the 'War Widows and Invalids' Society and at my private Relief Bureau at our Palace, the first one in the country to have launched the practice of home visiting in order to ascertain needs and to apportion the necessary help to each case.

Quoting from my diary:

2 JANUARY 1920

Our charity organizations are extraordinarily vast; no one has any idea what a lot we do and that hundreds are helped each day.

Mme Popp, with her usual energy, had organized the 'Gouttes de lait' and the school canteens with the voluntary services of French and Romanian doctors, under the supervision of the French Legation. The babies of destitute mothers received free pasteurized milk and free medical care, while the pre-school and school-age children had one hot meal a day. I remember visiting, at Christmas time, one of these 'Gouttes de lait' and school canteens at the 'Grivitsa Station' district, mostly inhabited by railway workmen and their families. Mme Irene Butculescu and Mme Popp accompanied me, for we had also to stop and see the orphanage at the Bucharest Town Hall. There was a touchingly simple ceremony; no crowd, which was an intense relief to me. While distributing with unwearying hands sweets and gifts to at least 500 children, accompanied by their mothers, my tired brain seemed to float in a haze of sadness, out of which rose innumerable visions of suffering and dying faces dancing around me like pale ghosts. In a few short years we had come such a long way, with grief leading us by the hand; and little Mircea lay cold in his grave.

'Trăiască Regina Mama Noastră' (long life to our beloved queen, our Mother), cried many little voices, bringing me back to reality, while large, astonished eyes gazed up at me out of livid, drawn little faces. Suffering everywhere and we could do so little in comparison to all the need there was!

It was in memory of my last-born, little Mircea, who had died at the beginning of the war, that, with Lia Brătianu and several altruistic doctors, we had started the society 'Principele Mircea'. Thanks to the collaboration of the American Red Cross, so efficient in this sort of work, we helped to begin building up the health of the future generation, by instituting baby clinics and child and mother welfare centres in as many towns and villages as possible. Although at first the work seemed hopelessly beyond our resources, today there are over 350 of these centres in Romania, carrying the name of Mircea as a blessing to thousands of destitute children who looked up to his picture as to the face of a precious little friend.

The country had paid a tremendous toll in men to the war and to the black typhus, which killed as many as the enemy on the battlefields. It was imperative to fill the holes made in the population, to fight starvation and infant mortality, which were decimating the growing generation, especially in the villages.

Peasant folk and workingmen kept pouring into the capital to organize their papers, their pensions and their claims, and to find work. The government had promised special help to war invalids, and everyone felt a right to the state's protection. The main Bucharest station was thronged with crowds of people, sleeping pell-mell on the floor of the waiting room, and even on the pavements. A 'Triaj bureau' and an overnight shelter had to be organized, together with a 'Deparasitation station', as the epidemic of exanthematic fever was still threatening to regain its wartime virulence. Attached to the overnight shelter was an Employment Agency, whose sole propose was to provide work for the unemployed and vagrants. We had to try to sweep the country clean of that pernicious tendency of always accepting charity without any work in exchange for the service received. We hoped to build a new mentality as well, a self-respect which would approximate the Anglo-Saxon ideal.

In connection with this difficult educational work of the masses, I should like to mention the marvellous contribution of General Ioan Manolescu,[3] founder of the 'Casele Naţionale'. This institution started during the war, aimed at endowing every Romanian village with a community centre, where all the welfare, recreational, cultural and social activities of the peasants could be concentrated in order to awaken the peasant from his traditional inertia, to link his life with the progress of the urban sections, and to find adequate outlets for the peasant arts, crafts and cottage industries: wool tweeds, hand-woven and hand-embroidered linen, national costumes, wood crafts and their kind.

General Manolescu had established a workshop for orphaned boys in Bucharest and a community centre at his home village, in Breaza, where we continued his efforts with the trained leadership of the American Red Cross personnel: Mrs Moran, Miss Le Gros, Miss von Kurowsky, Miss Elisabeth Cleveland and others. It was there that Mignon and I inaugurated the first health campaign in the schools and a model rural child welfare bureau.

129

Today General Manolescu's dream has become a reality, for under the impetus given by my son, King Carol,[4] the OETR (Office for the Education of Romanian Youth), with the general's able leadership is endeavouring to awaken in every village the spirit of civic responsibility, to carry out a programme of public health, to impart knowledge for life's national and international exigencies, and to raise the standards of living of the rural population.

Equally good educational work, but chiefly among the peasant women, was started by the 'Cercurile de Gospodine' (Good Housewives' Circles) under Lia Alimănishteanu and Simky Lahovary. The city ladies felt that their sisters in the villages should ameliorate their living conditions by taking care of their babies in accordance with new scientific methods, by cooking the proper food, by finding adequate occupation and recreation for them and by creating the appropriate outlet for their home industries.

But of course it was no good giving advice unless we were able to put at the peasants' disposal those things essential to everyday requirements. As the standards among the rural population were very low, it needed enormous efforts to stir them out of their lethargy, and to liberate them from centuries-old superstitions.

Much was also done in that direction by Elise Brătianu at the 'Albina' and Zoe Râmniceanu at the 'Ţesătoarea' to develop the national arts and crafts, weaving and embroidery, by encouraging the peasant women not to abandon the old secrets of vegetable dyes. They were directed to keep up the tradition of the beautiful design and colouring of ancient carpets and embroideries, instead of yielding to the devastating 'mauvais goût' which was sweeping through the villages with hideous modern innovations.

All kinds and varieties of social work sprang from under the spur of necessity, and it is impossible for me to speak of all of them without overtaxing the reader's patience. But I must not forget to mention the wonderful efforts of Mme Poenaru and of Dr Leonida, an eminent woman oculist, to set the 'Vatra Luminoasă' (the Luminous Hearth), the home for the blind, on its feet again. This had been Carmen Sylva's pet dream for which, with marvellous self-abnegation, she had sacrificed both money and energy, almost breaking her heart over the many vicissitudes which had hampered its complete realization.

During the war the 'Luminous Hearth' had completely crumbled, but Mme Poenaru, who had been Queen Elisabeth's last lady-in-waiting, got it back into working order. I can only hope that, in this world of short memories, someone may be found who in my memory may one day uphold a good work in which I had believed. It was a beautiful proof of fidelity for which I bless the dear old lady and her valiant collaborator, both of them today no longer of this world.

The praiseworthy work of Mme Butculescu and of her mother, Mme Pherekyde, at the 'Obolul' and the 'Patronaj', cannot be forgotten either. The latter has been the first institution of its kind to help wayward, vagabond and retarded boys get a chance in life. The director has been a splendid pioneer educator in that field.

But as I said a while ago, there was such a blossoming forth of institutions that it is impossible to speak of each of them in particular, although my heart goes out in gratitude to every one of them.

Although I have spoken in previous chapters of the marvellous work done by the American Red Cross and the American Relief Administration, and too long descriptions may be mere repetition, I feel an urge to mention some of our most devoted helpers: Major Toose in Buzău, Major Spratt at Jassy, Mrs Moran and Captain W. Wildman in Dobrudja, Major Treadwell in Transylvania, Mr Reed and Miss Hawkes in Oltenia, who started in every rural district of the country thousands of canteens for destitute civilians: children, mothers and the elderly.

I have no head for statistics, so I cannot state the amount of clothing and food supplies distributed by the American Relief Administration and the American Red Cross. I have already spoken of Colonel Amant, the Texan, and Colonel Anderson, the Virginian. Their assistants did a stupendous amount of work in relieving the famine-stricken population. By the autumn of 1919, when the emergency period was over, the American Red Cross was persuaded to continue its work for another year. Dr Kendall Emerson and Mr

Horace Morrison, the successors to Colonel Anderson, focused their attention on child welfare, thus giving most valuable advice and help to the 'Principele Mircea Society', which was in its infancy. They also gave medical, surgical and dental supplies to our Ministry of Health, and Mrs Morgan and a small unit were left to carry out the Junior Red Cross idea throughout the secondary and normal schools as well as the orphanages. I was, myself, much taken with the idea of strengthening the ties of international friendship among the young, and I encouraged Ileana to preside over the Romanian Junior Red Cross. Thus, at the age of ten, she had her first real official responsibility. She was growing fast into an enthusiastic social worker and has remained so ever since.

Soon another American organization was to occupy much of Ileana's and my own time. Thanks to Lady Waldergrave's splendid unit of six secretaries, headed by Miss Hodgkin, an American who was just the sort of woman we needed to make things happen, came to start the Romanian YMCA. Within a month, in spite of great difficulties and almost incomprehensible opposition, the first club for young girls was started, and ever since then Ileana has taken a vivid interest in the work, setting a good example to the young girlhood of her day.

At the same time a training school for nurses was organized by English and Canadian nurses who came to us through the kindness of Lady Paget and Mme Pantazi, while the YMCA launched its work with soldiers and gradually moved into work with students. The country's youth needed a spiritual vision, a real renaissance, and the Americans and Canadians were pouring new inspiration into their hearts.

All this work of welfare and educational restoration was finally concentrated under the wise and efficient supervision of the Ministry of Labour, a new State Department inaugurated during the Averescu government, which owed its initial creation to Mr Grigore Trancu-Iaşi,[5] our first minister of labour, with whom I still work today in spite of many changes, with unabated enthusiasm.

TWELVE

Trying to Quiet Unrest

Looking through notes written down at that time, I find that there was such an agglomeration of hard work that it would hardly make good reading. And yet it was, in spite of a somewhat chaotic state of affairs, very interesting from a queen's point of view. I find among them this rather amusing description of myself.

I am living through a curious phase of my life, full of surprises. I have come to the conclusion that I myself am part of the general 'anarchy' I deplore. I am forced by circumstances into a position that is not rightly mine. It is our want of 'men' which has brought this about. Little by little I have been drawn into the vortex by those who did not know who to turn to. So they turned to me, in whom they found, if not academic knowledge, at least a never-failing good will, coupled with a courage and energy upon which they never called in vain. So by degrees I was dragged into a field of action much more vast than I had ever dreamt of. Every question is urgent, has to find an immediate solution. I always give all the strength I have, often, I fear, too rashly, in a way which would have made methodical old Uncle Carol,[1] my austere teacher, turn in his grave.

But the difficulties are heaping up, every day more and more, and these shoulders must be broad enough to carry the burden laid upon them. They have no choice. My fearlessness, added to the faculty of never showing weariness or depression, makes people of every category count upon me in a crisis.

I feel that I am not '*dans la légalité*', an expression our politicians like hurling at each others' heads when in opposition. But I am just a product of the unruly times to which we belong. Energy, courage and brains are mine, so it comes naturally to others to call upon

133

them at a moment's notice, neither they nor I pausing to consider if I am being exploited beyond my strength. I myself was quite ignorant of my inexhaustible resources, until I had to draw upon them every day more and more. I may succumb in the effort, but it will be like an old horse who dies in harness, pulling his load to the bitter end.

The crux of my difficulties was that everything had to be accomplished by persuasion, as no absolute power was mine; I had no official right to give orders. Everything was expected of me, but a hundred spokes were eternally being stuck into my wheels.

What nearly 'broke the camel's back' was that household and family complications absorbed the hours when I should have rested from my public duties. There were also a thousand private petitioners, full of misery, to whom I had to lend an ear. The moment when I returned to my room, it was invaded by complainers, by Job-like tales of woe.

The heating of the house was not working properly, the servants were out of control, the cook was stealing, the head coachman was getting too old; he neglected his horses, the gardener had not sufficient spades, the hot-house glass was broken, and today glass was beyond price. The maids were quarrelling; the liveries of the footmen were becoming shabby. All materials needed to replace what had been destroyed during the war could be had for neither love nor money.

Nicky had measles at Eton; Mignon, at Heathfield, unaccustomed to unheated rooms, had an attack of rheumatism and, to cap it all, was desperately homesick. Communications were still hopelessly slow – telegrams did not reach their destination, and letters took weeks to arrive. Mrs X had lost her situation, Mrs Y wanted to place her niece in a private school, Mrs Z had buried her child and wanted to dig it up again to bury it elsewhere, the authorities refused permission, would the Queen please give orders to the public officials, and so on, and so on.

There was perhaps a certain bitter humour in all this; in a play it might have been very funny, but in real life, it meant daily exasperation. And here comes General Nicoleanu, the prefect of police. Worried about Bolshevik propaganda, he had sent out a cry of alarm, but those over busy politicians lent him a deaf ear, although the danger was real enough. 'If no steps are taken against their underhand machinations, there might be a blow-up any day. Would Your Majesty help me in my task? Her voice is generally listened to. Your Majesty is so popular! Would our Gracious Queen visit the centres of unrest? Her presence would work miracles.' So I visited the centres of unrest: factories, popular canteens, eating-houses, poor-hospitals. This strategy was successful: instead of being kissed, I was received with confidence. I listened to complaints, I spoke words of good cheer. I can still see the faces of the rough workmen who stepped out from behind the machines they were handling to offer me dropping little winter-flowers, the best they had. And I can still smell the heavy odour of cabbage and onions pervading the canteens.

Mr Lupu,[2] the socialist minister of the interior of the Vaida Voevod government,[3] was unruly. Would I have a talk with him and try to calm him down? He was fond of me in spite of his ultra-left ideas; perhaps I could influence him. Yes, why not? So I sent for Dr Lupu, who in 1913 had worked with me in the cholera camp of Zimnicea. Ever since then we had kept a sneaking liking for each other, although we represented opposing forces.

'Mr Lupu, are you not going a little too quickly ahead? I have also heard that you are not particularly respectful in your attitude towards the King.'

'But we need reforms, this is an era of democracy, the hour of the masses, we are opening doors into a new world . . .'

'But Mr Lupu, have you thought about this seriously? Don't you think it is a mistake to pull down and overthrow before knowing what are you going to put in place of what you are trying to uproot? If you uproot me, for instance, I shall no longer be able to help. I think you like me, don't you?'

'Yes, everybody likes you; you have bravely done your share and I am convinced we still need the King. But what am I to do? I have made all sorts of promises to my partisans and they are a noisy, impatient lot!'

In Lupu's eyes burned the flame of the fanatic, they looked hot and restless and could not always meet mine. He was a product of

135

our new times. Sincere up to a point, up to a point also an idealist, but dangerous, because, although full of desire for improvement, he was too ready to shake the existing order of things without being sufficiently strong or capable to carry through a constructive plan, for it is far easier to talk and rant than to build.

'Are you red constructive elements?' I sweetly asked.

Lupu passed an impatient hand through his unruly hair.

'No they are not! That is exactly the trouble. They are a rowdy, impatient lot, and now that I am "en function" I see that they are obstructors. With you one can talk as a human being. To be quite frank, my former associates are somewhat of a nuisance!'

'Why don't you shake yourself free of them if they hinder your work?'

'But I can't, that is the trouble!' Perspiration was now running down the doctor's cheeks. 'Too long have I howled with the wolves. They know too much about me and can beat me with my own theories of yesterday. If I become more conservative, they will howl me down!'

The man was evidently at his wit's end, torn to pieces between a newly emerging common sense and his former demagogy. If he tried to talk reason to his candidates they would clamour against him and avenge themselves by revealing things from his past, best left in the dark.

'I'm caught between two currents; I have nothing solid to lean upon. Although you are Queen, and queens are against my principles, I feel that somehow you understand me.'

I did understand him, wishing that I could help him. He belonged to the man of tomorrow, but he had no routine. He longed to do his share, but he was evidently not yet ripe for office, in spite of all his colourful talk, which whetted unhealthy appetites. He was no doubt a living force, but a dangerous one, unless redirected into the right channels. This conversation, which lasted over an hour, threw a light on 'les moeurs politiques' which was strangely revealing and not a little uncomfortable.

Vaida Voevod's ministry, which had succeeded Văitoianu's (Maniu having refused to form a cabinet), was mostly composed of

Transylvanians. To my astonishment Averescu had at first accepted the interior portfolio, an arrangement which was not long-lived. Lupu replaced him, introducing certain rowdy elements finally conducive to the fall of the cabinet.

I was told that there were even comic scenes in parliament, when Iorga, our great historian, then president of the Chamber, tried to bully this unassimilated crowd of turbulent deputies, like an enormous classroom, presiding over them with uplifted finger and sharp repartees. It was Professor Iorga's[4] habit to treat everybody as through they were his pupils. I was no exception, and I still chuckle today over a miscellaneous crowd of my new subjects: jurists, deputies, professors, schoolmasters and budding patriots, in my Golden Salon at Cotroceni. With real professional gusto and pedagogical watchfulness he put me through my paces, wondering if the Queen would know how to handle such an embarrassing social development. I did my best and my sense of humour was vastly tickled by his attitude of one who hoped to find fault even with the lady on the throne.

Personally I was very fond of Vaida; he was sincere, well-meaning and had a lot of common sense. He did his very best to hold his own at home as well as at the Peace Conference, and was liked in England. But parliament having got out of hand because of too many not yet focused elements, Vaida could not keep afloat. His government fell while he was abroad, to be replaced by General Averescu[5] who was, as mentioned before, the public favourite at that time. People expected wonders of him and he was very convinced that he was up to the situation.

Except for that tragic interlude in 1918, during the end of the war, when the general accepted to treat with the Germans, he and I had always been friends. A great protégé of old King Carol I, who considered him one of his most able generals, Averescu had in earlier years once commanded my regiment, the 4th Roşiori. So my contact with him had been constant and we had never lost sight of each other.

There was certainly a look of triumph on his face when on 15 March 1920 he came to present to me the members of his cabinet, asking to be received in a private audience immediately afterwards.

He began by thanking me for his nomination.

'I did not nominate you, dear General, it was the King.'

With the rather sly smile which characterized him, he made a little military bow and quoted:

'Ce que femme veut, Dieux veut.'

'This is not always the case,' I protested.

'But this time it is,' insisted the general.

'This time General, it was public opinion that chose you, and this is your triumph; now it is up to you to justify people's trust in you. I shall certainly uphold you and second your efforts whenever you feel that I can be of any use, but do not minimize the difficulties you will have to cope with; they are very great because all things will crush in upon you at once.'

'If I can be certain of having your Majesty's support for me, then half the battle is won.'

As gracefully as possible I acknowledged the compliment. I felt he really desired to have me as an ally. Often before, I had already sensed how much Averescu desired to work with me. Something in his nature, I believe, made him wish to work with a woman, with the Queen rather than with the King. This put me on my guard because I was unwilling to be forced into a thing a little sly about Averescu. He had a colossal memory and never forgot a word once said, even in jest. At any hour he was ready to hold it against one with a cunning not always quite canny. Rashly outspoken myself, I was, however, when debating with him, particularly careful not to give myself away, to play into his hands, even if I occasionally quite enjoyed our little fencing bouts.

As Queen, my attitude could only be one of strictest equity showing no favouritism of any kind, no preference in one direction or the other. I had to stand above all things, my ear always attentive, my mind free from prejudice, ready to help, if a man deserved help, but never admitting that I could have any private understanding upon which the most glaring delight could not fall. The general's speech was over full of insinuations which I professed not to understand, gradually steering him towards discussion of his political programme and ambitions.

He was full of confidence. Like all beginners he imagined he could bring about miracles just because he had come into power. I did not discourage him; others would see to that soon enough!

In Romania success is not appreciated; even the chosen favourite would soon have to learn this to his own detriment. It was always my theory that the belief of others could make a hero even out of a quite ordinary man, whilst it needs exceptional strength not to be crippled by irony and disbelief.

Life was confronting him with intricate problems, almost as challenging as my own. Everywhere upheaval, disorganization, lack of money. I felt that I must continually replenish my energy so as to uphold the courage of others fighting their way, and try to quieten, with all the reserve, strength and unflinching perseverance God granted me, all personal, social and national unrest.

There are only a chosen few who find their strength in opposition and who like to battle with destructive criticism and unjustified insults.

Averescu was no hero, but he had a genuine belief in himself. If those who had so noisily pushed him to the fore had stuck loyally to him, he would no doubt have been able to accomplish much more than he actually did. But hardly had the King given him the power others have demanded for him than those very supporters began to sap the basis of their idol, sapping his self-assurance with their sceptical criticism.

He would not like to hear me say this, but there was something naive about Averescu, for all his ruses. I have had to deal with him at times when he was genuinely bewildered and mortified by the way he was being treated, unable to believe that his good intentions could be so cruelly misunderstood. We have stood face to face at so many critical moments that, being profoundly human, I have sometimes pitied him deeply.

The Coronation of King Ferdinand and Queen Marie

Following the creation of Greater Romania, the coronation ceremony of King Ferdinand and Queen Marie took place at Alba-Iulia, the ancient capital of the newly acquired province of Transylvania, on 15 October 1922. The royal couple and the Liberal government considered that this symbolic act was necessary to seal the union of all Romanian lands. Queen Marie was not in favour of a hurried ceremony because she wanted to follow the English coronation ceremony as closely as possible. Due to the specific conditions, including those arising from King Ferdinand's Catholicism, the ceremony was different in many ways. Queen Marie reported the events in her journal:[1]

> We could not adjust ourselves to post-war conditions at once. It took me all of two years to settle into the new order, understand the new problems, the new viewpoints, the reversals of much that was on an even keel before.
>
> It was not until 1922, on 15 October, that we felt able to undertake the coronation with all the preparation and expense it entailed. But on that date at Alba-Iulia in our regained Transylvania this ceremony took place and Ferdinand and Marie were crowned King and Queen of Greater Romania.
>
> I was forty-seven, a more mature woman than the frail and timid creature who had come in 1893 as the bride of Romania's Crown Prince.

SUNDAY 15 OCTOBER 1922, ALBA-IULIA: OUR CORONATION DAY

> Rain! That was the first impression, but not heavy rain – just a spluttering against my window-pane, little long lines and far between,

140

happily, which meant that there were only drops. On the line of the horizon I saw a pale sun rising, for I was restless and woke early, although I had slept well during the night, which I do in the train as elsewhere. I sleep splendidly, but I do not need much sleep, which adds to my good humour on my life's path as I never dislike that moment of getting up human beings have to go through every morning.

I do not think that many queens have had to dress in a train for such a big ceremony as their coronation, but we could not organize it otherwise. The coronation itself had to be at Alba-Iulia and there was no accommodation there for us. Luckily I didn't have to get out of the train in crown and mantle because those were put on during the ceremony. I emerged in my red-golden underdress, a crimson-velvet mantle lined with silver-blue on my shoulders, and on my head a golden veil bound round my forehead with a golden ribbon over which the crown was to be placed, my 'grand cordon' and star! It looked well enough, but of course plain beside all the other princesses and queens who already had their diadems on.

They all looked perfect and were all pretty, which is rare. My two queenly daughters were a joy to the eye, each in her own way. Lisabetha was in a sort of golden moiré, which looked like a lizard-skin, with a mantle of the same tissue. On her head was a golden veil and a small diadem of pearls and diamonds. She looked very frail but very beautiful, with her wonderful classical refined features. But she still walks with a stick as she has trouble with her knee, and has a pained expression, which makes her look older than her years.

Mignon was also in gold, with an orange-velvet mantle which she had ordered especially as it is my favourite colour. Her dress was perfect in a wonderful golden tissue, a sort of golden jersey that had something of *la côte de mailû* [chain-mail] of olden days. On her head was a golden veil and her superb emerald and diamond diadem which Sandro [Alexander] had given her for her wedding. She looked beautiful, tall, upright and blooming, with her sweet, frank, happy expression – a great contrast to Lisabetha, which keeps people speculating which of the sisters is lovelier. Generally Lisabetha has the greatest reputation for beauty, but some passionately prefer Mignon's face. Mignon has an adorable mouth with an irresistible, lovable expression like a cupid's. Lisabetha has something disdainful which does not make her popular with women of her family. The one who surpassed herself yesterday was sister Baby. She was all in gold, with a long court-train of Russian coral pink and gold brocade trimmed with white fox.

But it was especially her headdress which was stunning. She had an opaque veil of gold which she had draped about her face Egyptian-wise, with her rag-shaped diamond diadem placed rather high above it and long emerald 'pendentifs' hanging on both sides of her face. Some superb emeralds and diamonds completed her attire with her violet and white Spanish grand cordon. I felt really proud of my women-folk.

Ileana was utterly sweet in her golden dress and blue velvet mantle, and Sitta[2] and Tim[3] all dressed the same – all three lovely girls in their way. My ladies wore the same blue velvet mantle over silver-grey, and all of them looked good.

The guests drove to the church ahead of us to await us there. Nando and I followed in our closed state carriage with four horses. The sky was spluttering, the roads very muddy; but at least it was not pouring. Carol and Sitta followed in a second carriage.

Alba-Iulia is charmingly situated. It is a quaint little old fortified town within whose battlements the former government (Averescu's) built the little cathedral where the coronation was to take place. It lies in the centre of a square enclosed by a building like a convent. It has been much criticized and certainly has mistakes, but the whole looks extremely pretty and affective and was beautifully trim and tidy.

We arrived at the church, where all the guests had already taken their places. Nando and I were opposite each other on thrones.

The service was fine, dignified, not too long, the choir excellent. The inside of the church, though not big, is imposing, the frescoes good. The church service over, Nando and I, followed by those carrying our crowns and mantles, stepped out into the open to the great square beyond the church where a dais had been erected with a baldachin over it. All the guests took their places around this dais, where Nando and I stood alone.

Old Pherekyde as head of the Senate and Orleanu, head of the Chambers, stepped up with our crowns. General Lupescu had His Majesty's mantle; General Popovici had mine. They were assisted according to my own wishes by the colonel and the youngest sub-lieutenant of our respective regiments, so that on this day of days I had my Roşiori[4] close beside me.

Pherekyde stepped up to His Majesty with the steel crown after the generals had hung our cloaks, or rather our royal mantles round our shoulders, mine all in the red-gold I have already described and Nando's in royal purple, both of them embroidered with the different arms of united Romania. Nando took the crown from him after he had made a very loyal speech and put it on his own head. Then Orleanu stepped up to me with my crown and made a very pretty speech indeed. I then knelt down before Nando, who put the great heavy crown on my head, while all present cheered with all their might and the military bands played the National Anthem.

I think it must have been a fine sight, and I hope that His Majesty and I played our part well and looked as well as we could in our somewhat overwhelming get-up. Alas, the real Romanian sun was wanting to give colour to the ceremony and the picturesque background. Such a pity, but at least it did not rain.

Walking very slowly under our baldachin, which was carried by officers of our respective regiments, we proceeded to the palace (which is built like a monastery, round the square of the church), followed by our family and guests. We slowly mounted the staircase and then proceeded to the centre of the open colonnade from where we bowed to the people beneath while they acclaimed us with colossal cheers.

Then everybody, beginning with the family, came to congratulate us and kiss our hands.

It all went off as well as anything in our country can go off, where all great ceremonies are difficult to arrange, for many reasons. The principal one is that the tradition does not exist,[5] it all has to be invented by those who know a little about it. But the whole ceremony was picturesque, dignified and at the same time unpretentious.

We were led to our apartments and there our crowns and mantles were removed, and we were left for a rest while all the guests were conveyed to the big banqueting hall, there to await our royal arrival.

I put on my diamond and sapphire diadem and hung the same red velvet cloak I had on for the arrival while the others sat smoking around me and our different maids fussed around us, ministering to our various needs.

Lisabetha stood it all better then we dared expect, and expressed her wish to take part in the great banquet.

It was an extraordinarily well-arranged meal, very quickly served, and excellent food. It lasted no longer than one and a half hours, which is remarkable when one considers that there were about 400 people present.

The banquet over, we went back to the palace, where we changed our clothes, I for my uniform, the others into smart hats and cloaks for the big review.

I put on my Roşiori uniform and over it the big green cloak in which I had made my entry in to Bucharest.

Carol had invented a sort of grey opossum busby or high hussar cap, which the cavalry regiments are to have. I inaugurated the first and it suited me astonishingly well, making me look almost indecently young. I had almost more success in my fur cap than in my crown.

I rode my beautiful 'Austral', who was absolutely perfect and carried me with a sort of noble pride. I thought of my good old Uncle Joe, who had given him to me in the hope I would ride him on my coronation day and I did, but I could not let him know this, not knowing where he was since he had started off on his mad journey into seething Russia to liberate one of his men whom he had sent there.

Nando was on Mr Joe, who looked a picture.

We rode out to a vast field where all the troops stood in a mighty square against a background of hills, the quaint old fortified town seen admirably from there, all gay with flags. The weather behaved, though it was fearfully muddy under foot. The temperature was just perfect and there was no wind.

Austral behaved magnificently; I could ride him right into the music and under the flags without his winking an eye. Also, he carries his head high and has a buoyant tread.

The turn of the enormous square ended, we rode back to the square in front of the town where the tribunes had been erected and His Majesty there reviewed his troops for a second time in a long but glorious march-past. I stood beside him on my proud Austral.

Nicky marched past with his 1st Vânători looking young and slim and altogether aristocratic, and was a tremendous success.

It was a long, long parade. Towards the end came my 4th Roşiori and, leaving my royal spouse's side, I went to meet them so as to ride past at their head. I decidedly took their fancy in that altern upon my noble grey horse. And if there is one thing I can do, it is ride!

This ended our day in Alba-Iulia, and we all left again on our different trains. Lisabetha was very tired, and Sitta and Tim, thinking of their father's sad fate while we were thus being honoured, were constantly near to tears, which I so well understand. The contrast seemed so cruel. Poor Tino![6]

Ileana took a little supper with me alone in my cabin while Lisabetha went to bed and Queen Mignon helped her father with the dinner in the dining car.

All day long I kept thinking of my Mircea, who ought to have been there, the youngest of my proud family. I thought of him sleeping so quietly in the old Cotroceni[7] with all the days he did not live, neither the good ones nor the bad ones. He neither grieves nor trembles nor rejoices with us any more. Now he would have been a quite big boy. Perhaps he would have held my train for me . . . Little Mircea, where are you? Little life, bud that was not to bloom.

MONDAY, 16 OCTOBER 1922, BUCHAREST

Carol's birthday and the day of our solemn entry into our capital. Alas – bad weather, lowering clouds, a wicked grey, leaden sky and a nasty wind. Our train was stopped at Pantelimon[8] and I had a quiet breakfast in bed. Early I sent a card of myself in coronation robes as birthday greetings to Carol into his carriage, then slowly I dressed myself in all my glory chosen for today. Another golden dress, but this time of another tint – dazzlingly yellow-gold in a wonderful tissue as soft and supple as the velvet of today, made quite plain with several rows of golden cord round my waist and hips and large broad sleeves of dark brown fur. Over this dress a superb cloak of red velvet stamped with gold and a large collar of the same brown fur, on my head a *kokoshnik* [a tiara in the Russian style] of a material that seemed all set with rubies, a hat which looked like a diadem.

Lisabetha, who drove with me in the first carriage, was in a lovely dress of golden lace with a beautiful fur coat.

All the gentlemen rode and I followed in a glass carriage drawn by four horses, with Lisabetha and Tim sitting opposite. I was annoyed to see that they had sent me a closed carriage, but later I had to agree that they had been wise because it began to rain and then to pour and ended, alas, by being a really wet day, so rare in Romania. In the second carriage drove Mignon and old Tomasso[9] of Genoa. In the third, Baby, Sitta and Ileana. Sitta has not been very well lately – a sort of nicotine poisoning from smoking too much. Today I lent Austral to Ali,[10] who loves the horse.

The decorations were all tastefully done and the public was frantically enthusiastic, roaring with joy, and nothing dampened by terrible weather.

We finally reached the metropole, Lisabetha on the verge of exhaustion as it was a long way from the Mogoşoaia[11] railway, the same road we had taken on our entry after our two years' exile. That day I rode into town with Nando and there were both French and English troops to receive us, all along the *chaussée*.

The Te Deum was beautiful and the silence of the dark, candle-lit church was very soothing after the roaring crowds.

All the gentlemen were very wet, and afterwards there were great discussions about whether to postpone the big popular march-past the next day or not. As all was mapped out for the next day and I knew that it would be impossible to find another time to do it, I strongly voted to proceed. All the people, the thousands and thousands of peasants, were waiting to march past; it would have been almost impossible to let them all know, besides they too were wet and it was better to let them warm themselves with their own enthusiasm for marching past. I had rather a heated discussion with the males of my family but was well sustained in my opinion by my guests and officials, so after a good cold lunch in the Parliament, a small necessary visit to the metropolitan's quarters, we went to our usual parade place under the shadows of Mihai cel Mare's statue and had a tremendous *défilé*.

First a very well arranged historical pageant and then an enormous march-past of peasants from every quarter of Romȃnia Mare [Greater Romania].

It rained part of the time and the nice costumes, even beautiful costumes that had been prepared, were all soaked. There were moments when it did not rain, but it remained ugly weather all the time. Such a pity!

Finally at about half past three we all reached Cotroceni safely. All our guests were put up here and they all felt very comfortable, were pleased with their rooms and enjoyed warm baths, then a big tea at the round table before my studio fire.

Lisabetha did not take part in the big banquet we had in the evening, for which Reburhn had beautifully decorated our table around Papa's[12] magnificent collection of silver and gold ships, which I was using for the first time. Before I dressed for the banquet, Barbo[13] came to see me to bring me his personal congratulations. He had not been able to approach me yesterday though he had been there.

We thought of all the terrible days of anxiety while we were fighting for *Romȃnia Mare*. Today certainly, and especially yesterday, was indeed a crowning of our great efforts and a recompense for the many tears shed in exile after my Mircea had been laid in his grave.

TUESDAY, 17 OCTOBER 1922, COTROCENI

Weather still dull and ugly but at least no rain, but not at all the beautiful sunshining autumn weather we are accustomed to in Romania in October, which is generally still a beautiful month.

Our day began at half past ten with deputations, congratulations and so on. We stood in the throne room, on the steps of our thrones. It was neither very lengthy nor tiring. But afterwards came the great ordeal. His Majesty and I arranged ourselves for a second time in our mantles and crowns to drive through the streets, so that the population of our capital should get a glimpse of us thus attired.

We drove to the big 'arènes' of the Carol Park, where the two thousand mayors from all the communities of Greater Romania were united to give us a welcome – and what a welcome! We appeared in full

147

'Ornat'[14] upon the open space which crowns the building and stood there in full view of our united people as crowned King and Queen.

The enthusiasm was delirious, tumultuous, thunderous – a magnificent and stirring reception while huge choirs sang the national anthem, which was entirely drowned out by the cheering.

Corbescu, mayor of the city of Bucharest, finally made a speech when the crowd consented to be quiet for a moment, and Nando answered very well from his height. Then the roaring and acclaiming all began again and would have gone on for ever had we not turned to go.

We waited for a while in the small room there and then, having removed our crowns and mantles, we circulated through the four huge sheds which had been erected in all the long avenues to give a repast to the many peasants.

It really was a triumphant procession. We marched down the centre of the tables, which were stood in two lines leaving a passage between them. Luckily the path had been sanded so it was not muddy, though damp and cold. I was still in my golden underdress, golden veil and silver cloak, or rather a silver mantle lined with *bleu de roi* velvet, still very gorgeous and queenly.

I walked along ahead of Nando, followed by sister Baby and Ileana (my little queens had gone home) and preceded by Angelescu and our ADCs.

All the peasants took the flowers from their tables, threw them before my sheet and showered them over me with enthusiastic, delirious delight. It was indeed a heart-warming occasion: soul enjoyed it immensely and certainly walked several kilometers thus.

We returned to Cotroceni for lunch at three o'clock, and still had all the heads of our deputations for the meal. The table was again decorated with my ships and all our Byzantine glasses, and looked exceedingly fine. I confess to having felt rather tired, but the meal was decidedly cheerful. Sitta was not well and did not come to anything, feeling giddy and sick.

I had barely an hour's rest, then had to go back to the palace to receive more deputations. An hour's rest and then dressing in the same way as for the Alba-Iulia banquet. The theatre was overflowing with a delightful and select public. The second act of the *Fliegender Hollander* was very well given, and afterwards an allegorical piece by Mircea Rădulescu very prettily done. In the entr'acte we received the occupants of the boxes, who congratulated us with exuberance.

Everybody seems enchanted and particularly impressed by the beauty of the ceremonies, and especially of the female members of the family and their clothes and jewels. Certainly not one of us women was ugly, which is so rare, and we had clothed ourselves artistically in glorious tissues, wonderful colours and dignified, unusual shapes of dresses and unduthy which gave the whole thing '*un cachet très special*'.

Lisabetha stood all the fatigue much better than anyone dared hope. Finally, amidst colossal cheers, we left the theatre.

WEDNESDAY 18 OCTOBER 1922, COTROCENI

[. . .] For lunch we were a smaller party, more or less only those who were in the house with a few suites en plus, but old 'Tomato', as we call him, the Duke of Genoa was at his own legation. Dear old 'Tomato' is really old; one can hardly understand what he says. He had a tremendous appetite and a kindly, gracious way, but we do not find very much to say to each other and he has been at my right hand through all the ceremonies.

After lunch we young ones, that is to say; I (feeling young though I am not), Bertie, Baby, Ali and Ileana, took a good ride. I mounted them all splendidly, myself riding Kiraliff, and we had excellent gallops on a muddy but soft ground. Bertie and Ileana have become extraordinary chums.

THURSDAY 19 OCTOBER 1922, COTROCENI

A morning sacrificed to the photographers, as we wanted to have souvenirs of the three queens together, as we were on the day of the coronation. So Mama queen and her little queens were photographed together, successfully. I hope as this time so that each should have something to sell, we used the 'Mandy' and finally I let 'Julietta' take a few of me, as he[15] was nearly succumbing to jealousy because we had given that honour to the Transylvanian woman and not to him . . .

And so, the coronation over, another corner was turned, another road stretched ahead, teeming with life and human problems, new ways, new demands on all who travel it.

Postscript

After the First World War only three of Queen Victoria's granddaughters remained on European thrones: Marie in Romania, Maud in Norway and Ena in Spain. On the continent other grandchildren had different fates: Alexandra the Tsarina of Russia had been murdered; Kaiser Wilhelm II had gone into exile in the Netherlands, and Sophie, Queen of the Hellenes, had gone into exile in Switzerland, though she returned to Greece in December 1920.

Marie had inherited from her uncle, King Edward VII, a taste for politics and diplomacy. She also emulated her grandmother, Queen Victoria, in the idea that international alliances are not complete without dynastic marriages (even if the events of 1914 had demonstrated the limits of this policy, with Germany ending up in bitter confrontation with Russia and Britain).

THE MOTHER-IN-LAW OF THE BALKANS

The Queen engineered some matrimonial alliances with Greek monarchs when George, Crown Prince of Greece, married Princess Elisabetha of Romania in February 1921[1] and the Crown Prince of Romania married Helen, Princess of Greece, in March the same year.[2] Another one was completed with the Kingdom of the Serbs, Croats and Slovenes[3] in June 1922, when King Alexander married Princess Marie (Mignon) of Romania.[4] After these alliances Queen Marie acquired the nickname of the 'mother-in-law of the Balkans', a title she was glad to accept. These matrimonial links complemented superbly the Romanian government's policy of regional alliances such as the creation of the Little Entente in 1921, and the Balkan Entente in 1934.

151

Marie had another project of matrimonial alliance, without results, however – the marriage of her son, Prince Nicolae, with Princess Giovanna, daughter of King Victor Emmanuel III of Italy. The project would never be accomplished due to the rivalry between the Italians and Yugoslavs over the Adriatic Sea, reflected in the fact that the Italians did not appreciate the marriage of Princess Marie (Mignon) to King Alexander of Yugoslavia. Later in 1930 Giovanna would marry Boris, the Tsar of Bulgaria. In the end Prince Nicolae had a morganatic marriage[5] with a Romanian from a gentry family.

In 1931 Princess Ileana married, at Sinaia, Anton Archduke of Austria: in this case Queen Marie didn't manage to conclude a political marriage, although there was talk of her marrying Tsar Boris III of Bulgaria or Prince of the Asturias, heir of Spain, in the late 1920s, and also there was an unfortunate short betrothal with a minor German prince.

DIPLOMATIC TOUR

In the spring of 1924, King Ferdinand and Queen Marie undertook a diplomatic tour of France, Switzerland, Belgium and the United Kingdom. They were thus the first monarchs to visit the headquarters of the newly established League of Nations in Geneva.

The visit to England meant very much to Marie, where, beyond the official meetings, it meant a return to her home country. It also meant an official recognition of the prominent role she had played in the war. At Buckingham Palace, King George V declared: 'looking back upon the strife and endurance of the Great War, we see how new and stronger links of fellowship were forged by common suffering in a common cause. But apart from the common aims, which we pursue, there are other and dear ties between us. Her Majesty the Queen, my dear cousin, is British born.'[6] Queen Marie remembered also in her journal the arrival day as 'a great day for me, one of emotions, sweet, happy and the same time glorious emotions to come back as Queen to my own country, to be received officially, in all honour and enthusiastically into the bargain – to feel your heart swell with pride and satisfaction, to feel your heart beat and tears start into your eyes, while something gave you a lump in your throat!'[7]

The visit of Ferdinand and Marie in 1924 was a symbolic recognition of Romania at that time and a reflection of the prestige the country had gained during the First World War. The family links that strengthened the relationship were also important. The royal visit of March 1924 is less familiar to those interested in the history of the Romanian monarchy or in the personality of Queen Marie. For Romania it was more important than Marie's visit to the United States in 1926. The considerable attention she received from the American press strongly influenced all subsequent writing about her, though the tour of 1924 by King Ferdinand and Queen Marie had a much bigger impact, consisting of state visits to the former Allies.

THE DOWAGER QUEEN

After the death of King Ferdinand and of Prime Minister Brătianu in 1927, Queen Marie exerted a certain influence over political life during the Regency, when Michael[8] was a minor king.[9] Some had wanted to co-opt Queen Marie into the Regency in October 1929, after the death of one of the regents, but she refused because two members of the royal family[10] could not be simultaneously members of the Regency. Marie did not want to replace her son, Prince Nicolae, or find herself enmeshed in fights between the political parties. In October 1929 she wrote to her friend Roxanne Weingartner: 'Many wanted me to be a member of the Regency, while for others this would not have been comfortable, because this would have meant control and the introduction of the old atmosphere during Rexford [Ferdinand], without which they are already used, and from this many contradictory discussions started, polemics and God knows what else.'[11] The Romanian Constitution of 1923 (art. 77) forbade the succession of women to the throne, but it did not forbid women belonging to the royal family to act in the Regency.

After Prince Carol returned to Romania and was proclaimed king in June 1930, he began to isolate Queen Marie from political life.

She lived in increasing seclusion in the Cotroceni Palace or at her residences in Bran, Balcic, or Pelishor. After prolonged illness, Queen Marie died in July 1938.

THE DYNASTY IN ROMANIA AFTER THE QUEEN'S DEATH

After the queen's death in 1938, Europe was aflame again and on the eve of a new war. In the summer of 1940 Romania lost Bessarabia, Northern Transylvania and the Cadrilater (Southern Dobrudja). On 6 September 1940 King Carol II abdicated in favour of his son, Michael, who reigned between 1940 and 1947. Marshal Ion Antonescu, a dictator who took the country into war on the side of Nazi Germany, ruled Romania until August 1944. After a coup d'état on that date King Michael I arrested Antonescu and put Romania on the side of the Allied powers. Under Soviet pressure, Romania gradually moved to a communist regime.

On 30 December 1947 King Michael was forced to abdicate by the communists. He left Romania on 3 January 1948, together with the Queen Mother, Helen. Princess Elisabetha of Romania (former Queen of Greece), Ileana, princess of Romania and archduchess of Austria, and her children and husband, Anton, archduke of Austria, left the country on 12 January. The dynasty thus scattered into exile. King Michael I settled in Switzerland, having lived for a while in the United Kingdom in the early 1950s. Queen Mother Helen went to Italy. King Carol II went into exile in September 1940 for a short period in Spain, then to Mexico, Brazil and finally to Portugal. Prince Nicolae lived in Italy, Switzerland and then in Spain, having being exiled previously by Carol II due to his morganatic marriage. Princess Elisabetha settled in France. Princess Ileana sought exile in Switzerland, Argentina and then in the United States. Queen Marie of Yugoslavia (born Princess of Romania) moved to Britain.

After almost forty-five years of exile, King Michael, together with his wife, Queen Anne (née princess of Bourbon-Parma), visited Romania,[12] with the approval of the Romanian government, for the first time in the spring of 1992. After many disagreements with the Romanian authorities, Michael returned to Romania in 2001. He now lives there, having recovered some proprieties such as Săvârşin Castle, in Arad county, the house at 32 Caragiale Street in Bucharest. Elisabetha Palace is used now as his official residence in Bucharest. In December 1997, on the fiftieth anniversary of his forced abdication, King Michael announced a new dynastic law which recognized the male primogeniture among the siblings, but also allowed the succession of females to the throne. He made known his eldest daughter Margarita as Crown Princess of Romania and heir apparent.

The descendants of Queen Marie and King Ferdinand had sat on the thrones of Romania, Yugoslavia and, for a short period, of Greece. However, all these countries are now republics, and their former kings, queens and heirs have no kingdoms to rule. It remains to be seen whether historians will have to rewrite their stories.

Appendix:
Select List of Queen Marie's Writings

BOOKS

The Lily of Life, London: Hodder & Stoughton, 1913

The Dreamer of Dreams, London: Hodder & Stoughton, 1915

Four Seasons out of a Man's Life, Bucharest, 1915

The Story of a Heart, Craiova, 1915

The Naughty Queen, Bucharest, 1916

My Country, London: Hodder & Stoughton, 1916

The Stealers of Light. A Legend, London: Hodder & Stoughton, 1916

Mon Pays, Paris: Georges Crès & Cie, 1917

À mon people! De mon âme à la sienne, Paris: Jouve, 1917

The Child of the Sun, Iaşi: Editura 'Versuri şi proză', 1918

Minola. Povestea unei mici regine triste, Iaşi: Tipografia serviciului geograic al armatei, 1918

Peeping Pansy, London: Hodder & Stoughton, 1919

Gânduri şi icoane din vremea războiului, Iaşi, 1919

Dor nestins, Bucureşti, 1920

Ilderim. Poveste în umbră şi lumină, Bucureşti: Editura literară a casei scolilor, 1921

The Story of Naughty Kildeen, London: Oxford University Press, 1922

Kildine, Historie d'une méchante petite princesse, France: Maison Alfred Mame et Fils, 1922

The Voice on the Mountain. A Story for Those Who Understand, New York: Alfred A. Knopf, 1923

The Voice on the Mountain. A Story for Those Who Understand, London: Duckworth, 1924

The Queen of Romania's Fairy Book, New York: Frederick A. Stokes, 1923

Why? A Story of a Great Longing, Stockholm: Svenska Tryckeriaktiebolaget, 1923

A Legend from Mount Athos, Bucureşti: Editura librăriei I. Hertz, 1923

The Lost Princess. A Fairy Tale, London: S.W. Partridge & Co., 1924

The Country that I Love. An Exile's Memoirs, London: Duckworth, 1925

What Vasile Saw, Boston: D.C. Heath, 1925

Kandi Klara Kalandjai, Cluj, 1925

The Queen of Romania's Fairy Book, London, T. Fisher Unwin 1925

Ilderim. A Tale of Light and Shade, London: Duckworth, 1925

The Story of Naughty Kildeen, New York: Harcourt, Brace and Co., 1926

Păsări fantastice pe albastrul cerului, Bucureşti: Editura atelierelor grafice ale ziarului Universul, 1928

How I came to Tenha Yuvah, Cernăuţi, 1928

The Magic Doll of Romania. A Wonder Story in Which East and West Do Meet, New York: Frederick A. Stokes, 1929

Crowned Queens. A Tale from out the Past, London: Heath Cranton, 1929

My Dream Houses, Bucureşti, 1930

Stella Maris. The Smallest Church in the Land, Bucureşti, 1930

Copila cu ochi albastri, Bucureşti, 1931

Ce-a văzut soldatul Vasile. Poveste din timpul războiului, Bucureşti, 1932

The Story of My Life, vols I–III, London: Cassell, 1934–35

The Story of My Life, New York: Charles Scribner's Sons, 1934

Ordeal: The Story of My Life, New York: Charles Scribner's Sons, 1935

Masks. A Novel, London: Duckworth, 1935

Masks, New York: E.P. Dutton & Co., 1937

Măşti, Bucureşti: Editura librăriei Socec, 1938

Historie de ma vie, Paris: Plon, 1937–38

Regine încoronate. Povestire din trecut, Bucureşti: Adevărul, 1944

A Christmas Tale, New York: Aldus Printers, 1957
The Story of My Life, New York: Arno Press, 1971
Miracle of Tears, Woodside: Bluestar Communications, 2001
Kildine – povestea unei mici principese răutăcioase, Bucureşti: Corint, 2003

ARTICLES, EXTRACTS OF WRITINGS PUBLISHED IN PERIODICALS

'În numele tău' (In your name) and 'Lacrimi' (Tears), *Calendarul Regina Maria pe 1918 (Queen Marie's Calendar)*, Iaşi: Tipografia serviciului geografic, 1918
'A Queen in a Crisis: "It is No Sinecure to be the Queen of a Country"' in *Ladies' Home Journal*, December 1918
'Un Martyr de la Grande Tragédie: Le Tsar Nicolas II', in *Revue des Deux Mondes*, septembre 1919
'The Vanished Tsarina', *The Living Age*, October 1919
'Some Memories of the Russian Court', *The Living Age*, October 1919
'The Fallen Czar', *Woman's Home Companion*, July 1920
'A Resurrected Army', *The Living Age*, July 1921
'Modern Fashions', *The Living Age*, February 1925
'Lulaloo – A Fairy Tale Told by a Queen', *Good Housekeeping*, March 1925
'Une reine regarde la vie', *Excelsior*, Paris, June 1925
'Making Marriage Durable', *New York World*, May–June 1925
'My Journey to America. Impressions of America', *The World*, New York, 1926
'Is Royal Blood a Blessing?', *Pearson's Magazine*, 1927
'My Life as Crown Princess', *The Saturday Evening Post*, December 1933–June 1934
'My Mission', *Cornhill Magazine*, October–December 1939

MANUSCRIPTS

The Real Regina Maria. The Story of a Soul; A Book of Remembrances; The Future of Monarchy; New Queens for Old;

Clothes; About Beauty; About Marriage; About Women; Woman's Dress and Woman's tongue as Influence on the Marriage Problem; About men; About Fidelity; A Queen Prayer; The Virtue of Perseverance; Be Yourself; Americans I have met; Scrisă când am devenit Regină (Written when I became a Queen), Paginile mele românești (My Romanian pages), București (Bucharest), Pagini scrise in decembrie 1916 (Pages written in December 1916); London under three reigns; The Woman of Tears; An English princess amongst Foreigners; What it feels to be exiled; Greeting written for Mr. de St. Aulaire; Written for the Romanians in America; Defence against a horrible article written in America; At Grand-mama's Court; Upon the Education of Royal Children; What Life has taught me; What Romania means to its Queen; The Problem of Happiness; Article written for the coronation – 'The Bells are Pinging'; Colonel Boyle; Ioan Brătianu; Back to Kind Old London. (Romanian National Archives, Bucharest, Regina Maria)

EDITIONS OF *THE STORY OF MY LIFE*

The Story of My Life, London: Cassell, vol. I – 1934; vol. II – 1934, vol. III – 1935. The volumes had several reprints in the late 1930s.

The Story of My Life, New York: Charles Scribner's, 1934. Reprinted in the same period.

Ordeal: The Story of My Life, New York: Charles Scribner's, 1935

Histoire de Ma Vie, Paris: Plon, 1937–9 (3 vols)

Editions in Romanian: *Povestea Vieţii Mele*, 1934–6, 3 vols, București: Adevărul Publishing House. Reprinted in 1990–1 and 1998 (publishing houses: Eminescu, Moldova, Porţile Orientului).

Editions in the late 1930s in German, Polish, Czech, Swedish, Italian and Hungarian

The Story of My Life, New York: Arno Press, 1971

Private printing late 1970s in New York (facsimile)

1: Romanian Royal Family – House of Hohenzollern

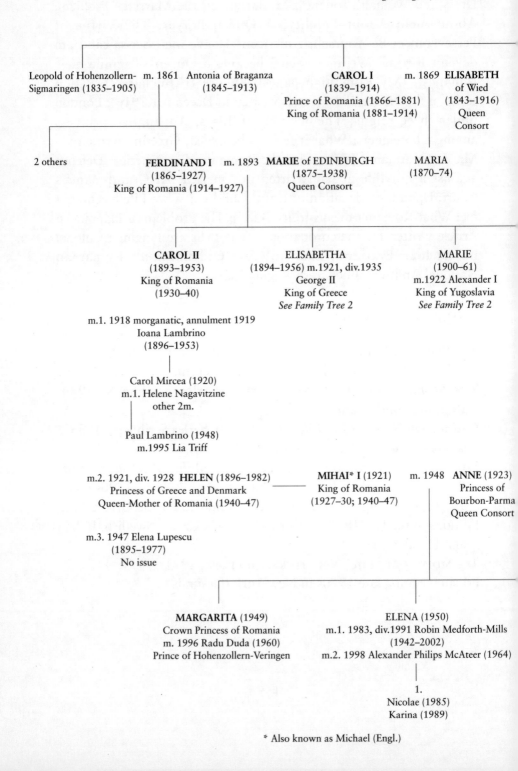

KARL ANTON of Hohenzollern-
Sigmaringen (1811–1885)

Leopold of Hohenzollern-   m. 1861   Antonia of Braganza
Sigmaringen (1835–1905)   (1845–1913)

CAROL I   m. 1869   ELISABETH
(1839–1914)   of Wied
Prince of Romania (1866–1881)   (1843–1916)
King of Romania (1881–1914)   Queen
                                        Consort

2 others

FERDINAND I   m. 1893   MARIE of EDINBURGH
(1865–1927)   (1875–1938)
King of Romania (1914–1927)   Queen Consort

MARIA
(1870–74)

CAROL II   ELISABETHA   MARIE
(1893–1953)   (1894–1956) m.1921, div.1935   (1900–61)
King of Romania   George II   m.1922 Alexander I
(1930–40)   King of Greece   King of Yugoslavia
                    See Family Tree 2   *See Family Tree 2*

m.1. 1918 morganatic, annulment 1919
Ioana Lambrino
(1896–1953)

Carol Mircea (1920)
m.1. Helene Nagavitzine
other 2m.

Paul Lambrino (1948)
m.1995 Lia Triff

m.2. 1921, div. 1928 **HELEN** (1896–1982)   **MIHAI* I** (1921)   m. 1948 **ANNE** (1923)
Princess of Greece and Denmark   King of Romania   Princess of
Queen-Mother of Romania (1940–47)   (1927–30; 1940–47)   Bourbon-Parma
                                                                  Queen Consort

m.3. 1947 Elena Lupescu
(1895–1977)
No issue

MARGARITA (1949)   ELENA (1950)
Crown Princess of Romania   m.1. 1983, div.1991 Robin Medforth-Mills
m. 1996 Radu Duda (1960)   (1942–2002)
Prince of Hohenzollern-Veringen   m.2. 1998 Alexander Philips McAteer (1964)

1.
Nicolae (1985)
Karina (1989)

* Also known as Michael (Engl.)

m. 1834 JOSEPHINE OF BADEN
(1813–1900)

Marie of Hohenzollern-   m. 1867 Philip of Flanders and   3 others   Romanian Royal Coat
Sigmaringen (1845–1912)   Saxe-Coburg   of Arms
                                   (1837–1909)

Albert I Saxe-Coburg   m.1900   Elisabeth of Bavaria
(1875–1934)   (1876–1965)
King of the Belgians

ROYAL HOUSE OF BELGIUM

NICOLAE (1903–1977)   ILEANA (1909–1991)   MIRCEA
Co-Regent of Romania (1927-30)   m.1. 1931 Anton Archduke of   (1913–16)
m.1. 1931 Ioana Dumitrescu   Austria, Habsburg-Toscana
(1909-1963)   m.2. 1954 Ştefan Issărescu
m.2. 1967 Theresa Lisboa Figueira de Mello   *See Family Tree 2*
(1913-97)
No issue

IRINA (1953)   SOPHIE (1957)   MARIA (1964)
m. 1983 John Kruger (1945)   m. 1998 Alain Biarneix of   m. 1995, Casimir Wieslaw
                                Laufenbourg (1957)   Mystkowski (1958)
                                                                 officially separated 2000

Mihai (1985)   Elisabeta-Maria
Angelica (1986)   (1999)

2: QUEEN MARIE'S DAUGHTERS AND THEIR DESCENDANTS

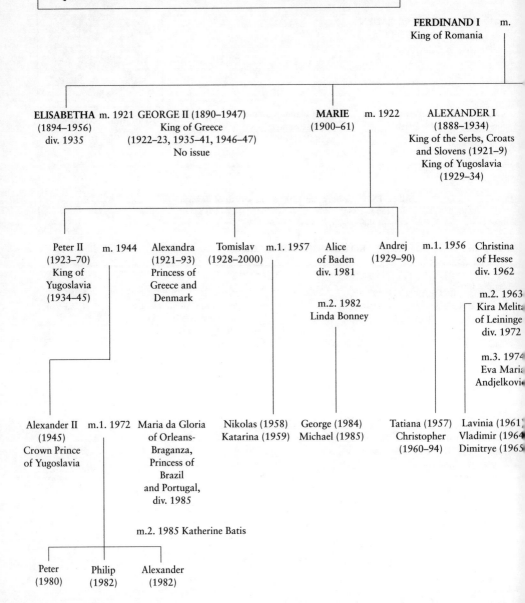

FERDINAND I   m.
King of Romania

ELISABETHA m. 1921 GEORGE II (1890–1947)
(1894–1956)   King of Greece
div. 1935   (1922–23, 1935–41, 1946–47)
                              No issue

MARIE   m. 1922   ALEXANDER I
(1900–61)   (1888–1934)
                           King of the Serbs, Croats
                           and Slovens (1921–9)
                           King of Yugoslavia
                           (1929–34)

Peter II   m. 1944   Alexandra   Tomislav   m.1. 1957   Alice   Andrej   m.1. 1956   Christina
(1923–70)   (1921–93)   (1928–2000)   of Baden   (1929–90)   of Hesse
King of   Princess of   div. 1981   div. 1962
Yugoslavia   Greece and
(1934–45)   Denmark   m.2. 1963
                                                                      m.2. 1982   Kira Melita
                                                                      Linda Bonney   of Leininge
                                                                                                              div. 1972

                                                                                                              m.3. 1974
                                                                                                              Eva Maria
                                                                                                              Andjelkovi

Alexander II m.1. 1972 Maria da Gloria   Nikolas (1958)   George (1984)   Tatiana (1957)   Lavinia (1961)
(1945)   of Orleans-   Katarina (1959)   Michael (1985)   Christopher   Vladimir (1964
Crown Prince   Braganza,   (1960–94)   Dimitrye (1965
of Yugoslavia   Princess of
                              Brazil
                              and Portugal,
                              div. 1985

                     m.2. 1985 Katherine Batis

Peter   Philip   Alexander
(1980)   (1982)   (1982)

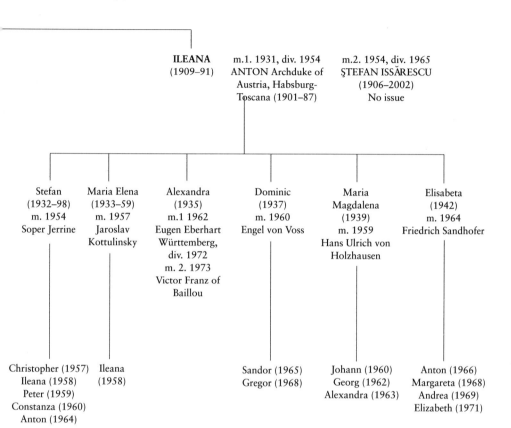

MARIE
Queen of Romania
(née Princess of Edinburgh)

ILEANA
(1909–91)

m.1. 1931, div. 1954
ANTON Archduke of
Austria, Habsburg-
Toscana (1901–87)

m.2. 1954, div. 1965
ŞTEFAN ISSĂRESCU
(1906–2002)
No issue

Stefan
(1932–98)
m. 1954
Soper Jerrine

Maria Elena
(1933–59)
m. 1957
Jaroslav
Kottulinsky

Alexandra
(1935)
m.1 1962
Eugen Eberhart
Württemberg,
div. 1972
m. 2. 1973
Victor Franz of
Baillou

Dominic
(1937)
m. 1960
Engel von Voss

Maria
Magdalena
(1939)
m. 1959
Hans Ulrich von
Holzhausen

Elisabeta
(1942)
m. 1964
Friedrich Sandhofer

Christopher (1957)
Ileana (1958)
Peter (1959)
Constanza (1960)
Anton (1964)

Ileana
(1958)

Sandor (1965)
Gregor (1968)

Johann (1960)
Georg (1962)
Alexandra (1963)

Anton (1966)
Margareta (1968)
Andrea (1969)
Elizabeth (1971)

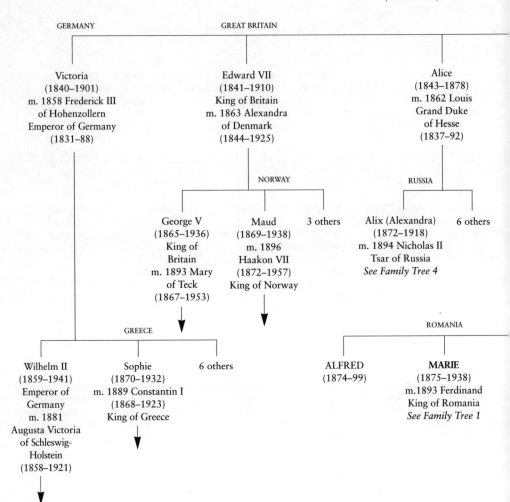

QUEEN VICTORIA OF BRITAIN
(1819–1901)

GERMANY   GREAT BRITAIN

Victoria   Edward VII   Alice
(1840–1901)   (1841–1910)   (1843–1878)
m. 1858 Frederick III   King of Britain   m. 1862 Louis
of Hohenzollern   m. 1863 Alexandra   Grand Duke
Emperor of Germany   of Denmark   of Hesse
(1831–88)   (1844–1925)   (1837–92)

                                              NORWAY   RUSSIA

                   George V   Maud   3 others   Alix (Alexandra)   6 others
                   (1865–1936)   (1869–1938)   (1872–1918)
                   King of   m. 1896   m. 1894 Nicholas II
                   Britain   Haakon VII   Tsar of Russia
                   m. 1893 Mary   (1872–1957)   *See Family Tree 4*
                   of Teck   King of Norway
                   (1867–1953)

       GREECE   ROMANIA

Wilhelm II   Sophie   6 others   ALFRED   MARIE
(1859–1941)   (1870–1932)   (1874–99)   (1875–1938)
Emperor of   m. 1889 Constantin I   m.1893 Ferdinand
Germany   (1868–1923)   King of Romania
m. 1881   King of Greece   *See Family Tree 1*
Augusta Victoria
of Schleswig-
Holstein
(1858–1921)

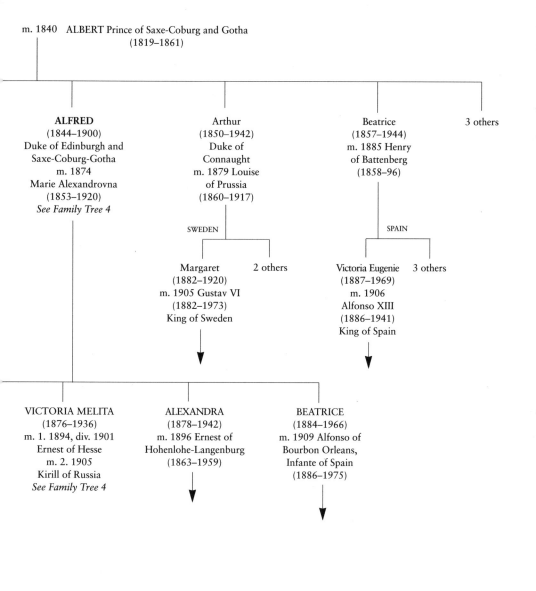

m. 1840   ALBERT Prince of Saxe-Coburg and Gotha
(1819–1861)

ALFRED
(1844–1900)
Duke of Edinburgh and
Saxe-Coburg-Gotha
m. 1874
Marie Alexandrovna
(1853–1920)
See Family Tree 4

Arthur
(1850–1942)
Duke of
Connaught
m. 1879 Louise
of Prussia
(1860–1917)

Beatrice
(1857–1944)
m. 1885 Henry
of Battenberg
(1858–96)

3 others

SWEDEN

SPAIN

Margaret   2 others
(1882–1920)
m. 1905 Gustav VI
(1882–1973)
King of Sweden

Victoria Eugenie   3 others
(1887–1969)
m. 1906
Alfonso XIII
(1886–1941)
King of Spain

VICTORIA MELITA
(1876–1936)
m. 1. 1894, div. 1901
Ernest of Hesse
m. 2. 1905
Kirill of Russia
See Family Tree 4

ALEXANDRA
(1878–1942)
m. 1896 Ernest of
Hohenlohe-Langenburg
(1863–1959)

BEATRICE
(1884–1966)
m. 1909 Alfonso of
Bourbon Orleans,
Infante of Spain
(1886–1975)

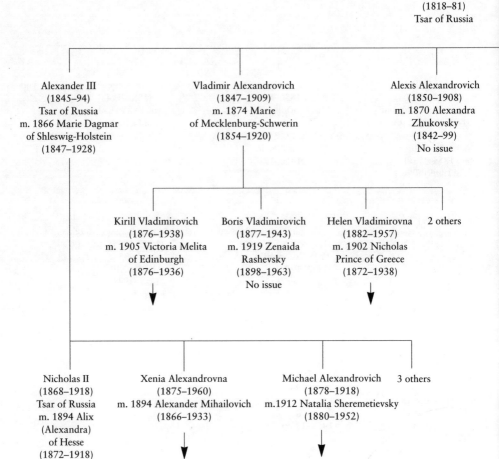

ALEXANDER II
(1818–81)
Tsar of Russia

Alexander III
(1845–94)
Tsar of Russia
m. 1866 Marie Dagmar
of Shleswig-Holstein
(1847–1928)

Vladimir Alexandrovich
(1847–1909)
m. 1874 Marie
of Mecklenburg-Schwerin
(1854–1920)

Alexis Alexandrovich
(1850–1908)
m. 1870 Alexandra
Zhukovsky
(1842–99)
No issue

Kirill Vladimirovich
(1876–1938)
m. 1905 Victoria Melita
of Edinburgh
(1876–1936)

Boris Vladimirovich
(1877–1943)
m. 1919 Zenaida
Rashevsky
(1898–1963)
No issue

Helen Vladimirovna
(1882–1957)
m. 1902 Nicholas
Prince of Greece
(1872–1938)

2 others

Nicholas II
(1868–1918)
Tsar of Russia
m. 1894 Alix
(Alexandra)
of Hesse
(1872–1918)

Xenia Alexandrovna
(1875–1960)
m. 1894 Alexander Mihailovich
(1866–1933)

Michael Alexandrovich
(1878–1918)
m.1912 Natalia Sheremetievsky
(1880–1952)

3 others

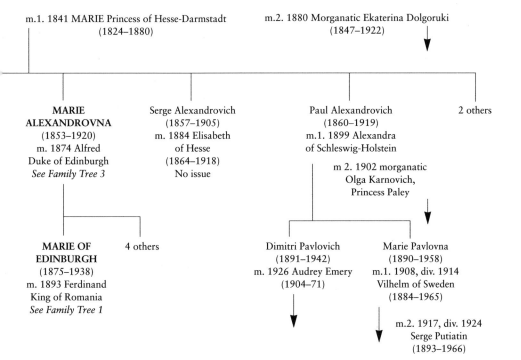

m.1. 1841 MARIE Princess of Hesse-Darmstadt
(1824–1880)

m.2. 1880 Morganatic Ekaterina Dolgoruki
(1847–1922)

**MARIE
ALEXANDROVNA**
(1853–1920)
m. 1874 Alfred
Duke of Edinburgh
See Family Tree 3

Serge Alexandrovich
(1857–1905)
m. 1884 Elisabeth
of Hesse
(1864–1918)
No issue

Paul Alexandrovich
(1860–1919)
m.1. 1899 Alexandra
of Schleswig-Holstein

m 2. 1902 morganatic
Olga Karnovich,
Princess Paley

2 others

**MARIE OF
EDINBURGH**
(1875–1938)
m. 1893 Ferdinand
King of Romania
See Family Tree 1

4 others

Dimitri Pavlovich
(1891–1942)
m. 1926 Audrey Emery
(1904–71)

Marie Pavlovna
(1890–1958)
m.1. 1908, div. 1914
Vilhelm of Sweden
(1884–1965)

m.2. 1917, div. 1924
Serge Putiatin
(1893–1966)

Notes

Introduction

1. See Paul Minet, 'Even More Reading Between the Lines. Some final Interpolations by Miss Grizel Gray of Walmer', *Royalty Digest. A Journal of Record*, vol. XI, no. 10 (Ticehurst, April 2002), p. 298.
2. Prince Carol renounced his rights as crown prince and heir to the throne in December 1925 due to a love affair with a commoner, Elena Lupescu.
3. See Romanian National Archives, Bucharest (RNA), Regina Maria, private papers, correspondence with Prince Nicolae and Queen Marie of Yugoslavia.
4. Librarian at the Foreign Office.
5. Stephan Gaselee, typewritten letter to Queen Marie of Romania, signed 15 October 1937, London; RNA, Regina Maria, III/469.
6. Diana Fotescu (ed.), *Americans and Queen Marie of Romania*, Iaşi–Oxford–Portland: Center for Romanian Studies, 1998, p. 259; Ray Harris Baker to Queen Marie, 11 January 1938.
7. *Cornhill Magazine*, vol. 160, nos 958, 959, London, 1939.
8. Ibid., No. 959, p. 433.
9. Ray Harris Baker, *A Collection Concerning Marie Queen of Romania and the Romania of 1866 to 1941*, Washington, 1942, pp. 2–3.
10. Marie, Queen of Romania, *The Story of My Life*, vol. II, London: Cassell, 1935, fifth edition, p. 333.
11. Queen Marie, 'Souvenir of Alfred's last stay with us', October 1898, autographed manuscript, RNA, Regina Maria, III/97.
12. Constantin Bacalbaşa, *Bucureştii de altă dată, 1901–1910*, vol. III, Bucureşti: Editura ziarul Universul, 1936, edition II, p. 75.
13. She wrote under the pen name Carmen Sylva.
14. Queen Marie, 'A Book of Remembrance', typewritten manuscript, RNA, Regina Maria, III/62, p. 242.
15. Ray Harris Baker, *A Collection*, p. 3.
16. RNA, Queen Marie's Journal, III/120; see *Însemnări zilnice (decembrie 1918–decembrie 1919). Maria Regina României*, ed. V. Arimia, vol. I, Bucureşti: Editura Albatros, 1996, p. 336; Mărioara Voiculescu, Romanian actress.

17. William T. Ellis, 'Rumania's Soldier Queen', in *Century Magazine*, vol. 96, July 1918, p. 338.
18. Queen Marie, 'The Real Regina Maria. The Story of a Soul', 1922–3, autographed manuscript, RNA, Regina Maria, III/100, 3 vols.
19. RNA, Regina Maria, III/330, London, 13 December 1927.
20. Ibid., III/371, London, 5 November 1929.
21. Ibid., III/395, London, 21 August 1933.
22. Ibid., III/ 411, London, 16 April 1934.
23. D.V. Barnoschi, *Recenzie. Maria, Regina României. Povestea Vieţii Mele*, Bucureşti: Cultura românească, 1936, p. 18.
24. Ch. Scribner, typewritten letter to Ray Harris Baker, signed 5 November 1941, New York, Kent State University Library Archives, Special Collections, Queen Marie's Collection.
25. Stephan Gaselee, typewritten letter to Queen Marie, signed February 27 1935, Madeira, RNA, Regina Maria, III/439.
26. Press cuttings from a British newspaper, RNA, Regina Maria.
27. Pelesh Museum Archives, Posada, 123–133, 12 January 1938; Georges Dilmare's letter to Queen Marie of Romania.
28. Queen Marie, 'The Story of a Good Man. King Ferdinand of Romania', autograph manuscript, RNA, Regina Maria, III/58, pp. 97–8.
29. Mary M. Colum, 'The Queen and Mr. Wells', *The Forum*, vol. 93, no. 2, February 1935, pp. 86–7.
30. Queen Marie's letter to Miss Beckley, p. 50, Cotroceni, 16 February 1929, typewritten letter, RNA, Castele şi palate – Regina Maria, 105/1929.
31. Marie, Queen of Romania, *The Story of My Life*, vol. I, London: Cassell, 6th edition, July 1936, p. 5.
32. Queen Marie's letter to Miss Beckley, Cotroceni, 16 February 1929, p. 51, typewritten letter, RNA, Castele şi palate – Regina Maria, 105/1929.
33. Ibid.
34. *Story of My Life*, vol. I, pp. 8–14.
35. Queen Marie, 'How it feels to be exiled' (fragment from a version of the first volume of memoirs), typewritten manuscript, RNA, Regina Maria, III/7, p. 110.
36. *Story of My Life*, vol. I, pp. 50, 51.
37. Prince George's letter to Princess Marie, 13 March 1888, autograph letter signed, RNA, Regina Maria, V/ 981.
38. RNA, Regina Maria, III/7, p. 112.
39. Bessarabia was under tsarist rule from 1812; Bessarabia was a Romanian county situated in northern Romania between the Prut and Nistru rivers.
40. See Diana Fotescu, 'The Marriage of Princess Marie of Edinburgh and Ferdinand Crown Prince of Romania', *Royalty Digest. A Journal of Record*, vol. X, no. 11, Ticehurst, May 2001, p. 334.

41. Queen Marie of Romania, 'A Book of Remembrance', p. 91, typewritten manuscript – a version of 'The Story of My Life', RNA, Regina Maria, III/62. For comparison, see *Story of My Life*, vol. I, p. 287.

42. Queen Marie's letter to Miss Beckley, p. 51, Cotroceni, 16 February 1929, typewritten letter, RNA, Castele şi palate – Regina Maria, 105/1929.

43. Ibid.

44. Queen Marie, 'The Story of a Good Man. King Ferdinand of Romania', autograph manuscript, RNA, Regina Maria, III/58, p. 64; see also RNA, Regina Maria, III/7, p. 105.

45. RNA, Regina Maria, III/7, p. 105.

46. Ibid., p. 107.

47. Ibid., p. 106.

48. Review of *The Story of My Life*, volume II: A Rumanian Crown Princess, *Times Literary Supplement*, 18 October 1934, p. 703.

49. Ibid.

50. Queen Marie to Miss Beckley, p. 51, Cotroceni, 16 February 1929, typewritten letter, RNA, Castele si palate – Regina Maria, 105/1929.

51. Marie, Queen of Romania, *The Story of My Life*, vol. III, London: Cassell, 3rd edition, April 1935, p. 4.

52. Review of *The Story of My Life* by Marie, Queen of Romania, volume III: Wartime Rumania, *Times Literary Supplement*, 14 March 1935, p. 151.

53. *Illustrated London News*, 6 April 1935, p. 582.

54. Marie, Queen of Romania, *The Story of My Life*, vol. III, London: Cassell, 3rd edition, April 1935, p. 25.

55. Ibid., p. 26.

56. Ibid., pp. 153–5.

57. Saint-Aulaire, Auguste Felix Charles de Beaupoil, *Confession d'un vieux diplomate*, Paris: Flammarion, 1953, p. 399.

58. I.G. Duca, *Memorii. Războiul*, vol. IV, Bucureşti: editura Machiavelli, 1994, p. 130.

59. See V. Drăguşanu, *Regina eroilor*, Iaşi, 1918.

60. Marie, Queen of Romania, *The Story of My Life*, vol. III, London: Cassell, 3rd edition, April 1935, p. 222.

61. Ibid., p. 295.

62. Ibid.

63. Saint-Aulaire, *Confession*, p. 440.

64. Marie, Queen of Romania, *Ordeal: The Story of My Life*, New York: Ch. Scribner's, 1935, p .326.

65. 'Marie, Queen of Conquered Romania, Defies the Kaiser', *Literary Digest*, 57: 56–9, 8 June 1918.

66. See RNA, microfilm USA, R. 26, T.136–89, S.A. Rumanian No. 1/15, vol. 2, Ministerul de externe german, secţia A: Acte secrete privind familia regală, 22 August 1918.

Notes

67. Ibid.

68. *Story of My Life*, vol. III, p. 445.

69. RNA, Regina Maria, III/50, p. 1.

70. Ibid., p. 3.

71. Fotescu (ed.), *Americans and Queen Marie*, p. 185, Ray Baker Harris to Queen Marie, 16 September 1934.

72. RNA, Regina Maria, III/118, pp. 104–106.

73. See G. Găvănescul, *Ocolul pământului în şapte luni şi o zi*, Bucureşti, 1923, 4 vols.

74. The sultanate was formally abolished on 1 November 1922 by the parliament. Mehmed VI made several attempts to re-establish himself as caliph in the Hejaz. He died in 1926 in San Remo.

75. Law 1/1920; see Diana Fotescu, *România, Mitteleuropa şi Balcanii*, Bucureşti: Pro Transilvania, 1999, p. 57; F. Dareste, *Les Constitutions Modernes*, vol. II, Paris, 1932, pp. 49–67.

76. Thereafter he lived in Coburg, dying in 1948.

77. Prince Wilhelm of Wied was appointed by the Great Powers as the first king of Albania in March 1914. In September the same year he left Albania and never returned. He died in Sinaia, Romania, in 1945. The prince was a nephew of Queen Elisabeth of Romania (née princess of Wied).

78. Queen Wilhelmina of the Netherlands refused to extradite him to the Allies following the armistice. He died in 1941.

79. See Hungary, Law 47/ 6 November 1921.

80. See G.A. Pordea, *Ardealul şi Habsburgii*, Madrid, 1956, p. 16.

81. After the death of King Ferdinand in 1927, trouble ahead was heralded by Carol's renunciation of his right of succession to the throne. A regency which guided the minor King Michael, his son, then led the country. Carol returned to the throne spectacularly in 1930. This is the period when Queen Marie published *The Story of my Life* and started *The Later Chapters*.

82. RNA, Regina Maria, V/5195.

83. Queen Marie, Journal, 1919, autograph manuscript, RNA, Regina Maria, III/116, notebook XV, pp. 11, 26, 43.

84. Queen Marie, Journal, 7/20 March 1919, London, autograph manuscript, RNA, Regina Maria, III/116, notebook XV, p. 170.

85. Nicolae Iorga, *Istoria Românilor. Întregitorii*, vol. X, Bucureşti, 1939, p. 425.

86. Queen Marie, Journal, 7 March 1919, Paris, autograph manuscript, RNA, Regina Maria, III/116, notebook XV, pp. 113–14.

87. Ibid.

88. Queen Marie, Journal, 8 April 1919, Paris, autograph manuscript, RNA, Regina Maria, III/117, notebook XVI, p. 68.

89. Queen Marie, Journal, 7 March 1919, Paris, autograph manuscript, RNA, Regina Maria, III/116, notebook XV, p. 138.

90. Marie, Queen of Romania, 'My Mission. Paris Again', *Cornhill Magazine*, vol. 160, no. 960, December 1939, p. 739.

91. See Diana Fotescu, 'Queen Marie in Paris and London (1919): A Diplomatic Event', *Romanian Civilization*, vol. II, no. 2/1993, p. 26; and The National Archives (Public Record Office), FO 371/3597, 12 May 1919.

92. Marie, Queen of Romania, 'My Mission. Paris Again', *Cornhill Magazine*, vol. 160, no. 960, December 1939, p. 726.

93. Ibid., p. 750.

94. She had been so called by the *Daily Mirror*.

95. See 'Obituaries. Queen Marie's Life. Active, Eventful', *New York Times*, 19 July 1938.

96. RNA, Casa Regală, 27/1920.

97. Queen Marie, Journal, 24 May 1919 – Bichis-Csaba, autograph manuscript, RNA, Regina Maria, III/117, notebook'XVI, p. 160.

98. Ibid., p. 161.

99. *Treaty between Her Majesty and the Emperor of all the Russias for the Marriage of His Royal Highness the Duke of Edinburgh with Her Imperial Highness the Grand Duchess Marie Alexandrovna of Russia*, signed at St Petersburg, 22 January 1874 – presented to both Houses of Parliament by Command of Her Majesty 1874, London, printed by Harrison and Sons.

100. Queen Marie's letter to Nancy Astor, 14 July 1938, autograph letter, signed, Reading University Library, Archives and Manuscripts – Nancy Astor Papers. She left Dresden for home on the following day, 15 July.

Chapter One

1. Cotroceni royal palace church, built by the Wallachian Prince Serban Cantacuzino in seventeenth century in Bucharest.

2. Prince Mircea (1913–16), son of King Ferdinand and Queen Marie.

3. Prince Mircea.

4. General Ernest Ballif was King Ferdinand's aide-de-camp, and from 1916 acted in the same position for Queen Marie.

5. Nickname of King Ferdinand of Romania (1865–1927).

6. Prince Nicolae (1903–78), Marie's second son; regent between 1927 and 1930. He completed his studies at Eton College and Wembley Naval School in England, 1926. On 9 April 1937 he was forced to renounce his princely prerogatives and took the name Nicolae Brana, because of a morganatic marriage in 1931.

7. N. Mişu (1848–1924), Romanian diplomat, minister of Romania in London between 1919 and 1921.

8. Joseph (Joe) Whiteside Boyle (1867–1923), Canadian colonel in the First World War, who had an important role in securing the return of the Romanian MPs and other refugees detained in Odessa by the Bolsheviks.

9. George V, King of Great Britain (1867–1936); in 1893 married Victoria Mary, born princess of Teck (afterwards Queen Mary).
10. Iuliu Maniu (1873–1953), Romanian politician; member of the national committee of the Romanian National Party, deputy in Hungarian parliament before Transylvania became a part of Romania; president of the Romanian National Party in Transylvania, and then of the Peasant National Party. Prime minister in 1928–30 and 1932–3, when he retired from the leadership of the party and of the government. In 1947 the communists arrested him and he later died in the Sighet prison.
11. Alexandru Vaida Voevod (1872–1950), lawyer, Romanian politician, one of the leaders of the Romanian National Party in Transylvania and the Peasant National Party. Prime minister in 1919–20, 1932 and 1933. In 1935 he set up the 'Frontul Românesc' political party.
12. Vasile Goldiş (1862–1934), historian and politician; member of the Romanian Academy.
13. Ştefan Ciceo-Popp (1865–1940), politician, economist. In 1917 he was one of the founders of the Labour Party.
14. Miron Cristea (1868–1939), the first patriarch of the Romanian Orthodox Church; in 1927 he was a member of the Regency; 1938 in and crown counsellor in 1938–39.
15. Iuliu Hossu (1885–1970), uniate bishop; senator.
16. Paul, Grand Duke of Russia (1860–1919), Marie Alexandrovna's brother.
17. Town in north-eastern Romania; the Romanian spelling is Iaşi.
18. Bela Kun (1886–1939), the leader of communist Hungary between March and August 1919. After 1919 he went in exile in Vienna, and then in Russia.
19. Henri Mathias Berthelot (1861–1931), French general; between 1916 and 1918 he was the commander of the French Military Mission in Romania.
20. Walter Holworth Greenly (1875–1955), general, the commander of the British Military Mission in Romania (1916–19).
21. King Ferdinand of Romania ruled between 1914 and 1927.
22. Woodrow Thomas Wilson (1856–1924), professor, governor of New Jersey (1910), president of the USA, 1913–21, promoter of the League of Nations.

Chapter Two

1. Marie Putiatin (1890–1958); first marriage concluded with Wilhelm, Prince of Sweden; her second marriage was with Serghei Putiatin. Cousin of Queen Marie of Romania.
2. Princess Paley (1866–1929) married Grand Duke Paul in 1902; she wrote *Memories of Russia 1916–1919*, Herbert Jenkins, 1924.
3. The village hospital during the First World War.
4. Alexandrina (Didine) Cantacuzino (1881–1944), a Romanian aristocrat; she was a publicist, a feminist militant and founder of the National Society of the

Christian-Orthodox Romanian Women (1910). During the First World War, as a member of the Red Cross, she led the biggest hospital in Bucharest. She was a founder of the popular canteens, and in 1927 founded 'The Woman House'.

5. Alexandru (Alecco) Constantinescu (1859–1926), agriculture and estates minister in the liberal government from 1914 to 1916.
6. Ion (Ionel) I.C. Brătianu (1864–1927), president of the Romanian Liberal National Party (1909–27), several times minister and prime minister.
7. Constantin Coandă (1857–1932) Romanian general, prime minister and foreign affairs minister in 1918, president of the Senate (1920–1; 1926–7).
8. Nickname for Prince Nicolae of Romania.
9. Pimen Georgescu, Orthodox bishop of Moldavia.
10. General Nicolae Petala (1869–1935), in 1925 appointed General Inspector of the Romanian Army; Senator.

Chapter Three

1. Elise Brătianu (1870–1957), wife of Prime Minister Ion I.C. Brătianu and the sister of prince Barbu Stirbey.
2. Victor Antonescu (1871–1947), Romanian politician; liberal MP, several times minister of justice, finance, and foreign affairs; minister at Paris and Geneva.
3. Princess Elisabetha (1894–1956), the eldest daughter of Queen Marie; in 1921 married King George II of Greece, divorced in 1935.
4. Nickname of Princess Marie (Mărioara) of Romania (1900–61), Queen Marie's daughter; in 1922 married King Alexander I of Yugoslavia.
5. Princess Henriette of Belgium (1870–1948), elder sister of King Albert I of Belgium; married Emanuel of Orleans, Duke of Vendôme and Alençon (1872–1931).
6. Lahovary.
7. Procopiu.
8. Princess Anna Elisabeta Brâncoveanu Noailles (1876–1933), a French poetess of Romanian extraction. In 1922 she was appointed as the first woman member of the Royal Academy in Belgium, and in 1925 became an honorary fellow of the Romanian Academy.
9. Georges Clemenceau (1841–1929), prime minister of France (1906–9; 1917–20), leader of the Radical Party, president of the Peace Conference, Paris, 1919–20.
10. Nickname for Alexander Mikhailovich Romanov, Grand Duke (1866–1933), in 1894 married Xenia Alexandrovna Romanov, Grand Duchess of Russia.
11. Grand Duchess of Russia, Xenia (1875–1960), daughter of Alexander III, Tsar of Russia.
12. Eulalia de Asis de la Piedad, Infanta of Spain (1864–1958), sister of King Alphonso XII of Spain; married Antonio de Orléans y de Bourbon, Infante of Spain. She was the mother-in-law of Queen Marie's sister: Beatrice (Baby).

13. 'Both my jewels and legal tender of the country to the amount of 7 million gold francs were sent by the National Bank of Romania, together with many artistic treasures, to Moscow and were never returned' – Queen Marie's note.
14. Raymond Poincaré (1860–1934), French politician. Prime minister in 1912, 1922–4 and 1926–9; president of France between 1912 and 1920.
15. Stephen Pichon, French politician and diplomat, journalist; several times minister of foreign affairs in 1906–9, 1913 and 1917 and 1920.
16. President of the French Academy.
17. Aristide Briand (1862–1932), French politician and diplomat. Prime minister and minister of foreign affairs; he was one of the organizers of the Locarno Conference from 1925 and co-authored the Briand–Kellog Pact from 1928.
18. Woodrow Wilson.
19. David Lloyd George (1863–1945), British politician, leader of the Liberal Party, prime minister between 1916 and 1922.
20. Lord Robert Cecil, British politician, Conservative MP, Foreign Office secretary at the start of the First World War.
21. Lord Arthur James Balfour (1848–1930), British politician; prime minister 1902–5; Foreign Office secretary between 1916 and 1919.

Chapter Four

1. Ileana, Princess of Romania (1909–91), Queen Marie's daughter; in July 1931 she married Archduke Anton of Habsburg (1901–87) and divorced in 1954; a second marriage was concluded with Dr Ştefan Issărescu (1906–2002).
2. George V (1865–1936), reigned 1910–36; in 1893 married Victoria Mary von Teck, the future Queen Mary, known as May.
3. Mary of Teck (1867–1953), Queen consort of George V, known before her marriage as Princess Mary.
4. David Edward, Prince of Wales (1894–1972), future King Edward VIII (1936); he had been on the throne for nine months; abdicated and married Mrs Wallis Simpson, an American twice-divorced commoner; subsequently assumed the title Duke of Windsor.
5. Albert George, Duke of York (1895–1952), future King George VI between 1936 and 1952; in 1923 married Lady Elizabeth Bowes-Lyon, the late Queen Mother.
6. Mary, Royal Princess (1897–1965); in 1922 married Lascelles Henry George, 6th Earl of Harewood.
7. Waldorf William Astor (1879–1952), married to Nancy Langhorne Shaw.
8. Queen Victoria.
9. Queen Alexandra (1844–1925), born Princess of Denmark; married Edward, Prince of Wales, later King Edward VII.
10. Queen Amélie of Portugal (1865–1951), born Amelie d'Orléans of Paris; married in 1886 Saxe-Coburg-Gotha, Carlos I, King of Portugal.

11. Arthur, Duke of Connaught, Marie's uncle (1850–1942); in 1879 married Louise Margaret of Prussia.
12. Lady Carisbrooke.
13. Victoria Melita, Grand Duchess of Russia, née Princess of Edinburgh (1876–1936); first marriage in 1894 with Ernst Louis, Grand Duke of Hesse and Darmstadt, divorced in 1901; second marriage in 1905 concluded with Kirill, Grand Duke of Russia (1876–1938).
14. Sir Winston Churchill (1874–1965), prime minister in 1940–5 and 1951–5; leader of the Tories.
15. In 1913 the first Romanian boy scouts groups were set up in Bucharest, Sinaia, Braşov and Blaj. In 1914, the Boy Scouts Association was founded under the leadership of Crown Prince Carol.
16. Pauline Spender Clay, née Astor (1880–1972); married to colonel Herbert Spender-Clay.
17. Lady Nancy Astor (1879–1964); wife of Waldorf Astor; the first woman MP in the UK in 1919 (Conservative).
18. Prince of Wales, afterwards Edward VIII.
19. Henry Peter Hansell was, in 1919, at Eton, the tutor of Prince Nicolae (Nicky) of Romania. Before that he was also a private tutor to the children of Arthur, Duke of Connaught.

Chapter Five

1. Ferdinand Foch (1851–1929), French general; president of the International War Council of the Allied Troops.
2. Henri Pétain (1856–1951) French army commander.
3. Albert I (1875–1934), King of Belgium from 1909, the son of Philippe, Earl of Flanders; married to Elisabeth of Bavaria (1876–1965).
4. On 10 January 1893.
5. Nelson Cromwell (1854–1948) focused on philanthropic institutions after the First World War. He was the founder of the Society of Romania's Friends in New York. In 1926 he organized a reception in honour of Queen Marie's visit to the USA.
6. King Ferdinand and Queen Marie were the first monarchs to visit the League of Nations in Geneva (1924).
7. Beatrice, Infanta of Spain, née princess of Edinburgh (1883–1966); married Alfonso (Ali), Infante of Spain in 1909; her nickname was Baby Bee.
8. Minister of Great Britain at Bucharest during the First World War.
9. She arrived in Paris on 10 April 1919.
10. Duchess of Saxe-Coburg-Gotha, born Marie Alexandrovna, Grand Duchess of Russia.
11. Loie Fuller (1862–1928), American dancer, Queen Marie's friend. After the First World War she helped Romania through a high-profile charity campaign in the USA.

12. Samuel Hill (1857–1931), American entrepreneur. He founded 'Maryhill Museum', inaugurated in 1926 in the presence of Queen Marie of Romania.
13. Ignacy Paderewski (1860–1941), Polish pianist, composer and politician; prime minister of Poland in 1919.
14. Marie left the French capital on 16 April 1919.

Chapter Six

1. The future King Alexander of Yugoslavia (1888–1934). In 1922 he married Marie (Mignon), Princess of Romania, Queen Marie's daughter.
2. Town in north-eastern Romania.
3. Resurrection.
4. Joseph Breckrindge Bayne (1880–1964), American doctor, volunteer in Romania during the First World War. When first greeted by Queen Marie at work in hospital he simply answered, 'How do you do?' Thereafter, he was referred to as 'Dr How-do-you-do'.

Chapter Seven

1. The visit took place between 23 May and 1 June 1919.
2. The old frontier between Transylvania and Romania (until 1918), 3 February 1893 was the first time that Marie crossed it as a crown princess of Romania.
3. Mihail Pherekyde (1842–1925), Romanian politician, member of the Liberal Party; several times minister, and MP.
4. I.G. Duca (1879–1933), Romanian politician, member of the Liberal Party; MP and prime minister in 1933; assassinated by the 'Legionars' (members of the 'Garda de Fier', a Romanian fascist movement).

Chapter Eight

1. Town in the Transylvanian Alps, the place of the royal castles Pelesh, Pelishor and Foishor.
2. Alexandru Averescu (1859–1938), Romanian general and politician; leader of the party 'Liga Poporului' (People's League); prime minister in 1918, 1920–1 and 1926–7; crown counsellor in 1938.
3. Take Ionescu (1858–1922), Romanian diplomat and politician, member of the Conservative Party; several times minister in 1920–1, 1926–7, 1931–2; prime minister in 1939, crown counsellor in 1938–40.
4. Constantin Argetoianu (1871–1952), Romanian politician and diplomat; the leader of the Agrarian Party.
5. Heathfield school, Ascot.

6. Eton College.
7. The Cotroceni Palace in Bucharest.
8. 1919.

Chapter Nine

1. Marie Alexandrovna, Duchess of Saxe-Coburg-Gotha (née Grand Duchess of Russia).
2. Beatrice, Infanta of Spain.
3. Prince Barbu (nickname Barbo) Stirbey (1872–1946), head of King Ferdinand's household; member of the Liberal Party, prime minister in 1927.
4. Maria (nickname Maruka) Cantacuzino, née Rosetti-Tetcani; first marriage to Mihail Cantacuzino and the second in 1936 to George Enescu.
5. George Enescu (1881–1955), Romanian classical composer.
6. Olga, Queen of Greece (1851–1926), née Olga Constantinova Romanov, Princess of Russia; married 1867 to Schleswig William, George I of the Hellenes, King of Greece.
7. Ellen (1882–1957), daughter of Grand Duke Vladimir; married 1902 to Schleswig Holstein Sonderburg, Nicholas, Prince of Greece.
8. Ador Gustave (1845–1928), President of Switzerland in 1919.
9. Nickname for Queen Marie's daughter, Elisabetha.
10. Nickname for Queen Marie.
11. Nickname of Alfonso Maria de Orleans y de Borbon, Infante of Spain (1886–1975); married 1909 to Beatrice, Princess of Edinburgh.
12. King Alfonso XIII of Spain (1886–1941), acceded 17 May 1886, abdicated 14 April 1931; in 1906 married Victoria Eugenie (Ena) of Battenberg.
13. Victor Emmanuel III (1869–1947), King of Italy from 1900; in 1946 he abdicated in favour of his son Umberto II; in 1896 he married Petrovic-Njegos, Helen of Montenegro, the daughter of King Nicolas I of Montenegro.
14. Helen, Queen of Italy, née Princess of Montenegro (1873–1952).
15. Moscow coronation of Tsar Nicholas II in 1896.
16. Benito Mussolini (1883–1945), fascist dictator, prime minister and 'capo del stato' in Italy, 1922–43.

Chapter Ten

1. Arthur Văitoianu (1864–1956), Romanian general and minister of internal affairs in 1918, 1922–3 and minister of war in 1918–19; prime minister in 1919 and crown counsellor in 1938.
2. In 1919.
3. This refers to Crown Prince Carol's desertion from the army in 1919, a consequence of his love affair with Ioana (Zizi) Lambrino.

Chapter Eleven

1. Pen name of Queen Elisabeth of Romania (1843–1916), born Princess of Wied; in November 1869 she married Carol I of Hohenzollern, King of Romania.
2. Princess from the Romanian aristocracy (1884–1971), the daughter of Prince Alexandru Mavrocordat; in 1908 married Prince Mihail Sturdza, the nephew of the Moldavian prince M. Sturdza; in 1918 she created in her palace in Miroslava an orphanage called 'Princess Olga Sturdza', which became in 1919 the Superior School of Agriculture.
3. Ioan Manolescu, general and journalist; he was the president of 'Casele Naţionale' (National Houses), and general director of the Romanian Scout Movement.
4. King Carol II (1893–1953), Marie's eldest child; king of Romania between 1930 and 1940; he had a morganatic marriage with Ioana (Zizi) Lambrino; in 1921 he married Princess Helen of Greece; a third marriage was with Elena Lupescu. He died in Portugal and on 14 February 2003 his remains were brought back to Romania and reburied at the royal tomb in Curtea de Argeş.
5. Grigore Trancu-Iaşi (1873–1940), Romanian politician, economist; founder of the Labour Party; first minister of labour and social security between 20 March and 16 December 1921.

Chapter Twelve

1. King Carol I of Romania (1839–1914), the founder of the Hohenzollern Dynasty, reigning between 1866 and 1914.
2. Dr Nicolae Lupu (1876–1947), Romanian politician; MP, member of the Peasants' Party (1924–36).
3. On 1 December 1919 and 13 March 1920.
4. Nicolae Iorga (1871–1940), historian, member of the Romanian Academy; prime minister 1931–2; crown counsellor 1938–40; murdered by the far right movement, 'Garda de fier' (Iron Guard).
5. Averescu's government (March 1920–December 1921).

The Coronation

1. RNA, Regina Maria, III/136, an unpublished text from Queen Marie's diary
2. Nickname for Helen – Elena – (1896–1982), Princess of Romania, born princess of Greece; married in 1921 to Crown Prince of Romania, Carol (future King Carol II), divorced in 1928; she became Queen Mother of Romania (1940–7) during the reign of his son, King Michael I (Mihai I).
3. Princess Irene of Greece (1904–74); married in 1939 to Savoy, Aymon Margherito Mario, the 4th Duke of Aosta.
4. Regiment 4, Red Hussars.

5. During the Middle Ages there were coronation ceremonies for the princes of Moldavia and Wallachia. Here Queen Marie refers to the royal ceremony and the traditions of a dynasty, as she was familiar with them from her childhood in the UK. There was a Coronation ceremony in 1881 in Bucharest for King Carol I and his wife Queen Elisabeth. This particular ceremony of which Marie writes took place in Greater Romania at Alba-Iulia and it was much better and minutely organized, being for Romania a benchmark for these kind of ceremonies.

6. King Constantin I of Greece, Schleswig-Holstein Sondenburg-Glucksburg (1868–1923); ruled Greece from 1913–17 and 1920–22.

7. Cotroceni church, built in the seventeenth century by prince of Wallachia Şerban Cantacuzino.

8. Near Bucharest.

9. Prince Tomasso of Savoy, the 2nd Duke of Genoa (1854–1931); married Princess Marie Isabella of Bavaria (1863–1924).

10. Alfonso, Infante of Spain.

11. Mogoşoaia at that time was a village close to Bucharest.

12. Alfred, Duke of Edinburgh, Earl of Kent and Ulster, Duke of Saxe-Coburg-Gotha (1844–1900); in 1874 married Marie Alexandrovna (née Grand Duchess of Russia).

13. Prince Barbu Stirbey.

14. The full Regalia.

15. I. Klinsberg, royal photographer in Romania.

Postscript

1. On 27 February 1921 in Bucharest.

2. On 10 March 1921 at Athens.

3. From 1929 called Yugoslavia.

4. On 8 June 1922 in Belgrade.

5. Concluded on 28 October 1931 with Ioana Dumitrescu.

6. See Ştefan Meteş, *Regele Ferdinand al României*, Institutul de arte grafice Ardealul, Cluj, 1925.

7. RNA, Regina Maria, III/148, 12 May 1924, London, p. 66.

8. Mihai in Romanian.

9. His father, Prince Carol, renounced his rights as crown prince and heir to the throne in December 1925. In January 1926 King Ferdinand proclaimed Michael heir to the throne.

10. The institution of the Regency was composed of three members, one of the regents being Nicolae.

11. See RNA, Regina Maria, V/5629, 15 October 1929.

12. The first attempt was made in December 1990 when he came with a Danish diplomatic passport but was deported by the Romanian authorities.

Select Bibliography

Archives

Kent State University Library, Kent, Ohio
National Archives, The Public Record Office, London
Pelesh Museum Archives, Posada
Reading University Library, Archives and Manuscripts, Reading
Romanian National Archives, Bucharest

Books

GENERAL

Almanach de Gotha, London, vol. 1, 2003

Aronson, Theo, *Grandmama of Europe. The Crowned Descendants of Queen Victoria*, London: John Murray, 1973

Bacalbaşa, Constantin, *Bucureştii de altă dată*, Bucureşti, 1935–36

Dormer, P.G., *The Edinburghs at Eastwell*, Ashford: Eastwell Publications, 1992

Eilers, Marlene A., *Queen Victoria's descendants*, New York: Atlantic International Publications, 1987

Fotescu, Diana, *România, Mitteleuropa şi Balcanii*, Bucureşti: Pro Transilvania, 1999

Hindley, Geoffrey, *The Royal Families of Europe*, London: Constable, 2000

Kline, Charles, *To Her Majesty Marie Queen of Romania*, Pennsylvania, 1926

Lieven, Dominic, *Empire. The Russian Empire and Its Rivals*, London: John Murray, 2000

Marie, Queen of Romania, *The Story of My Life*, vols I–III, London: Cassell, 1934–35

Meteş, Ştefan, *Regele Ferdinand al României*, Cluj: Institutul de Arte grafice 'Ardealul', 1925

Monteoru, Argentina, *Măriei Sale Reginei-poete Maria a României cu ocazia primei sale poeme tipărite*, Bucureşti, 1915

Mordacq, Général, *Le Ministère Clemenceau, journal d'un témoin*, Paris: Plon, 1931

Potra George, *Din Bucureştii de ieri*, Bucureşti: Editura Ştiinţifică şi Enciclopedică, 1990

Select Bibliography

Rose, Kenneth, *King George V*, London: Phoenix Press – Orion Group Ltd, 2000

Romanian Monarchy, European Monarchies Series No.1, Royalty Digest (ed.), Ticehurst, 1999

Saint-Aulaire, Auguste Félix Charles de Beaupoil, Comte de, *Confession d'un vieux diplomate*, Paris: Flammarion, 1953

Summers-Devere, A., *War and the Royal Houses of Europe in the Twentieth Century*, London: Arms and Armour Press, 1996

Tzigara-Samurcaş, Al., *Muzeografie românească*, Bucureşti, 1936

Van der Kiste, John, *Crowns in a changing world. The British and European Monarchies 1901–1936*, Stroud: Alan Sutton Publishing, 1993

——, *Princess Victoria Melita. Grand Duchess Cyril of Russia 1876–1936*, Stroud: Alan Sutton Publishing, 1994

Van der Kiste, John and Jordaan Bee, *Dearest Affie. . . . Alfred, Duke of Edinburgh. Queen Victoria's second son, 1844–1900*, Stroud: Sutton, 1995

Vopicka, Charles, *Secrets of the Balkans: Seven Years of a Diplomat's Life in the Storm Center of Europe*, Chicago: Rand McNally & Co., 1921

Zeepvat, Charlotte, *Queen Victoria's Family. A Century of Photographs 1840–1940*, Stroud: Sutton, 2001

BIOGRAPHIES OF QUEEN MARIE

Arimia, Vasile (ed.), *Însemnări zilnice (decembrie 1918–decembrie 1919). Maria Regina României*, vol. I, Bucureşti: Editura Albatros, 1996

Bolitho, Hector, *A Biographer's Notebook*, London: Longmans, Green and Co., 1950 (chapter 'Queen Marie of Roumania's letters to her "American friend"')

Daggett, Mabel Potter, *Marie of Romania. The Intimate Story of the Radiant Queen*, London: Brentano's, 1927

Drăguşanu, Vasile, *Regina Eroilor*, Iaşi 1918

Elsberry, Terence, *Marie of Romania. The Intimate Life of a Twentieth Century Queen*, London: Cassell, 1973

Fotescu, Diana (ed.), *Americans and Queen Marie of Romania*, Iaşi–Oxford–Portland: The Center for Romanian Studies, 1998

Gauthier, Guy, *Missy, Reine de Roumanie*, Paris: France-Empires, 1994

Iorga, Nicolae, *Regina Maria. Cu prilejul încoronării*, Bucureşti: Cartea românească, 1923

Marcus, Della, *Her Eternal Crown: Queen Marie of Romania and the Baha'i Faith*, Oxford: George Ronald Publisher, 2001

Morris, Constance Lily, *On Tour with Queen Marie*, Foreword by Queen Marie, New York: Robert McBride, 1927

Oprişan, I. Gr., *Rolul Reginei Maria în viaţa României*, Bucureşti, 1938

Oudard, Georges, *La Reine Marie de Roumanie*, Paris: Plon, 1939

Pakula, Hannah, *The Last Romantic. A Biography of Queen Marie of Romania*, London: Phoenix–Orion Books, 1996

Panaitescu, Emil, *Marie, Reine de Roumanie*, Bucureşti, 1939

Pravilă, Nicolae, *Majestatea Sa Regina Maria a României Însemnări biografice*, Bucureşti, 1916

Rosetti, Gen. Radu, *Amintiri despre Regina Maria*, Bucureşti, 1942

Sălălceanu, Grigore, *Regina Maria*, Cernăuţi, 1939

Volbură, Poiană Năsturaş, *Regina României*, Baia Mare: Tipografia Astra, 1919

NEWSPAPERS AND PERIODICALS

Century Magazine

Cornhill Magazine

Daily Mail

Daily Mirror

Illustrated London News

New York Times

Punch

Realitatea Ilustrată

Royalty Digest

Times Literary Supplement

The Times (London)

Universul

Index

Queen Marie of Romania is referred to as QM

of, xxxiv; Imperial Treasury in Moscow, xxxiv; letter for QM, 76; marriage treaty, xxxiv; old traditions, 76; QM on, 76

Marie (Mignon), Princess of Romania, later Queen of Yugoslavia, xxv, 26, 82; diadem of, 141; exile of, 154; at Heathfield school, 134; marriage of, 151, 152; passion for England, 84; Romanian coronation, 141, 142, 145, 146

Marie, Queen of Romania:
arrival in England, 44, 152; at the Grand Opera , 65; at the Elysée with Poincaré, 33, 34, 41; at the opening of the Parliament, 122; attitude as queen 36, 38, 49, 119, 138; audiences of, 31, 52, 53, 67, 70; autobiography, xiv, xvi; banquet, 6, 7, 85, 102, 103, 144, 147, 149; birthplace (Eastwell Park), xiii, xix; Celtic traditions, xxiv; charity organizations/work, xxvi, 126, 127, 129; Collette Willie and first orchids, 24; coronation of, 141–3, 146, 148; cousin Marie Putiatin, 8, 12, 13, 44, 84; and David, 44, 50, 61; death of, ix, xi, xxxiv, 154; diadems of, 144, 146; (her) diary/diaries (journal), ix, x, xv, xxv, xxxi, xxxiv, 9, 24, 32, 39, 44, 57, 60, 61, 63, 68, 72, 74, 78, 97, 110, 127, 140, 152; distress commingled with festivities, 18; distress, continual, 6, 11, 44, 75; encounter with Clemenceau, 29, 30, 31, 41; English traditionalism, 47; exile in Jassy, 9, 19, 20, 75, 77; fashion, 13, 27, 29, 32, 67, 76, 77, 122, 141, 142, 146, 148; fear of Bolshevism, 9, 10, 15, 65, 72, 82, 88; fears of Carol's intrusions, x;

flying visits, 19 (Jassy), 74 (Reims), 118 (San Rossoro); First World War (Great War), xiii, 38, 97, 152; hide her private papers, x; jewels stolen by the Bolsheviks in Russia, 32, 67, 149; Hoover and, xxxii, 35, 36; life at Buckingham Palace, 47; lunch given by Paderewski, 85, 86; (and) Marie Alexandrovna, xxi, xxxi, 76, 113–18; medal from the British Red Cross, 59; military honours in Paris, 30, 33, 34; military honours in Switzerland, 113, 115; 'mother-in-law' of the Balkans, 151; (and) Nicky at Eaton, 8, 9, 26, 45, 46, 62, 134; official lunch given by the Lord Major, 57; photographers and, 25, 27, 150; the Press and, xii, 28–30, 59, 60, 153; propaganda made by, xxxii, 58, 66, 70; Queen Alexandra and, 53; Queen Mary and, 44, 46–8, 54, 56, 62, 84; reception at Paris station, of 24, 25; reception at the 'Academie des Beaux-Arts', 34; receives Transylvanian deputations, 8; receives the foreign ambassadors in Paris, 58; (her) Regiment 4 Roşiori, 137, 143–5; royal mentality of, 90; royal welcome at Victoria station, 44; (and) Samuel Hill, 80; Spanish flu, 7, 8; special mission at the Peace Conference, xi; xxxi, xxxii, 16, 19, 21, 23, 39, 41, 50, 51, 60, 87, 89; *Story of my Life, The* (memoirs), ix, xiv, xvi–xxviii, 3, 61, 159; sugar distribution to the poor, 13, 14; talks with Lupu, 135–6; varied visitors: Lord Derby, Albert Thomas, 31; visits her aunts and cousins in England, 54; visits the King and Queen of Italy, 118; visiting the French battlefields and